Carl P. Mc
750 Del
Punta Go   P9-DTQ-381

100

WITHDRAWN

Captive of the Rising Sun

Captive
of the
Rising Sun

The POW Memoirs of
Rear Admiral Donald T. Giles, USN

*Edited and with Additional Material
Provided by* Donald T. Giles, Jr.

Naval Institute Press
Annapolis, Maryland

© 1994
by the United States Naval Institute
Annapolis, Maryland

All rights reserved. No part of this book may be reproduced
without written permission from the publisher.

Library of Congress Cataloging-in-Publication Data

Giles, Donald T., 1898–1983.
    Captive of the Rising Sun : the POW memoirs of rear admiral Donald
    T. Giles, USN / edited and with additional material provided by
    Donald T. Giles, Jr.
        p. cm.
    Includes bibliographical references and index.
    ISBN 1-55750-320-6
    1. Giles, Donald T., 1898–1983. 2. World War, 1939–1945—
Prisoners and prisons, Japanese.   3. Prisoners of war—Japan—
Biography.   4. Prisoners of war—United States—Biography.
5. World War, 1939–1945—Personal narratives, American.   6. World
War, 1939–1945—Campaigns—Guam.   I. Giles, Donald T., 1924–
II. Title.
D805.J3G54   1994
940.54′7252—dc20   93-37042
                                                              CIP
Printed in the United States of America on acid-free paper ∞

9 8 7 6 5 4 3 2

First printing

This book is dedicated to my mother,
Virginia Basil Giles,
the quintessential Navy Wife.

Contents

✳ Illustrations

Maps

Photographs and Figures

✳ Acknowledgments

This book would not have been possible without the interest and kind support provided by Captain Paul R. Schratz, USN (retired). Captain Schratz was a former shipmate and close lifelong friend of my father, and although he never said so, I believe Captain Schratz shared an interest with me in seeing my father's story told. His assistance went far beyond what was deserved and cannot be forgotten.

I also want to thank Lieutenant Reginald W. Reed, USN (retired), for providing me with a copy of an unpublished manuscript he had written describing his experiences on Guam and at Zentsuji. This manuscript, "Saga of a Sacrificial Goat, USN," provided additional information substantiating what my father had recorded.

Additional information and photographs of Zentsuji and Roku Roshi were lent to me by Mrs. Nancy Cross, daughter of the late Colonel Donald Spicer, USMC. These data provided an additional dimension to my narrative and were greatly appreciated.

I also thank Mr. Joseph McDermott and Mr. Charles Ikins, legislative assistants to former Congressman Ben Blaz of Guam, for information on the history of Guam; Ms. Laura F. Brown of the University of Baltimore Library (Steamship Historical Society Collection) for her research regarding the *Argentina Maru* and *Lisbon Maru;* and the reference librarians of the Alexandria Library for their assistance in obtaining background information for inclusion in the book.

Above all others, I must thank my wife for being a supportive and understanding "computer widow" while I spent what must have seemed like endless hours in research and writing.

 # Preface

It was early morning when they were herded together and marched at bayonet-point to the harbor where a ship lay at anchor waiting to take them to prison. Except for the less fortunate who received special attention from a Japanese bayonet, it was not a long march, as such things go. It was not a long march unless you happened to be one of the prisoners—professional military men, some of whom felt and would feel for years thereafter that they had failed: that they had failed their country, their flag, and the traditions of the naval service; that they had failed the natives who had been entrusted to their care; that they had failed in their careers. For them it was a long march indeed as they carried the burden of their failure deep inside, struggling valiantly to hold their heads high in the face of degrading insults shouted in Japanese. What a terrible psychological price was levied by the American people and by our Congress—a price long in the making in Pacific policies, and terminating on that dismal day in 1942.

Because the garrison on Guam was small and virtually unarmed, it was unable to hold out long against the vastly more numerous and better-equipped attackers. It is probably because of this that little has been written about what happened on Guam. When the island went off the air on 8 December 1941, the world was engrossed in far more earthshaking events as war erupted throughout the Pacific region. Nevertheless, the defense of Guam offered scores of examples of loyalty and courage as the island fell to the overwhelming forces of a brutal and treacherous enemy.

My father was Rear Admiral (then Commander) Donald T. Giles, USN. He was one of those marched at the point of a Japanese bayonet, and he survived four years of indignity and suffering in Japanese prison camps.

While in prison he kept a diary recording how they were treated by the Japanese. Among other things, the diary detailed four years of starvation, psychological harassment, and brutality. Knowing how severely he would be punished if the diary were to be found, he kept it sewn into the lining of his clothes. Unfortunately, just before he was repatriated, the diary was lost.

Realizing how difficult it might be for him to discuss his capture and imprisonment after he returned home, I was reluctant to ask many questions, and he volunteered little information. Because of this, I knew only a few details of his capture, and much less of what had transpired in prison camp.

Much later, several years before he died in 1983, he started to write a book about his experiences as a POW, basing it in part on recollections of what he had recorded earlier. For one reason or another he completed only a draft manuscript and never offered it for publication. I knew that the manuscript existed, but he never showed it to me.

After my father died I tried to fill a void in our family history by researching the capture of Guam and the experiences of its garrison as prisoners of war. Hearing that I was doing this, Captain Paul R. Schratz, USN (retired), a former shipmate of my father aboard the USS *Wichita* and a lifelong friend, sent me a copy of the manuscript that my father had sent to him for review. I am unable to express adequately my thanks to Captain Schratz for this kindness. Without it, much of the story of my father's life on Guam and as a prisoner of war would have been lost.

This book is based in large measure on information contained in that draft manuscript. In order to flesh out the details of what happened, I have added material based on research from other sources in the United States and in Japan. The Prologue ("Background to Defeat"), Epilogue, and endnotes were written entirely by me, and I compiled Appendix A. In the remaining chapters, where my father's personal story is told, material that I have added has been set off by an ornament preceding and following the text.

If I were allowed only two phrases with which to describe my father, they would have to be that he was fiercely patriotic and that he was an ardent supporter of the U.S. naval service.

Although he never expressed it, I always felt that his presence on Guam was the result of a mistake in the Navy Department. After graduating from the Naval Academy as a member of the class of 1921, he received postgraduate education in engineering and had several progressively responsible tours of sea duty in engineering and two tours of shore duty in engineering. He was an engineer. Yet with our entry into the Second World War almost a certainty, he was ordered to an administrative billet on Guam where his engineering skills would be wasted and where it was almost certain he would be killed or captured.

Unfortunately, after returning from prison camp his life was not entirely happy. Two years after being repatriated, his wife (my mother), Virginia Basil Giles, died after a long and painful illness.

During the four years he had been in prison, the navy passed him by. Ships were different, tactics were different, the navy that he loved was different. The only thing that remained the same was his ardor for the service. In June 1947, as he and I stood at Annapolis Roads and watched the Midshipmen Cruise Squadron get under way, he commented—almost to himself—how much he wished he had command of one of those ships and how his career had been wasted.

This book has been written to tell what happened on Guam, to describe the loyalty and courage displayed by her defenders both during the capture of the island and during the four years they spent in prison. The siege and capture of Guam and the four horrible years that followed were not isolated events. They must be viewed in light of the pacifist sentiments that abounded in our country during the years prior to the Second World War and in light of the response of our Congress to those sentiments.

This book has also been written for Peter Barclay Giles and Kathryn Elizabeth Giles, so that they will know the courage, spirit, and patriotism displayed by their great-grandfather during four years in hell and will understand the meaning of "Duty, Honor, Country."

Captive of the Rising Sun

✳ Prologue
Background to Defeat

Guam is a tropical island in the Marianas, part of Micronesia. Strategically located relative to Japan, the Philippines, and New Guinea, it is in the western part of the Pacific Ocean, 1,450 miles from Tokyo, 1,500 miles from Manila, and 3,350 miles from Honolulu. For over four thousand years Guam and the other islands of the Marianas were inhabited only by the friendly, peaceful, and industrious Chamorro. The peaceful isolation of the Marianas ended in the latter part of the sixteenth century, when the Spaniards arrived and took possession of the islands.

The U.S. presence on Guam began after the end of the Spanish-American War in 1898. Although that war had been supported enthusiastically by most Americans, many disapproved of our new status as a colonial power and argued strenuously against provisions of the Treaty of Paris by which we were ceded Guam, Puerto Rico, and the Philippines. This anti-imperialist sentiment was so strong in the Senate that the treaty was ratified by a margin of only one vote. On 23 December 1898 President William McKinley issued an executive order placing Guam under the control of the Navy Department, and he commissioned a naval officer as governor.

By 1898 all of the neighboring Micronesian islands had been annexed by foreign powers that were anxious to expand their colonial possessions in the western Pacific. From that time until the beginning of the First World War, colonial ownership of these islands became

1

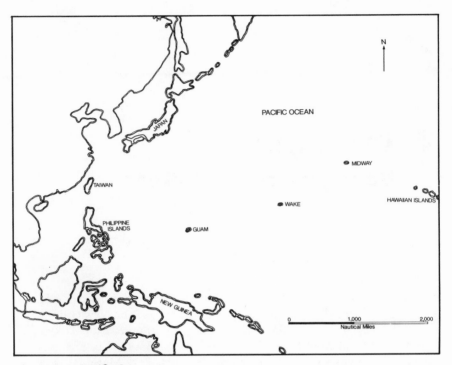

The western Pacific Ocean

concentrated among Germany, Great Britain, and the United States, with Germany occupying the Carolines, the Marshalls, Palau, and the Marianas (less Guam) and Great Britain occupying the Gilberts.

In the early 1900s, at the same time that parts of Micronesia were being annexed by Germany, Great Britain, and the United States, Japan—alleging that it was suffering from overpopulation and a need for economic growth—embarked on a course of imperialism that included the domination of Micronesia. Except for Guam, however, the only remaining Mariana Islands of any importance to Japan were Rota, Tinian, and Saipan—islands that were owned by Germany. The Japanese expansion into Micronesia was facilitated during the First World War when, as an ally of Great Britain and the United States, Japan was able to occupy all of German Micronesia.

Why was Guam left virtually unarmed? I can suggest four possible reasons: (1) isolationism and pacifism in the United States following the First World War; (2) treaty provisions with Japan by which the United States, Great Britain, France, and Italy agreed not to fortify their

Far Eastern possessions; (3) a cost that would have been prohibitive; and (4) the fact that the United States' strategic plan for the Pacific did not include defense of Guam or of the Philippines. A thesis can be developed to support any one of these possibilities, although the best explanation probably includes elements of all of them. A more interesting question is, Why was a handful of military men left to defend what was indefensible?

In 1918 the U.S. Navy was strong and was engaged in a building program designed to provide an unmatched naval combat capability. At this time, however, memories of the First World War were fresh, and isolationist sentiment was strong. Many Americans did not want to become involved in foreign problems. Such sentiments—defended by pacifists, scholars, clergymen, and other politically powerful groups—greatly reduced popular support for developing any improved military capability or for maintaining a military presence overseas. The enthusiasm for disarmament can be understood when one realizes that such feelings had also prevailed after other wars. In the United States, pacifist sentiment traditionally follows a war.

The furtherance of world peace was a theme of great historical importance in the United States, and this theme provided an irresistible foundation upon which other arguments for disarmament could be laid. Armaments were described as being the primary cause of war. Building on this specious assumption, it was argued that disarmament could be expected to reduce if not end the threat of war for all time. Secondarily, to build and maintain a large, modern navy would require a significant capital expenditure—money that many people would prefer to have allocated elsewhere.

The disarmament movement was supported actively by the American press—though it is difficult to understand why—and abetted by propaganda provided by foreign governments whose interests would not be well served by a strong U.S. Navy. From immediately following the First World War until the mid-1930s, the United States pursued policies or permitted itself to be drawn into treaties that progressively weakened its navy and paved the way for catastrophe in 1941.

During negotiations leading to the Treaty of Versailles, President Woodrow Wilson argued against recognizing Japan's claim to the islands it had occupied in Micronesia. However, under British pressure to do so, he concurred in placing these islands under Japanese mandate after having obtained an agreement that they would be administered by a civilian rather than a military government. Americans on Guam had been surrounded by Germans before the First World War. Now they were going to be surrounded by Japanese. As explained by Louis Morton in *Command Decisions,* "The mandate to Japan of the German islands in the Central Pacific had given that nation numerous bases astride the U.S. Fleet's line of communication and made American defense of the Philippines in the event of war with Japan virtually impossible."[1]

During the administration of President Warren G. Harding, plans for upgrading the navy were altered substantially in favor of naval limitation agreements. At the 1921 Washington Naval Conference, the United States made the appalling offer to scrap all capital ships under construction—six battle cruisers and seven battleships—in addition to two battleships that had already been launched. To approach this sacrifice, we asked Great Britain to scrap four battle cruisers under construction and called upon Japan to scrap four battle cruisers and three battleships. It was calculated that after this was accomplished, the strength in capital ships left to the United States, Great Britain, and Japan would be in a ratio of 5–5–3.

Japan would not consent to this reduced strength in capital ships without an agreement to maintain the status quo in the fortification and facilities of naval bases in the Pacific. This agreement excepted Hawaii, the Japanese home islands, and some British possessions that were too distant to be a threat to Japan. By denying the United States naval bases in the western Pacific from which to operate, this agreement dramatically increased the effective capability of Japanese capital ships. And as in most of the agreements that were made, the United States followed the rules scrupulously while Japan violated them with impunity. Witness the lack of fortifications on Guam as compared with the Japanese military might that developed on such bases as Rota, Saipan, and Truk.

Soon after the Washington treaty limiting capital ships had been signed, Japan embarked on a large building program for cruisers and other combat auxiliaries. In order not to be outgunned in these classes of ships, Great Britain and France did the same. Because we were already reducing the number of our capital ships, these foreign building programs further reduced the relative naval strength of the United States. Had Congress wanted to appropriate funds for ships to counter these developments, it would have been prevented from doing so by the strong political influence of the pacifist movement in the United States.

Seeking to stem this growing inequity, in 1930 the United States called for a naval conference. Held in London, this conference resulted in a treaty limiting the number of cruisers, destroyers, submarines, and combat auxiliaries. The other powers would agree only to maintain the status quo, which included the additional ships of these types that they had constructed while we had refrained from ship construction; hence the treaty resulted in a further reduction in our relative naval strength.

In 1931 Japan invaded Manchuria. In 1933 it withdrew from the League of Nations, and in 1934 it abrogated the treaties—two years being required (technically) before the notice of abrogation would become effective. Even with these ominous turns of events signaling what was to come, the United States continued to embrace isolationism and rejected thoughts of rebuilding the navy.

In 1935 we called for yet another naval conference, again held in London. By this time militarists who were opposed to any arms limitation were firmly in control in Japan. They would hear only of equality with the other powers—a measure that, instead of merely guaranteeing equality, would have made the Imperial Japanese Navy vastly superior in the Pacific. When this demand was rejected, in January 1936, Japan walked out of the negotiations, and all treaty limitations on naval construction were allowed to expire as of the end of that year.

These actions should have come as no surprise. The balance of power in the Pacific had been shifting steadily in favor of Japan. Ever since the 1920s some Americans had suspected that Japan was secretly militarizing some of the mandated islands. Prior to leaving the League of Nations in 1933, Japan had closed its mandated islands in Micronesia to foreign travel. This made on-site inspection impossible and intensified suspicions that the islands were being fortified. Communications intercepts from Japanese naval training exercises in the 1930s contained references to attacks on Guam and the Philippines.

In December 1937 the Japanese further demonstrated their warlike tendencies when they sank the U.S. gunboat *Panay* in the Yangtze. The Japanese official inquiry into the sinking reported that the attack had been a mistake, although the facts that emerged refuted this claim. The attack occurred in clear weather from about six hundred yards. An American flag flew prominently from the mast; another was painted on the topside of the *Panay*. Samuel Eliot Morison described the American response thus:

> A United States Naval Court of Inquiry at Shanghai brought out unmistakable evidence that the sinking was deliberate. But the United States government was so anxious to avoid war that it accepted the "mistake" theory, together with an indemnity. . . . In a Gallup poll conducted during the second week of January 1938, 70 percent of the American voters who were interviewed and had an opinion on the subject favored a policy of complete withdrawal from China—Asiatic Fleet, Marines, missionaries, medical missionaries, and all.[2]

It was not until about 1938 that we became sufficiently alarmed about Japan's growing naval power and intentions in the Pacific to start changing our policies of isolation and arms limitation. Naval appropriations began to grow substantially, and funds became available for improving our overseas bases.

In 1938 the secretary of the navy appointed a board of five officers to investigate the need for additional naval bases, both in the United States and in its possessions. This board—called the Hepburn Board after its chairman, Rear Admiral A. J. Hepburn, USN—made firm recommendations to the secretary of the navy (who subsequently relayed them to Congress).

Regarding Guam, the *Hepburn Report* made the following observations and recommendations:

Guam is practically defenseless against attack by any first-rate power.

The island could be made secure against anything short of a major effort on the part of the probable enemy.

A strong advance base at Guam would assure practical immunity of the Philippines against hostile attack in force, would assure the most favorable conditions that could be brought about for the prosecution of naval operations in the western Pacific, and would reduce to its simplest possible terms the defense of Hawaii and the continental coast of the United States.

Guam is adapted naturally to development as a major advanced base. Detailed studies to this end have been made in the past, and plans adequate to the situation are in hand.

Such development, recommended in 1919 by the Joint Army and Navy Board, was forbidden by the Washington Treaty of 1922 that has now expired.[3]

Congress concurred in the Hepburn Board's recommendations regarding developing and improving naval bases in Alaska, Hawaii, Midway, and Wake, but nothing was done for Guam. Armchair warriors and analysts did not accept military reason as put forward by graduates of the War College, men who had devoted their lives and careers to the study of military strategy and tactics. To these civilians Guam was little more than a remote island of coconut palms inhabited by brown-skinned natives. Its future strategic value as a military outpost worth defending was discounted. Some felt that Guam was too close to some of the Japanese mandated islands to be defensible—assuming, of course, that the Japanese had developed bases there, a point that was still not agreed to in some quarters. And above all, the cost of fortifying Guam would be prohibitive. Unfortunately, many who were opposed to fortifying Guam wielded political influence in Congress.

In February 1939 a bill seeking appropriation of only $5 million— for dredging Apra Harbor, building a submarine base, and providing some additional facilities—was defeated in the House of Representatives by a vote of 205 to 168. Even at this late date some congressmen said that they were fearful of provoking or appearing to challenge Japan.

The final and perhaps overriding reason for our failure to arm Guam was that defense of the island was not included in War Plan Orange, the United States' strategic plan for the Pacific. American military planners had determined that the Philippines and Guam were indefensible against a sustained Japanese attack, and because of this, no additional money was allocated for improving their defenses. The hope was that the Philippines would be able to hold out long enough for the U.S. Pacific Fleet to fight its way across the Pacific and relieve the garrison. As described by Louis Morton in *Command Decisions,* "Actually, no one in a position of authority at that time [April 1941] believed that anything like this would happen. Informed naval opinion estimated that it would require at least two years for the Pacific Fleet to fight its way across the Pacific. . . . Army planners in early 1941 believed that at the end of six months, if not sooner, supplies would be exhausted and the garrison [on Bataan] would go down in defeat."[4] No one said how long Guam could be expected to hold out. With its lack of defenses, survival was impossible.

Had the recommendations of the Hepburn Board for developing the strategic capabilities of Guam been carried out promptly, forthcoming events in the Pacific might have been different. However, Guam was bypassed and its small garrison of unarmed military personnel abandoned to Japanese aggression.

1 ✳ Changed Career Plans

In 1939 I was ordered to duty as engineer officer of the USS *Wichita*. The *Wichita* was the flagship of Cruiser Division 7, and, more important to me, she was a new ship. My previous tours of sea duty had been aboard early S-class submarines, two elderly battleships, and a four-piper destroyer.

The *Wichita* was the navy's newest heavy cruiser, and I was responsible for installing her engineering plant, training members of the engineering department, and conducting dock trials prior to her commissioning at the Philadelphia Navy Yard in 1939. She was my ship, and I was justly proud of her engineering department and of the magnificent officers and men who made her run.

After commissioning, our first deployment was into the Caribbean on a shakedown cruise that included seemingly endless days of training out of Guantánamo Bay, Cuba, and a visit to the Dutch island of Curaçao for relaxation and to show the flag. Pro-German sentiment was strong in nearby Argentina, and the inhabitants of Curaçao were fearful that the Nazis might seek to extend their influence into the Caribbean, take over the petroleum tank farms on Curaçao, and establish a submarine base in the sheltered harbor of Willemstad. These concerns were quite real and were expressed frequently in the many small shops that bordered the main drag of Willemstad. War clouds were gathering in the Western Hemisphere, and although the United States was not at war, German submarines were reputedly operating

USS *Wichita* (*Naval Institute Collection*)

off our Atlantic coast and in the Caribbean. In response to the growing threat, President Franklin D. Roosevelt had established a neutrality patrol in the Atlantic, and the *Wichita* was assigned to that duty.

It seemed as though we were constantly steaming, and in early June 1940 we headed south again. This time it was to show the flag in support of the Brazilian government when a political crisis threatened to overthrow President Getulio Vargas. There was also some scuttlebutt that the Nazis had established a submarine base upriver in the Amazon, and that the *Wichita* was going to be ordered to "seek and destroy." This rumor was unfounded, but it provided grist for much discussion in the wardroom mess and produced consternation in the engineering department over problems inherent in the operation of small boats in shallow, weed-entangled waters.

✳ After the experience at Gallipoli, it was generally recognized that a fortified shore position could not be taken by assault from the sea. This assumption was not accepted, however, by members of the U.S. Marine Corps, who looked upon such "impossibilities" as part of their job description. During the 1930s some enterprising marines developed amphibious tactics and new types of landing craft designed to disprove the erroneous assumption. ✳

As the decade drew to a close, it became increasingly clear to our military that sooner or later we would need to land U.S. troops on for-

USS *Henderson (Naval Institute Collection)*

eign shores. With this realization, the Atlantic Fleet and FMFLant (Fleet Marine Force, Atlantic) pressed on with testing the new tactics and equipment and intensified the training of ground forces in their use.

Although the marines were well versed in amphibious operations and had received training in the new tactics as they evolved, the army was unfamiliar with shipborne operations. To assist in remedying this shortcoming, in addition to conducting the neutrality patrols, our cruiser division was to participate in interservice amphibious training, and in February 1941 we were assigned to participate in Fleet Landing Exercise No. 7 on Culebra Island, off the coast of Puerto Rico. Three marine and two army combat teams plus three marine combat companies were engaged in the exercise, which was supported by the 6- and 8-inch guns of our ships offshore.

In February, while engaged in this fleet landing exercise in the Caribbean, I received dispatch orders detaching me from the *Wichita* and directing me to proceed to San Francisco for passage aboard the navy transport *Henderson* to Guam. Although the situation in the Pacific looked threatening, concurrent travel was authorized such that my wife and son could accompany me. It was expected that the *Henderson* would sail for the Far East on or about 8 April.

Considering the imminence of war, I was not pleased with these orders. Had I been railroaded by Washington? All of my naval career had been focused on engineering and directed toward command at sea—the objective toward which all Naval Academy graduates expected to steer. Now, with the likelihood of war increasing every day, I was being ordered to an administrative billet on Guam. At a time when my specialized training and shipboard experience in engineering could come to fruition aboard a combatant ship during war, I was being ordered ashore.

I booked passage on a commercial ship from Puerto Rico to New York and traveled to Annapolis by rail—the last leg being from Baltimore on the old electric WB&A, the Washington, Baltimore, and Annapolis line, better known to generations of midshipmen and their drags as the Wobble, Bump, and Amble.

In Annapolis Don, Virginia, and I received typhoid shots at the Naval Academy dispensary, proceeded hurriedly to pack our household effects and personal belongings, and sent them on their way to meet the *Henderson* in San Francisco.

Although the detail officer might have misread the gathering war clouds, Admiral Thomas C. Hart, USN, commander-in-chief of the Asiatic Fleet, had not. Just prior to our departure from Annapolis I received a letter from the Navy Department informing me that although the families of U.S. Navy and Marine Corps personnel already serving on Guam would be allowed to remain until the end of their tour of duty, no other families would be allowed to accompany personnel to Pacific duty.

Although I agreed with Admiral Hart—and most other sensible people—that the Asiatic Station was probably going to be overrun by the Japanese, Virginia and I felt that I should not have to live out of a suitcase and with no amenities prior to whatever would occur. We decided that we would travel as a family to San Francisco, where we would attempt to divide the shipment, sending those things that I would not need on Guam back to Annapolis and letting the remainder of the shipment proceed. Knowing that we would be together as a family no further than the West Coast, we set out in mid-March on the long cross-continent drive.

✳ During our trip to California my father tried to do some of the things he would soon be unable to do from so far away. Along some of the straight stretches of road in the Midwest he let me take the wheel while advising me on how to be a good driver. One afternoon he gave an unscheduled chemistry lecture on the halogen family and continued to emphasize how important it was for me to apply myself in school. ✳

In San Francisco we checked into guest quarters at the Presidio and spent several days at the pier, where with the help of several white hats we divided our crated belongings into two piles: those that would be returned to the East Coast and those that would continue on to Guam.

Two things loaded aboard the *Henderson* were our conservatively black Chevrolet and our green Gulbransen upright piano with a hole in the back, which I had bought from the wardroom mess of the USS

Utah. Because Virginia did not drive and Don had not yet received his driver's license, it was appropriate that the car go with me. It had come equipped with a town-and-country horn. When the "town" setting was selected, the horn sounded like any automobile of that vintage. When the "country" setting was selected, however, every carabao on Guam would know I was coming.

✳ The Gulbransen piano was my father's pride and joy. I believe he even liked its horrible green color. This was before the days of "controlled" environments, and sometimes the wardroom of the *Utah* was very humid. To protect its inner workings from mildew and rust, a shipfitter decided to hang an electric light bulb inside the piano. Being a bit heavy-handed, he cut a hole through the back large enough for the entire light fixture to be passed through. Of course, this did nothing to improve the tone of the piano. Those who played it, however, were not concert pianists, and those who listened accepted the musical offerings without criticism. They could have done no better. My father's concerts would frequently open with "To a Wild Rose" and a recognizable rendition of "To a Waterfall." Then he would slide from Edward MacDowell into some Sigmund Romberg before ending with a few sing-alongs from the *Navy Song Book*. ✳

While we proceeded as best we could to sort our belongings amid the general pierside confusion, shipfitters were ominously installing machine guns and splinter shields on the *Henderson*'s weather decks. Apparently others were also aware of the deterioration of affairs throughout the Pacific.

✳ There used to be a book called *The Navy Wife*. It dealt primarily with the social customs and traditions of the service in which a Navy Wife is expected to excel, and it was pretty much on the required reading list for every bride-to-be at Annapolis. What it did not discuss, however, were the less glamorous aspects of this demanding lifestyle. My mother enjoyed a well-deserved reputation as a good Navy Wife. She had lived through countless separations, had traveled alone (more often than not) from one port to the next, had been primarily responsible for raising me, and had faced issues and made decisions by herself that in civilian life are normally made by families as a unit. The walls that separated the rooms at the Presidio were thin, and on one of our last nights together, for the first and only time in my life, I overheard my mother crying. Being faced with a separation that would almost certainly see my father killed or captured by the Japanese was above and beyond what any wife should be called upon to bear, good Navy Wife or not. ✳

Finally the time came to say farewell. Never an easy thing to do, it was made even more difficult this time by the uncertainty of when, if ever, we would be reunited. Without conversation, we drove across the Bay Bridge to Oakland and the train station. We arrived a good half-hour before train time. I wanted to be certain that Virginia and Don were well situated for the trip back across the continent to Annapolis, where they would await my return. We all tried to smile and "put on a happy face" for one another. Inside, however, we were filled with foreboding. What lay in store for us? The train pulled out, and I stood on the platform until it disappeared from sight. Then I returned to San Francisco and the *Henderson*. It would be a long tour of duty without my family. But how long, I really didn't know.

2 ✳ The Idyllic Island of Guam

In the early-morning twilight of Wednesday, 7 May, we rounded the southern end of Guam. As was my custom, I had risen early, had a cup of coffee in the wardroom, and was on deck to watch our arrival. The southern part of Guam is mountainous and appeared to rise directly out of the sea. As we approached the green-black landmass, I was aware of a reef well off our starboard side and could sense the presence of surf breaking in the distance. Proceeding partway up the western side of the island, the *Henderson* entered Apra Harbor and dropped the hook at about 0800.[1]

Going ashore immediately, I was greeted warmly by the officer whom I was relieving—the thought occurring to me at the time that he must be damned happy to be leaving this undefended island before the outbreak of war. After I had checked with the dockmaster about the offloading of my hold baggage and automobile, I was driven the five miles to Agana and to my temporary quarters outside of town. The two-lane macadam road to Agana paralleled the beach and ran through groves of coconut palms past small villages, ending at the Plaza de España in the center of town.

My first impression was that in many respects Guam looked like parts of Panama, where I had been stationed almost twenty years earlier aboard a submarine at Coco Solo. Outside of town, natives lived on small farms carved from the jungle that threatened to reclaim them, and the sight of someone driving a water buffalo along the road was

15

not uncommon. Houses were wooden, unpainted, and frequently only one story high. The appearance of Agana contrasted sharply with that of the surrounding area. In town, many houses were constructed of concrete; numerous automobiles were on the streets; and there were many small businesses and theaters.

That Wednesday afternoon the naval station was observing Rope Yarn Sunday—time allotted for people to tie up loose ends, take care of personal affairs, engage in recreation, or just be lazy. This was fortunate timing, because it allowed personnel arriving on the *Henderson* additional time before having to report to their new duty station.

The next morning I reported to the governor, Captain George J. McMillin, USN, and assumed my duties as vice governor of Guam and executive officer of the naval station. My initial thoughts on being ordered to Guam had not been happy, but by the time I arrived on station these reservations had abated somewhat, and I had convinced myself that this could be an interesting and rewarding experience for a career line officer.

I found that Guam, like Samoa and other tropical islands of the Pacific, was beautiful. Fine gray-coral beaches and reefs surrounded the island. The beaches were shaded by swaying coconut palms and luxuriant tropical growth. A temperature in the seventies and a gentle northeast trade wind welcomed my arrival. Flowering trees and shrubs abounded throughout the island, making it truly a paradise. Had my family been with me, this could have been an idyllic tour of duty.

The most imposing building in the center of Agana was Government House. It had been built in 1746 by Spanish priests and had served as the palace in Spanish times. A large plaza was in front of Government House, and in the center of this area stood our huge flagpole. Coconut palms, flamingo trees, and many other flowering shrubs bordered the plaza, their blossoms turning the area into a profusion of color. Their beauty was challenged only by the Governor's Garden behind Government House. This large garden was filled with lovely tropical plants and fruit trees of every sort. It was indescribably beautiful.

The architectural style of Government House might be described generally as tropic-colonial. The rooms had high ceilings and were separated by wide corridors. The thick stone exterior walls kept the temperature inside the building relatively constant and cool. To insure air circulation, the jalousie-covered windows were both high and wide. It did not detract in any way from the loveliness of the building, but the interior color scheme could only be described as austere. All of the walls were painted a flat white, and the wide wooden floorboards were stained a deep, dark oak.

Entrance to Government House from the plaza was through a pair of wide, dark mahogany doors that opened on to a large entrance hall. The ground floor consisted of several offices used in administering the island government. My office was in this area. It was very large, with a prominent, slowly revolving ceiling fan, and overlooked the Governor's Garden. From the entrance hall a wide, curved stairway led to the floor above. This floor included the governor's office, a large dining room, library, ballroom, and sleeping quarters for the governor and his family.

On the trip from San Francisco I had shared a stateroom on the *Henderson* with Dr. (Commander) William T. Lineberry, who was taking command of the Naval Hospital. We had enjoyed one another's company on board ship, and shortly after arriving on Guam we rented a tropical-style frame house together. Our house was located in a grove

Governor McMillin's birthday dinner at Government House on 25 November 1941. Shown left to right: Commander Giles, unidentified officer, Captain McMillin, and Dr. Lineberry. This was among the last photographs to leave Guam before its capture on 10 December 1941. *(Collection of Donald T. Giles, Jr.)*

of coconut palms, about fifty feet from the water and fronting on a lovely beach protected by a coral reef offshore. Our living and sleeping quarters were above an open ground-floor area that was used for cooking and laundry. As in all island-style houses of this type, the open breezeway under the house helped cool the living and sleeping quarters above. If the open breezeway were counted as a first floor, it could be called a two-story house.

For a modest cost we hired a cook, a maid, a part-time laundress, and a houseboy who proclaimed his given name to be Jesus but whom we chose to refer to as Sus. Social life on Guam could not be called a whirl, but we were a compatible group, and everyone did his bit. Although not gourmet-class, our cook was quite good, and we hosted a few small supper parties at our quarters, using Mrs. Lineberry's Minton china.

Considering that we were without our families, Bill Lineberry and I had as enjoyable a time as possible, and when time allowed in late afternoons we managed to get in some golf on the eighteen-hole course near the Officers Club on the bluff above Agana. We became good friends, and I used to kid him that in the Navy Medical Corps Monday and Tuesday are spent recovering from the effects of the previous weekend, Wednesday is "Ladies' Day," and Thursday and Friday are spent planning for the forthcoming weekend. Bill Lineberry's conduct did not fit this description at all. He was an outstanding and dedicated doctor. In the coming years his medical skills and dedication were proven repeatedly as with minimal resources he helped save the lives of countless fellow prisoners of war. He was also a good golfer, as our score cards would attest.

A high point in my unofficial life on Guam was an initiation into the Order of Carabao. Meetings of this group of officers were given over mainly to hijinks, and induction into their number entailed riding backwards on a carabao. Carabao are not particularly high-spirited animals, but I did approach the event with some trepidation. Inasmuch as my posterior had seldom been introduced to the back of *any* animal, this induction ceremony was probably as much of an experience for the carabao that participated as it was for me.

The most important part of U.S. Naval Station Guam was the small navy yard at Piti located several miles from Agana. It contained warehouses and repair facilities and served as home port for what we euphemistically called the Guam Fleet, which was moored at the navy yard piers. This "force" was composed of the USS *Penguin* (a minesweeper),[2] the USS *Gold Star* (a station ship), the USS *R. L. Barnes* (an oil barge), and two YP (yard patrol) boats. The *Penguin* was com-

USS *Penguin (National Archives)*

USS *Gold Star (Naval Institute Collection)*

manded by Lieutenant (later Rear Admiral) James Haviland III, USN. Jim had been a junior officer aboard the *Wichita*. It was good to see him again. The YPs, similar to subchasers used at previous times, were commanded by line chief petty officers.

The *Gold Star*, which we dubbed the *Goldie Maru,* was a freighter. She had a length of approximately 400 feet, drew 4,900 tons, and had a maximum speed of 12 knots. She spent about one-third of her time cruising between Guam, the Philippines, Japan, and China obtaining coal for the station power plant and rice and other commodities for the station and populace. A few cabins were always reserved aboard for "health cruises" by Guam-based personnel. Many of her crew were Chamorro.

Before arriving on Guam I had heard that it was unarmed. Now that I was on board and could assess the situation at firsthand, I was horrified by what *unarmed* really meant. In 1941 approximately four hundred U.S. Navy and Marine Corps personnel were stationed on Guam.[3] They included doctors, nurses, and others who were skilled in fields other than infantry tactics. The actual defense of Guam was entrusted to a contingent of 147 U.S. Marines augmented by an Insular Force Guard of about 100 Chamorro. The marine detachment, commanded by Lieutenant Colonel William K. MacNulty, USMC, consisted of 6 officers,[4] a warrant officer, and 140 enlisted marines, their barracks being in the town of Sumay on Orote Peninsula, about six or seven miles to the south of Agana. I was responsible for training the Insular Force Guard, delegating much of the actual training to Chief Boatswain's Mate Robert Bruce Lane, USN, who became my right-hand man, both during the defense of Guam and, I was soon to learn, while in prison camp.

We were armed with 15 Browning automatic rifles, 13 .30-caliber machine guns, 170 Springfield rifles (many of which were marked prominently FOR TRAINING ONLY—DO NOT FIRE), and numerous .45 Colt automatics. The *Gold Star* and *R. L. Barnes* were unarmed, and the *Penguin* and the two YPs might as well have been. The main battery of the *Penguin* was one 3-inch dual-purpose gun. Otherwise she and the two YPs were armed only with .30-caliber machine guns. With these motley forces and antiquated weapons we were to repel a well-equipped and highly trained enemy force of six thousand.

The other military facility on Guam was the Naval Hospital, staffed by nine doctors and dentists, five navy nurses, and several pharmacists and corpsmen. In addition to treating military personnel and their dependents, the Naval Hospital provided medical care to the natives. Constructed of white clapboard, the hospital had a tin roof on which a large red cross was prominently displayed. It could not have been mistaken for anything but a hospital.

My first priority after my car had been offloaded from the *Henderson* was to begin familiarizing myself with the island. It was about thirty miles long and four to eight miles wide, and although there were many dirt roads and trails that served individual farms, there was between eighty and ninety miles of paved road to be explored. I found that these roads were maintained in excellent condition by our Public Works Department.

The general configuration of the island might be likened to the shape of a sock. The southern part of the island is high and mountainous, with a range of hills along the west coast rising seven hundred to thirteen hundred feet above sea level. Numerous rivers and streams rise in these mountains and empty into the sea on the east coast. The highest single peak is Mount Lamlam, which the natives claim is the highest mountain in the world. Actually there is some truth to this claim, inasmuch as Guam is a mountaintop whose base rests over thirty-seven thousand feet below at the bottom of the Mariana Trench, one of the deepest parts of the world's oceans. The northern part of the island is a plateau that is generally about three hundred feet above sea level.

Although much produce was brought in by the station ship and by occasional navy transports, the government encouraged farming to make the island more self-supporting. This attempt must have been succeeding. During my frequent drives around the island I was impressed by the number of small farms that seemed to be flourishing, and by the variety of agricultural products that were being grown. The primary crop for export was copra, or dried coconut meat. In addition to this cash crop, farmers grew a wide variety of fruits and vegetables. The development of small island industries was also encouraged. These included the making of roof tiles, baskets, rattan furniture, woven fishnets, and shell jewelry.

Although the decision had been made not to develop our defenses, the commercial significance of Guam could not be denied. Guam was the overnight stop and refueling place for the weekly Pan American China Clipper flights. These seaplanes had been transiting the Pacific with mail, light cargo, and passengers since 1935. Flying from San Francisco to the Orient, they stopped at Honolulu, Midway, Wake, and Guam, using overnight accommodations on Guam in the PanAm Hotel at Sumay.

We looked forward to the arrival of these flights, both for the less-than-week-old mail they brought and, perhaps equally important, for the outside social contacts they permitted. Whenever a visiting dignitary or well-known passenger arrived, he or she was customarily invited to dine and spend part of the evening at Government House. Such visits were major social events on the island. The guest lists included Major General Lewis Brereton, U.S. Army Air Force, on his way to the Philippines; Mr. and Mrs. Ernest Hemingway; Henry Luce and his wife, Clare Boothe Luce; Russian statesman Maxim Litvinov; and *Life* photographer Margaret Bourke-White.

3 ✳ War Warnings

Guam, like the other Pacific islands, could have become a haven for tourists. Instead it became a military nightmare, an unprotected island surrounded by fortified Japanese bases. Standing on Mount Tenjo in southern Guam, one could make out the Japanese base on Rota, an anchor of Japanese defenses in the Pacific. Just thirty miles beyond Rota was Saipan, an island that Japan believed to be impregnable. On Guam we were literally under the guns of powerful Japanese forces. Had Guam been fortified and armed, as recommended years earlier by the Hepburn Board, the early war situation in the Pacific might have been different.

✳ As early as 1923 there were suspicions that Japan might be secretly arming its trust territories—the islands that had been mandated to it by the League of Nations. Unfortunately, using the intelligence-collection devices and techniques that were available at the time, this was difficult if not impossible to prove, and warnings of the possibility went unheeded. Some in the U.S. government might not have been concerned about Japanese intentions in the Pacific, but that group did not include the director of naval intelligence. In 1938 he directed the naval attaché in Japan to collect information regarding the possibility that Japan was militarizing the Marianas, contrary to the League of Nations mandate. Japanese activities in the far Pacific were still impossible to prove, but credence to the threat was provided by repeated roadblocks thrown up to prevent visits to the mandated islands by foreigners.

During the First World War the U.S. military began to develop an impressive capability for the collection and analysis of Communications Intelligence (COMINT). Some of this resulted in the collection of messages that, after being translated, provided the actual texts that had been transmitted by another nation. Some of the information collected was based on an analysis of the call signs of the transmitting and receiving stations, which when combined with directional data could reveal the locations of specific ships or commands. Other information was provided by traffic analysis, which revealed increases or decreases in ship movements by the volume of messages being transmitted from one location to another.

Much valuable intelligence was collected by communication intercepts of Japan's 1930 naval maneuvers. Until that time the United States was unaware of the tactics or communication techniques of the Imperial Japanese Navy. Analysis of messages collected and decrypted from these early naval maneuvers indicated that Japan's long-range war plans included the capture of Guam and the Philippines.

Some of the most indicative communication intercepts that were accomplished by the U.S. military in late 1940 identified the presence of Japanese military units on the mandated islands. Now it would be difficult for anyone to maintain that the Japanese were not a threat to peace in the Pacific. ✳

The Japanese did not like having an American outpost in the vicinity of their strongholds at Rota and Saipan, and throughout most of 1941 Japanese reconnaissance aircraft from Saipan kept us under scrutiny.

As the summer of 1941 drew on, radio and cable communications indicated a daily worsening of the international situation. This was of great concern to Governor McMillin and me. Although a reduction in the number of dependents on Guam was under way, many were still on station.[1] Actually, about half of the Americans on the island were noncombatants—families of service personnel, Americans who were married to natives, or the few Pacific Base Contractor personnel who had arrived to plan for the protection of Guam.

In the late summer Admiral Thomas C. Hart, commander-in-chief of the Asiatic Fleet, advised the governor that because the situation appeared to be worsening, he was sending all American dependents under his command back to the United States. Later in the summer the governor—whose orders placed him under the secretary of the navy, and not under Admiral Hart—did likewise, ordering the evacuation of all American families from Guam. Except for a few wives of nonmilitary personnel at the Cable Station and Pan American Airways plus a few others, the final contingent of families was shipped out on the last trip of the *Henderson* to the United States on 17 October. The only exception to the evacuation was Mrs. John Hellmers, the eight-months-pregnant wife of a chief petty officer. Under doctor's orders, she was allowed to remain until the birth of her baby. She and her newborn baby became prisoners of war with the others.

In the latter part of 1941, as they formalized their invasion plans, the Japanese intensified their reconnaissance activities. Their 18th Naval Air Unit from Saipan began regular flights, and they established a lookout post on Rota, watching for ship movements that could indicate a reinforcement of our garrison.

War clouds became progressively darker during November. On several occasions lone Japanese aircraft flew with impunity over Guam. Looking back upon what transpired, I realize that these must have been reconnaissance flights collecting information on which to base attack plans. They must have mapped and photographed the island down to the last inch.

While negotiations were being conducted between our State Department and the Japanese, we on Guam were kept apprised of the situation by Washington via our high-power radio station at Libugan. In addition to such officially provided information, we had one other source that was not generally known. By this time the navy was operating a rather complete network of communication listening posts located around the rim of the Pacific basin, one of the principal posts being on Guam. This was a labor-intensive operation in which operators manned headsets and manually copied down the messages that were intercepted. The information they collected was in Japanese and was not processed intelligence intended for our consumption. However, we did have a rudimentary translation capability, and some tidbits of the unprocessed intelligence information that was being collected did filter through to us—albeit unofficially.

In November Special Envoy Saburo Kurusu, flying back to Washington to confer with Ambassador Kichisaburo Nomura during the last negotiations, stopped on Guam for the usual overnight stay. Even though U.S. relations with Japan were strained almost to the breaking point, we extended the customary invitation to Kurusu to dine with the governor. Much to our surprise, he did not accept the invitation. This was the first time such an invitation had been refused, and it substantiated our view that war with Japan was near at hand.

During the final months of 1941 the diplomatic situation in the Pacific became more and more tenuous. Another worry: we were becoming increasingly concerned about the Japanese population on Guam. They were farmers and businessmen who had been living as respected citizens for many years and seemed to present no threat. However, some of the Japanese businessmen made frequent trips to their homeland to obtain items for sale in their stores and to negotiate agreements for the sale of our rice and products in Japan. It could have been the product of war paranoia, but these trips seemed to be occurring more frequently. Did we have an undetected fifth column in our midst?

Our war plans were specific. We would burn all classified material, destroy all equipment and supplies that could be of any possible use to the enemy, disperse the natives, and surrender. We had little or no protection. Wasn't this a horrible outlook for trained military people? We were expected not to resist, but to give up this unprotected island. We had to make sure that there were no casualties to the native population. Of course, we expected that our fleet would come and protect us.

In the very early morning of Sunday, 30 November, twelve of us gathered at the Officers Club.[2] Japan be damned—at that moment we had other pressing matters at hand. A crowd of ninety-eight thousand had gathered in Philadelphia's Municipal Stadium: the Army-Navy game was about to begin. Normally, at least a few bets could be expected. But on Guam we were all Navy, and no one could bet against the Blue and Gold. Radio reception was terrible.[3] The signal faded in and out. So drinks in hand, we gathered ever closer to the radio, trying to hear details of what was happening so very far away. Our team was sparked by All-American halfback Bill Busik, and he did not let us down. When the final gun was fired, we had prevailed. We had beaten Army, 14 to 6. This was to be the last event of our social calendar on Guam. For some, it would be their last social event ever.[4]

On 8 December 1941, all hell broke loose!

4 ✳ War Comes to Guam

Anticipating an attack by the Japanese, the USS *Penguin* and our two YP boats had been on patrol duty outside Apra Harbor for several months while negotiations were being conducted in Washington. As time passed and the situation became critical, the patrol activities and training they conducted became increasingly important.

During the latter part of 1941 I began to sense a growing uneasiness among our servants and among the local people I encountered. At first their questions were almost oblique, but as the end of the year approached, their concerns became more persistent. Bill Lineberry and I frequently interrupted discussions among our household staff about the Japanese who were on Saipan and Rota. We all knew that the Chamorro had a very effective grapevine, and I wondered sometimes if this network included islands other than our own. Could it be that they had a warning system more effective than ours? I dismissed these thoughts as paranoia.

Expecting that the ongoing negotiations with the Japanese in Washington would be unsuccessful, in early December we began to increase our readiness. All vehicle headlights were shielded by carbon paper or were painted black, leaving only a small slit in the middle to emit light as a warning to other vehicles or pedestrians. At this time we also began deploying our twelve .30-caliber machine guns. One was mounted on the hill above Agana for defense against air attack, one was given to the Insular Force Guard, one to the jail, and the remaining nine were given to the marines. Then on 6 December we initiated the first phase of our destruction plan, which included the burning of classified material and papers we did not want to fall into Japanese hands. On that evening we also increased our offshore patrol activity. On the evening of Sunday, 7 December (Guam time),[1] the *Penguin* put to sea for her dusk-to-dawn patrol off the west coast of Guam, making routine runs at steerageway speed while totally blacked out.

Monday, 8 December. At 0545 I was aroused at my quarters by an urgent telephone call. Governor McMillin had just received a warning message from Admiral Hart that Pearl Harbor had been attacked. This was a brief message, and it was too early for any assessment of the damage at Pearl Harbor to be included. I woke Bill Lineberry and told him the news. Then I dressed hurriedly and hastened to Government House, where I joined the governor and a small group of other officers. Although we had known that war was imminent, we were stunned, both because the target of the Japanese attack had not been foreseen with any accuracy, and because of the manner in which the attack had occurred. We were still fighting by gentlemanly standards and did not realize that war was no longer a gentleman's game.

Knowing that it would probably be only a few hours before part of the Japanese fleet would arrive and strike Guam, the governor and I alerted navy and Marine Corps personnel and activated our war plans immediately. The *Penguin* had just returned from her night-patrol activities and was moored to a buoy in Apra Harbor. Unable to raise her by radio, I sent a message by small boat to her commanding officer notifying him that we were at war, that we expected to be attacked, and that he should stand by to take appropriate action.[2]

Then we informed the senior civilian officials on Guam that hostilities had commenced. Because there was no civilian radio station on the island and because our mimeographed newspaper, the Guam *Eagle,* was not distributed until late in the afternoon, we could not inform the public directly.

I instructed the communications officer to burn all of the remaining classified documents and to have our coding machinery destroyed. The new fuel tanks on Cabras Island and much of our construction equipment was destroyed also, leaving only certain equipment that might be useful to us during the emergency. Even this was laced with dynamite so that it could be destroyed quickly. Finally, we ordered officials of the Bank of Guam to burn all of the paper money in their custody and to bag and deep-six all of their coinage.

As a preventive measure, Governor McMillin ordered the arrest of some Japanese nationals whose businesses could have permitted them to spy for the Japanese. This was a difficult and heart-wrenching thing to do. These people had been respected citizens on the island for many years. Under the circumstances, however, we were forced to suspect their loyalty. They were confined immediately in the concrete jail near the Plaza de España.[3]

At about 0630 the Insular Force Guard mustered at their barracks. They were armed and sent to the plaza to defend Government House and other government buildings.

Steps were taken to evacuate civilians from the more heavily populated areas to farms in the interior, where they would not be near any possible military objective. Schools were closed, and children were warned to stay close to their families.

Most of our marines took position at the butts of their rifle range near Sumay on Orote Peninsula, some seven miles south of Agana. This was to serve as their base of operations against possible enemy landings at Apra, the only port on Guam. Other marines were instructed to remain in the various small villages throughout the island to assist in village administration. Because they lived in these villages, they knew the residents and were familiar with the local terrain. These marines were our eyes and ears, serving as lookouts both prior to and during the forthcoming attack.

At about 0730 many of the telephone lines went dead. We assumed that the lines had been severed by Japanese nationals prior to their incarceration. This was extremely bad news, because our only other means of communication was a small radio station located near Government House. Because everyone had so many other duties to perform, it would not be feasible to locate where the lines had been cut. We were reduced to communicating via messengers traveling by automobile. What a way to fight a war!

The first attack on Guam came at about 0830, less than three hours after receipt of Admiral Hart's warning message. We had barely completed the preparations outlined above when a wave of nine fighter-bombers from Saipan arrived and commenced their attacks. The first attack was a low-level bombing run directed at our high-power radio station in the Libugan Hills in south-central Guam. Obviously the Japanese knew of this facility, its location having been gleaned from aerial reconnaissance or provided by Japanese nationals on Guam. The radio station was destroyed in short order—a tremendous loss, because it denied us our primary source of communications with the outside world. The USS *Penguin* had gotten up steam, and as attacking aircraft came into view, she slipped her moorings, got under way, and proceeded toward open water, where she could maneuver and better attempt to survive an attack while getting in a few licks of her own. Her crew had been planning a ship's party at Recreation Beach that evening, a party already delayed many times by their patrol activities. Now it would be delayed right off the calendar.

✳ At this time the Most Reverend Miguel Angel de Olano y Urteaga, bishop of Guam, was celebrating a high mass in the Agana cathedral. It was a high holy day, and the cathedral was crowded with worshipers. While the mass was in progress, the bishop was told that Guam was under attack. Turning to the congregation, he calmly advised them to leave the cathedral. Then he returned to the altar to complete the mass. ✳

In their first bombing runs, the Japanese concentrated on the Apra Harbor area, about six miles southwest of Agana. Targets in this area included installations on Orote Peninsula, the marine barracks at Sumay, the Piti Navy Yard, and Apra Harbor proper.

Major (later Colonel) Donald Spicer, USMC, the executive officer of our marine detachment, was heading toward the rifle butts when a dive bomber spotted him and commenced an attack. Spicer was in the open, crossing the Sumay golf course, when the bombs began to fall. As he ran, the first exploded well behind him. Hearing the second bomb whirring toward earth, Spicer hit the dirt on the number four fairway as it impacted, covering him with dirt and debris. Moments later, as the aircraft passed overhead, Spicer picked himself up and ran like mad toward the brush. The attack had lasted only a few minutes, but to Spicer it had seemed like an eternity.

✳ Major Spicer's prison notebook provides these additional remarks: "As I ran, I noticed the door to the radio shack was closed. I realized, with horror, that Corporal Anderson, the radio operator, always slept at that time, after his night's work. I started out of the brush to run the two hundred yards to him, but it was too late. Just then a bomb hit the lumber shed, ten feet from the radio shack, blowing in the side of the latter building. Later we found Anderson, unconscious on his mattress, which was half on and half off of his bunk. Whether he ever knew what hit him will never be known, for he died a few days later without regaining consciousness. One of the men in the brush near the shack said that he heard the key operating at high speed just before the bomb hit."[4] ✳

Turning from Sumay toward Apra Harbor, attacking aircraft bore in on the defenseless oil barge, the *R. L. Barnes,* and our two YPs, riddling all three vessels with shrapnel and machine-gun fire.

As the first dive bombers came screaming in from the south, the *Penguin*'s gunners opened fire. This was probably one of the strangest shoots in the annals of naval ordnance and gunnery. The *Penguin* had recently been resupplied, and her new ammunition had not been completely sorted in the magazines. Thus, when the gun-ners called for ammunition, whatever the handlers laid their hands on came up the hoist, into the breech, and out the muzzle: high-explosive shells, armor-piercing shells, star shells, some shells with tracers, some without. Two things were definitely accomplished: the *Penguin*'s gunners put a lot of steel into the air, and they got the attention of at least some of the Japanese pilots.

The firing of her 3-inch gun might not have been deadly accurate, but it did annoy the attacking Japanese such that some of their aircraft turned away from attacking Sumay and headed toward the gutsy little old minesweeper. Their first attack against the *Penguin* was aborted because of the sheer mass of shells that were exploding close to the diving planes. However, the next two attacks were more successful. By the time of the second attack, the *Penguin* had cleared the harbor entrance and was approaching Orote Point. During this attack, an aircraft managed to get through the *Penguin*'s 3-inch and machine-gun fire. This aircraft swooped in low and swept the topside with a hail of bullets. This succeeded in splitting the wooden foremast, fatally wounding the gunnery officer, Ensign Robert Gabriel White, USNR, and severely wounding several others.

The final attack was a high-altitude bombing run. Several of these bombs exploded along the port side, riddling the deck and water line with shrapnel. The *Penguin*'s war had lasted no more than half an hour, but the last bombing run had wounded her grievously. She was shipping water through shrapnel holes and was listing such that her 3-inch gun platform was no longer sufficiently stable for the gun to be fired.

Because of major damage to the vessel, particularly at the water line, the commanding officer, Lieutenant James W. Haviland III, ordered his ship to be scuttled and abandoned—a hard decision to make. During her short defiance of the Japanese the *Penguin* had succeeded in shooting down an enemy aircraft. Perhaps it was an uneven trade, a ship for an aircraft. But this was an uneven war, and any aircraft shot down meant fewer casualties to those who sought to defend the island against massive odds.

At about 0930, with the ship about one-half mile off Orote Point, all ports and watertight compartments were opened, the valves providing access through her hull were opened to the sea, and the *Penguin* was scuttled.

Both of our harbor patrol boats were also under way and were engaging enemy aircraft with their machine guns. After they had expended their ammunition, they turned north, away from Orote Point. By drawing enemy fire they provided an opportunity for the *Penguin*'s crew to abandon their sinking ship.

The *Penguin*'s motor launch was ashore when the attack occurred, and her motor whaleboat had been smashed in the skids by enemy machine-gun fire. Without any boats to use, the crew cast loose life rafts, into which they put their dead and wounded, and headed for the beach.

✳ The following anecdote was written by Lieutenant (then Signalman First Class) Reginald W. Reed, USN: "On the *Penguin* we had two mascot dogs, of doubtful ancestry. One, a large female puppy, was named Gertie. The other, named Jiggs, was half a dog high and a dog and a half long. At any rate, [L. J.] Pineault [coxswain, USN], who loved Gertie like a sister, took Gertie to a raft. Jiggs, on the other hand, jumped overboard after Magelssen [seaman first class, USN]. Jiggs was terrified and made shore under his own power, a good half mile."[5] ✳

During this brief engagement the *Penguin*'s crew had sustained the following casualties: one dead (the gunnery officer, Ensign White) and ten wounded (including the commanding officer and the executive officer, Ensign Edwin A. Wood, USNR). Of the wounded, E. M. Ratzman (seaman first class, USN) and R. E. Wilson (coxswain, USN) were the most critical. They had both been riddled by shrapnel, Ratzman in the intestines and Wilson in the lower abdomen. Miraculously, they both survived, a tribute to the surgical skill of our doctors on Guam.

About twenty-five men swam ashore, among them their commanding officer. Lieutenant Haviland's wrist had been shattered during the attack, and he swam with great difficulty, resting occasionally against the side of a raft as he made his way slowly toward the beach.

✳ After reaching the beach they faced another challenge, described here by Reed: "The cliffs were precipitous along the south side of Orote Point, making it very difficult to find any egress to the top. The volcanic rock of the cliff face cut like knives, so many had to bind their feet with life jacket material to make it at all. By slow, back-breaking, mule-hauling, the dead and wounded were hauled to the top of the cliff."[6] Not to be left behind, Jiggs and Gertie were among those helped to the top. ✳

After attacking Sumay and our naval vessels, the Japanese aircraft turned their attention on the Piti Navy Yard and Apra Harbor, where they bombed and strafed with impunity until about 1130, then headed back toward their bases to be rearmed.

Wounded were arriving at the hospital in Agana. A brave Chamorro sat quietly at a table in the emergency room, his head on his arms, his guts hanging out. Outside the hospital an American civilian, badly wounded in the back, was lying in a truck screaming for anaesthetic as the hospital corpsman fought desperately to open the narcotics safe. Like many things on Guam, its lock was overdue for replacement.

As word reached Agana of the bombing of Sumay and Piti, large numbers of people began to flee the city in panic. Pouring out of the cathedral and their homes, they began a mass exodus to the country-side. In large measure the panic was created by the arrival of refugees from the attacked areas, who brought frightening tales of the Japanese attacks: Sumay had been bombed and strafed severely and was in flames, and the hugh PanAm oil tanks were going up in smoke. And more dam-aging, there was a growing rumor that Agana would be bombed shortly. The picture was one of utmost confusion. The roads leading out of town teemed with humanity bent on escaping the Japanese onslaught. Family members got separated from one another and became hysteri-cal; confusion reigned. Suddenly, within the hour, an eerie quiet fell over the city. Agana was almost deserted.

In order to protect property from looting, we established security patrols in the deserted city, thereby further diluting our military capa-bility to repel an attack. An important housekeeping chore also inter-vened. It was noon, and hungry white hats and marines needed to be fed. Many of our mess cooks were natives who had already departed Agana for the boondocks. An informal mess was set up in an officer's quarters near the plaza, and the service club was thrown open for the use of all hands. Out of necessity, the mess had to feed in relays, and food was scanty. However meager it was, the meal was well received, and no complaints were heard.

Unfortunate and unexplainable events occur in any battle, and the attack on Guam was no exception. A case in point was the manner in which the heroes of the *Penguin* were received. After being bombed and strafed by the Japanese, evacuating ship, swimming or rafting ashore, and climbing up a sheer rock cliff to safety, many of the sur-vivors were virtually naked. Those uniforms that did remain were in terrible condition. Equally important, the survivors had lost all of their personal effects. They had not so much as a piece of soap, a razor, or a toothbrush.

Those who were practically naked were given clothing by members of the Insular Force Guard or by shore-based U.S. military personnel to tide them over until new clothing and effects could be issued.

Inexplicably, this never occurred. Although the stores-issuing room was well stocked, when members of the crew approached the native store-keeper, they were told that he was not authorized to issue them clothing, and that his only instructions were that in the case of invasion the storehouses would be destroyed. As base executive officer I accept responsibility for this gross injustice. However, some blame must be given the storekeeper, who was unable to exercise sufficient initiative even with a war closing in to cut through red tape on his own.

✳ No battle would be complete without at least some heart-wrenching stories. The following was provided by Major Spicer: "One of those unexpected things occurred during the bombing. It was of no importance but it affected me very strongly at the time.

"As I was coming out of the brush just after the first visit, a little fuzzy, light tan puppy came waddling toward me on his stubby little legs—crying piteously. I reached down to pick him up and he scrambled right up to my shoulder, put his head down against my neck and whimpered. Soon, he stopped and lay there quietly. Then, he wanted to get down but soon tired and begged to be picked up again. I held him during the next raid and then, having much to do, put him down by the storeroom. In the press of getting things organized, I forgot him. When I looked for him in the evening, he was nowhere to be found.

"Tuesday evening, when Jim Eppley [Lieutenant (Junior Grade) James Eppley (MC), USN] and I went up there again, we saw him stretched out on the pavement, in front of the storeroom, dead. He appeared not to be wounded but was probably killed by the blast of a bomb. Poor little fellow!"[7] ✳

At 1430 the aircraft returned to bomb and strafe Agana. The first bombs were wasted on several useless areas, hitting nipa houses and gardens. Later, one of the pilots flying in the vicinity of Government House must have assumed that this large house with the nearby radio towers was a command post. This was a correct assumption, because the governor maintained his post here throughout our defense.[8] Wheeling in our direction, the pilot aimed at our small radio station and dropped a string of bombs. One struck just behind the jail, and a second exploded several hundred yards from Government House. Although neither bomb hit the radio station, it sustained considerable concussion damage that put it out of commission.

Despite the bombing and strafing of the plaza area, we took no personnel casualties there, although the Governor's Gardens were chewed up and the area around the jail was damaged badly. Mrs. Takano, one of the supposed leaders of the Japanese on Guam and who was interned in the jail, cried out to be released, although at that time the concrete jail was undoubtedly the safest place on the island.

Periodically I had to leave Government House to visit other buildings, doing so at a dogtrot and trying to keep a very low profile on the "safe" side of the old Spanish-built walls surrounding the plaza. These excursions were frequently punctuated by machine-gun fire from strafing aircraft or by rock fragments thrown up by exploding bombs.

At about 1500, despite the large red cross painted conspicuously on its roof, a wing of the Naval Hospital was strafed by a low-flying single-pontoon seaplane. Fortunately, no one was hit. The tin roof deflected the bullets with a terrible din. Could this attack be explained away by the alleged poor eyesight of the Japanese? Eight years earlier another flight of Japanese aircraft had attacked and sunk the USS *Panay*—a neutral ship also prominently displaying the Stars and Stripes.

Outside Agana various naval installations continued to be bombed, and roads and villages were strafed regardless of the absence of military targets or personnel. In the town of Barrigada, about four miles to the east of Agana, an aircraft brutally strafed a group of small children. Unfortunately, they had been standing together and made an attractive target. Such a gallant foe we were facing!

Without telephones, communication with outlying areas was difficult, and reports to our command post by automobile frequently arrived late. The reports we did receive from scattered locations on the island were dismal. Our problems seemed insurmountable. We were unprotected, and the accuracy of the enemy bombing was improving.

✳ That evening, when they thought the bombing had ceased, Major Spicer and Lieutenant Eppley left cover to return to their quarters for food and clothing. Suddenly a single plane returned for some nighttime harassment. Major Spicer describes what transpired: "Each time he came over he bombed or strafed the barracks. Jim and I were in the brush, two hundred yards away. We were soaked by rain twice, and dried out again, before the guy finally went home. Then we went in and had three rum collins apiece and cooked up fried spuds and eggs, fried bread and ham and made coffee. After that we collected the rest of the food in the house, gathered up some clothes and returned [to the butts] to spend another night with the mosquitos."[9] ✳

Sometime after sunset we received a report from one of our patrols that a group of natives had landed in a canoe near Ritidian Point, at the foot of Mount Machanoa on the northern end of the island, and had disappeared into the jungle. I promptly sent a group of men to that area to search for the natives and apprehend them. After several hours of searching the difficult terrain, our search party was successful in capturing most (if not all) of these men and returned with them to Government House, where we interrogated their leader.

They were Chamorro from Saipan, he said, and the Japanese had forced them to come so that they would be on Guam ready to serve as interpreters after an invasion. He said that landings were scheduled for early on the morning of Wednesday, 10 December, and that they would occur in the vicinity of Recreation Beach and Dungca's Beach near the capital, and at other locations including Piti. He added that the Japanese were treating the people on Saipan like slaves, subjecting them to cruel exposure and beatings; there had been some deaths. Because of this, they were determined to tell us what they knew. All of the beaches that the leader had identified as potential landing sites were protected by distant coral reefs, making the details of the report suspect. Although we had no proof, we suspected these men from the beginning and made them official visitors in the island poky along with the incarcerated Japanese.

The information given by these men proved correct, although at the time we believed that it was a ruse to make us draw our marine forces away from Sumay and the harbor of Apra, where shipping could enter through openings in the coral reefs. If this supposed ruse had worked, the Japanese could have landed in the harbor unopposed and could have attacked both Sumay and the Piti Navy Yard with easy passage to Agana.

At this point we knew that it would not be long before we were captured or killed. Although we had heard that Pearl Harbor had been attacked, we did not know the extent of the damage suffered. We did know that no U.S. fleet could come to our aid. "Orphans of the storm," sacrificial lambs in the Pacific, we were helpless.

Thus the first day ended. What would tomorrow bring? Would the Japanese land? We could do little with our antiquated small arms against well-equipped and well-trained enemy troops. It was not until nightfall that we received reports from the marine patrols stationed at strategic lookout points throughout the island: no ships had been sighted. At least no landings were imminent. At sundown we had all of the city lights extinguished, giving the empty, moonlit city a ghostlike appearance. However, tensions ran too high to permit the luxury of contemplation or romanticizing.

The first night was a nightmare. There was no sleep as we assessed the damage and made plans for the coming day. The worst damage had been sustained in the harbor area, but there was very little in Agana. Reports were not encouraging. The *Penguin* had been sunk, and one of our YPs was burning. The Piti Navy Yard had sustained much bomb damage, where machine shops and warehouses of substantial construction had been demolished and the seams of the station oil barge opened, covering the harbor area with a heavy oil slick. Fuel supply dumps had been fired, barracks had been razed, housing projects and offices had been bombed and strafed.

I remained overnight in Government House, stretching out in my very rumpled linen suit on a sofa in my office. Several times during the night I was aroused with reports from one or more of the patrols concerning suspected activities in and about town, all of which were false alarms. Sleep was impossible; it was a long and restless night.

Tuesday, 9 January. At 0800 I joined the governor for coffee in his quarters, which were above my office. Before long we were joined by Lieutenant Colonel William K. MacNulty and Bill Lineberry to discuss possibilities. It was not a long discussion, because at about 0900 a flight of nine or ten fighter-bombers began a new attack. It was difficult during the two days of bombing and strafing to determine accurately how many aircraft were involved. Seldom arriving in a tight formation, they would appear, then wheel away for another run or return to their base for refueling and rearming.

Perhaps the pilots were less nervous than before, realizing now how defenseless we really were. For whatever reason, however, their bombing seemed to have become more accurate. This was true particularly in the Marine Corps area at Sumay and at the Pan American Airways compound. Because communications were difficult, damage reports were frequently unclear. There was little question, however, that the Japanese had succeeded in hitting the magazine at the marine barracks, causing much destruction in the surrounding area. And at the PanAm compound they completely destroyed what had been left by the first day's attacks. Although not confirmed, it was reported that one enemy aircraft had been downed in the Sumay area, trailing fire and smoke as it disappeared.

After attacking Sumay and the PanAm compound, they bombed and strafed Apra Harbor for about an hour before turning toward Agana and Agana Heights. Unless the attacking pilots had been ordered to turn Guam into a bloodbath, they were not well disciplined in their choice of targets. As on the previous day, they shot at almost anything that moved. Because of this, we kept out of the plaza and streets as much as possible.

Although there were few direct hits in Agana, a near-miss in the vicinity of the Catholic cathedral destroyed outbuildings, but there was little damage to the cathedral proper. One bomb did score a direct hit on Mrs. Mesa's house in back of the jail and blew the front out of the adjoining building, Underwood's store. The concussion from this bomb created havoc among the Japanese merchants who were incarcerated in the nearby jail. Their cries for release emanated from the lighting and ventilation slits in the concrete structure. Of course, they were not released. We were positive that these Japanese, who had been conducting business on the island for years, were responsible for our loss of telephonic communication. How else could the telephone wires have been so neatly cut in so many places? A little better aim on the part of the bombers would have wiped out Guam's fifth column.

While attacking targets in the center of Agana, the Japanese pilots must have spotted the Officers Club located on the bluff in back of Government House. This was a large, rambling white structure that they must have identified incorrectly as a command post. At any rate, for some time they gave their undivided attention to the clubhouse, severely damaging the structure and shooting up our "nineteenth hole."

We estimated that in their bombing runs they never flew lower than fifteen hundred feet. We assumed that this was because they wanted to keep out of range of our .30-caliber machine-gun fire, which was proving increasingly accurate. One aircraft was reported hit in the Agana area, but this was unconfirmed.

At about 1215 the planes turned away and headed back to base for rearming. We had no doubt that they would be back, but their departure provided me with an opportunity to return to my quarters outside of town, not knowing what I might find. Along the road leading from Agana there was much damage. Villages had been shot up, and there were many bomb craters along the way. However, arriving at what Bill Lineberry and I used to call "our beach," I found that our house was still pretty much intact. Then, as in a not-to-be-believed motion picture, Sus suddenly appeared.

Knowing that the end was near, I decided to make myself as presentable as possible for the inevitable. I don't know why, but I chose not to wear my uniform and instead changed into a fresh linen suit, the garb usually worn by the officers who conducted the civilian affairs of the government. Then, as if to remind myself that I was a naval officer, I put on my uniform cap. In the meantime I had instructed Sus to gather up our family flat silver and told him to bury it, pointing out an area in our nearby grove of coconut palms that I thought might be as safe as anyplace else. Then we parted company, never to meet again.

At about 1430 the Japanese returned for their second attack of the day. This time they flew first to the northern part of Guam, where they machine-gunned our lookout station at Ritidian Point. Then they flew south and strafed several scattered villages, where heavy damage and loss of life were sustained. Doubtless the Japanese bombs were being saved for more populated areas and assumed military targets.

Later that afternoon they started their third foray of the day, swooping low and strafing indiscriminately. Civilians were machine-gunned in the streets, and several passes were made against the Naval Hospital, where two wards and the hospital compound were strafed. Inasmuch as these were not bombing attacks, not much structural damage was done at the hospital complex, the attacks apparently having been intended as harassment. From the targets being struck and the nature of the weapons being used, it was apparent that many of the attacks were intended as "softening up" for a possible landing. But when? No sightings of enemy transports or combatant ships were reported to the command post.

At about 1630 the aircraft left, leaving us to lick our wounds and to contemplate what would befall us next. Rumors abounded that small units of Japanese had already landed at various locations on the island and had been hidden by the Japanese citizens before their incarceration. I felt that the circulation of such rumors was to be expected, considering the tension that prevailed and the acuteness of our situation. Mr. Shinohara[10] and Mrs. Sawada, whom we believed to be leaders of the Japanese sympathizers on Guam, had been in jail for a couple of days, and although we were certain that our loss of telephone communications was the result of their activities, we had no evidence of their involvement in any other form of espionage. Also, our patrols had found nothing suspicious up to the time the Japanese had been incarcerated. Because Guam was surrounded by many reefs, well offshore, the landing of anything other than a small boat would be difficult. Furthermore, our roving marine patrols were watching all of the possible landing spots on the island. These patrols were very alert and had reported nothing suspicious.

Later that Tuesday evening the invasion fleet appeared off Guam. By midnight the island was surrounded by Japanese naval craft. Although the *Penguin* had been sunk, we continued our offshore patrols using the one YP boat that remained. That night one of these vessels nearly collided with a Japanese warship. Being totally outgunned, the YP turned tail and returned at high speed over Luminao Reef. Whether or not she had been detected, we did not know. At that late date it would have been of little consequence. We were so totally outnumbered that there was no reason to maintain secrecy.

At 2000 the governor called me and several other senior officers to his quarters to make a damage assessment. The Japanese had destroyed our radio communications with the outside world, and many of the island telephone lines were dead. After a brief but gallant fight, the USS

Penguin had been scuttled. Japanese aircraft had laid waste to Sumay and destroyed the magazine there. We had no aircraft or antiaircraft guns to protect us, and enemy aircraft were bombing and strafing indiscriminately. An invasion fleet had arrived and was surrounding the island.

On the brighter side of the ledger, our marines were positioned and prepared to fight. When the governor mentioned surrendering after a token resistance, Lieutenant Colonel MacNulty remarked that that was contrary to the traditions of the Marine Corps. Semper fi! They were ready to fight to the last. As an adjunct force, the Insular Force Guard stood ready to demonstrate their newly acquired infantry skills; and the navy could muster a group of boatswain's mates, radiomen, and hospital corpsmen whose specialized skills did not include armed combat. We had a handful of machine guns and BARs, vintage Springfield rifles, and Colt .45s.

We could not communicate. We were outgunned, outmanned, and surrounded. Our situation was hopeless, but we stood by with courage and a determination to give our all.

5 ✳ The Japanese, Face to Face

At about 0300 on Wednesday, 10 December, members of the Insular Force Guard on beach patrol near Tamuning watched as ominous black objects approached Dungca's Beach. Materializing as a series of landing boats, the shadows drove onto the beach as soldiers leapt over their gunwales and splashed ashore. Seaman Second Class Juan Perez, a member of the beach patrol, opened fire on the lead boat and then turned with the other members of his outnumbered patrol and ran back toward Agana to spread the alarm: the invasion had commenced. At about this time flares were sighted just inland from Recreation and Dungca's beaches, and soon thereafter four hundred Japanese marines made a landing at Dungca's Beach.[1]

Simultaneously, a reinforced brigade of fifty-five hundred men slogged across the beaches at other locations along the west central coast at Apurguan,[2] Tumon, and Agat, and along the east coast at Togcha.[3] A force of about six thousand members of the crack Japanese 144th Regiment, 5th Defense Force, from Saipan was attacking our unfortified island. These troops were commanded by Colonel Masao Kususe and were part of an invasion fleet, commanded by Rear Admiral A. Goto, consisting of a heavy cruiser, four destroyers,[4] twelve transports, a seaplane tender, and a minelayer.

At 0400 word of the attack reached Governor McMillin. We immediately issued orders to carry out the remainder of our war plan: setting off the dynamite charges around all remaining useful equip-

41

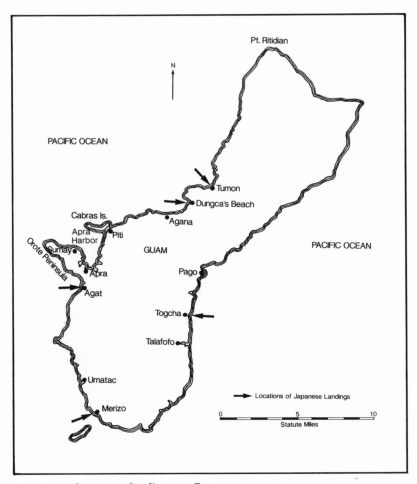

Locations of Japanese landings on Guam

ment. Before long, things began to get hot! There were no shore defenses at the landing points—or anywhere else, for that matter. Where were our defenses? There were none. No aircraft, no airfields—nothing but ancient small arms. All I had was my Colt .45. We were most poorly equipped to combat the seasoned, trained crack troops of our enemy. And after the surprise attack on Pearl Harbor, we were without hope of any relief from our fleet.

After crossing quickly through narrow bands of trees behind the beach line, the troops at Tumon and Dungca's entered a two-lane macadam road that skirted the coast in a southerly direction toward

Agana. The primary obstacle to progress was the narrow beach, which provided few staging areas for buildup of field pieces, ammunition, and support equipment. Except for a machine-gun nest the Insular Force Guard had emplaced near Apurguan, the Japanese movement toward Agana was unopposed.

Unfortunately, a group of natives fleeing Agana along this same narrow road for safe havens in the boondocks met the invading Japanese head-on. Without hesitation and without any warning, in a typically Japanese action, the invaders opened fire on the unarmed civilians, leaving the bodies of about twenty men, women, and children piled on the road beside their meager belongings. This was just one example of the wanton brutality we observed so frequently during the Japanese attacks on Guam. They did not display the slightest concern for the well-being of civilians, the wounded, or those attempting to surrender. Our contempt for the Japanese was just beginning.

Six beach patrol members on their way back to Agana from Dungca's Beach ran into an overpowering contingent of enemy troops and were killed. When their bodies were recovered later by a group of natives, it was found that they had been stripped to their underwear before being shot and bayonetted. Surrendering did not seem to be a reasonable alternative.

In Piti, along the coastal road south of Asan, an entire family was machine-gunned without warning, and a young woman was virtually cut in two, ripped by a bayonet from between her legs to her throat.

In the vicinity of Agat another group of Japanese soldiers moving north toward Agana attacked Bill Hughes, a Public Works foreman, who was driving with his wife and her sister, both natives, from their ranch in the country. Brandishing rifles with fixed bayonets, the soldiers jumped onto the running board of Hughes's car, yelling in Japanese what he assumed to be a command to stop. Having his wife and sister-in-law in the car, Hughes determined not to submit to the soldiers. Outguessing them, he gunned his engine, throwing them off the car. Unfortunately, his heroic act was insufficient. Before losing their grip on the careening vehicle, the Japanese bayonetted Hughes's wife, who was cut severely, and her sister, who died instantly. Hughes sustained a bad cut on his arm.

Approaching Agana, to the east of San Antonio and Padre Palomo, the same trigger-happy Japanese encountered more natives fleeing probable death only to meet certain death. Again the Japanese opened fire, killing some and wounding others, including the principal of the Padre Palomo school and his brother. Closer to town, near the San Antonio–San Nicolas Bridge, the "fearless" Japanese attacked a truck that was loaded with refugees, killing them all.

At about 0400 Hughes and his wife arrived at the Naval Hospital for treatment. Although hospital personnel had heard gunfire at various times, Hughes brought the first news that Japanese troops had landed. A little later Ensign Edwin A. Wood, who was a patient in the hospital after having been shot during the attack on the *Penguin,* went to the nurses' quarters and notified them that the Japanese had entered the city.

By 0500 lead elements of the attacking forces had merged, and about seven hundred members of the Japanese Special Naval Landing Force were advancing rapidly on the Plaza de España. Seaman Perez, who had opened fire on the initial boatload of Japanese as they landed at Dungca's Beach, was with a group of about one hundred Insular Force Guards and a small group of sailors and marines manning defensive positions around the palace grounds. Seeing a shadow moving stealthily across the plaza, Perez opened fire, flushing a large group of attackers from the darkness. As the Japanese ran for cover, a fierce firefight broke out.

This was our first encounter with the Japanese Special Landing Forces (sometimes called Japanese marines). These were crack troops, well-equipped and well-trained, quite businesslike in appearance but weird-looking. Their helmets were partially obscured by foliage, and their uniforms were covered with fishnet, to which more foliage was attached. Although this camouflage would later be seen frequently by our troops in the Pacific theater, to us it was a new experience. We were doubtless the first Americans to meet this special group.

We believed that our marines, sailors, and Insular Force Guard were superior to the Japanese. There was one difference, however. They were well armed; we were not. They outnumbered us ten to one, a force ratio twice what we seek in assaulting a well-armed garrison (which, of course, we were not). Furthermore, because they were not encumbered by unnecessary support, they traveled light and did not tire easily. They could subsist on rice and whatever else they could come by, living off the land. The number of Japanese soldiers who hid out on Guam for years after the war attests to their long-term ability to subsist without support.

At about 0600 gunfire was heard in the eastern San Antonio district of Agana. Anticipating that the attack had started, I ordered Chief Boatswain's Mate Robert Bruce Lane to deploy the Insular Force Guard and the marines and navy enlisted men who were attached to Government House behind the low stone wall shielding the plaza on that side, and behind upturned concrete benches around the bandstand. From these makeshift positions they prepared to repel the experienced, well-armed, and well-equipped Japanese special units. Lane also emplaced our few machine guns to guard the approaches to the plaza. Strapping on my Colt .45, I joined Lane behind the stone wall to command this pathetically equipped defense force.

In the early 1930s I had been executive officer aboard the USS *Dent*, a vintage four-piper destroyer home-ported in Coronado, California. Those were the days when midshipmen were schooled in landing-force tactics and in repelling boarders, a throwback to the days of Edward Preble and the Barbary pirates. In the *Dent* armory, just aft of the wardroom, stood a long rack of cutlasses. Foolish? Not really. Those were also the days when Chinese river pirates were known to board ships traveling up the Yangtze, and a ship steaming in Asiatic waters had to be prepared to use these ancient weapons and defend herself. That morning, as I crouched behind the low stone wall that I hoped would be between me and the attacking Japanese, I thought back to those landing-force drills in Annapolis, remembered that rack of cutlasses, and hoped that I would measure up to our defense against this special brand of pirates.

The Japanese approached rapidly from the San Antonio area through streets near the Naval Hospital. The suspense was terrible until the enemy appeared along three streets, crouching in attack formation. Upon sighting these troops at the plaza, I ordered our forces to commence firing. As the enemy rounded the corner by the church, one of our .30-caliber machine guns opened fire. Our attackers fell back momentarily. Shortly thereafter they made a second thrust, and again our fire was sufficiently accurate to stop them. Then they made a flanking movement to the right and burst into the plaza, some distance before us. Continuing to fire, we stood our ground, killing some of the enemy but suffering casualties ourselves.

The Japanese quickly established a machine-gun position in front of the church on San Ramón Avenue and wheeled field artillery pieces into position. As they zeroed in on us, their gunfire became devastating, and I knew that we had to retreat or be wiped out. Bullets were thudding into the wall behind which we crouched; others whistled overhead and impacted into the plaza to our rear. With the firepower that was being directed against us and the increasing number of Japanese troops that were approaching, continued defense of our position in the plaza appeared hopeless.

While our firefight was going on, Lieutenant Graham P. Bright, USN, a young supply officer attached to our administrative group, attempted to join us from his position in back of the Officers Club on the bluff above town. Hopping into his car, he headed toward the plaza. It was not a long drive—even less so that morning for Bright, because as he rounded the corner of the club he ran into a platoon of enemy soldiers who riddled his car with machine-gun bullets. Then they dragged him from the car and bayonetted him to death.

At about 0700, still holding on after twenty minutes of heavy firing on both sides, we received information from patrols that additional Japanese forces had landed at Pago, Talafofo, Inarajan, Merizo, and Umatac in the southern part of Guam.[5] These must have been intended as a second echelon, although one hardly seemed needed, in view of our increasingly desperate position. Then we learned that other troops were approaching from our flank and, worse yet, from our rear.

I called to the governor at his command post in Government House, and told him that I felt the jig was up and we would soon be wiped out. His reply to my assessment was that we should surrender. With what little we had to fight with, I felt that we had made a good showing. Receiving the governor's reply, I left the firing line and ran crouched over at a dogtrot to my Chevrolet, which was parked nearby. Carefully opening the door so as not to be targeted by the Japanese, I sounded three blasts on the horn, a signal recognized by anyone in the military as meaning "Secure." Hearing my signal, our men stopped firing immediately; the enemy continued to fire for a bit longer.

Soon, noting that we had ceased firing, someone from their side yelled, "Come!" Although the Japanese had not ceased firing at that point, Chief Lane and I started walking across the plaza toward the Japanese lines, the sound of shells crackling over our heads. It is a wonder that neither one of us was hit. As we approached their lines the Japanese fire stopped, and we met our foe, face to face, on the opposite side of the plaza.

Naval Academy class rings are noted for being prominently large. I was proud of having graduated from Annapolis and was particularly proud of my ring, which had a sapphire-blue stone set in its gold mounting. As Lane and I walked to meet the Japanese, I turned my ring around with its large face turned in toward my palm so that it would not be obvious and, I hoped, would not be taken from me. I wore my Naval Academy class ring this way for the entire time I was a prisoner of war, turning it around again only on the day I was repatriated.

Twenty-two thousand Chamorro, nationals of the U.S. government, had looked to us, the U.S. military on Guam, for protection of their lives and property. Much to our disgrace, we had let them down. Or had we? No, we had not. Sadly, the U.S. government had left us practically helpless. That was the shame of Guam. To this day I cannot help but think about these facts. We couldn't possibly have protected them with the inadequate means at our disposal, particularly against the large numbers of handpicked Japanese troops who were approaching us from three sides. With the meager means at our disposal, we had resisted for about twenty minutes—at which time it was evident that further resistance was futile and would result only in needless loss of life. Thirteen American officers and men and four members of the Chamorro Insular Force Guard had been killed, and thirty-eight had been wounded. Enemy losses were indeterminate.

The Japanese commander, who could not speak a word of English, placed Lane and me under a strong guard of combat-fit troops with bayonets fixed to their rifles. Fixed bayonets seemed to be customary with the Japanese while in action, and they used them frequently. We were soon to find out that the bayonet was not restricted to use against armed personnel. From the plaza Lane and I were marched to their landing site, where we were met by other forces under the command of Commander Hiromu Hayashi, Imperial Japanese Navy. Hayashi's English was as deficient as that of the other officer, and no interpreter was available at this time. The natives from Saipan who had been infiltrated to act as interpreters and whom we had jailed the night before had not yet been released from jail. Under these circumstances, a strange and strained conversation was conducted in sign language. The Japanese commander held up one finger and pointed directly at me. I shook my head and held up two fingers and pointed at myself. With an inquiring look on his face, the Japanese commander asked in sign language, "Where is your number one man?" I pointed in the direction from which we had just come, indicating that the governor was there.

With guns and bayonets still bristling and with some shoving, we were marched back under the same heavy guard to the plaza and Government House. Lane was wearing his chief petty officer's uniform, but I was still in my linen suit. Returning to the plaza, we found all of our officers and men stripped of all clothing except for their undershorts and lined up with Japanese soldiers pointing machine guns at them from positions at each end of the line of prisoners.

The Japanese asked repeatedly where our main force was deployed. Their aerial reconnaissance had located our high-power radio station and had been used effectively to identify landing beaches. Their intelligence had been grossly deficient, however, in estimating our strength.[6] They had expected to be met in force at the beaches and to have to fight their way to Agana. They had not believed that the United States would be so foolish as not to fortify Guam. Because of this error, they had allocated over five thousand well-trained troops armed with modern equipment to face our small force of ill-equipped defenders.

From the plaza Lane and I were marched into Government House, where we found the governor stripped of his linen suit, in his underwear, and under guard. We were still unable to communicate with our captors—a situation that the governor and I tried to remedy by pointing out the window to the jail and indicating in sign language that there were Japanese civilians inside. Upon obtaining this information, the Japanese commander had the jail opened and the prisoners released. Shortly thereafter Mr. Shinohara was brought to Government House to act as our interpreter during the surrender proceedings that followed.

Mr. Shinohara owned a large general-merchandise store in Agana and was one of the most prominent Japanese on the island. He had always been especially friendly to the officers, and frequently hosted colorful Japanese tea parties and sukiyaki suppers to which we were invited. Perhaps it was a lurking sixth sense, but many of us suspected him of having close connections with mainland Japan (the source of much of the merchandise that he sold in his store). We made a practice of politely refusing his frequent invitations.

Speaking through the interpreter, the governor indicated that although he was not anxious to do so, he felt that he must surrender in order to prevent additional bloodshed at the hands of such an overwhelmingly powerful force. A lengthy discussion followed regarding terms of the surrender, and Chief Yeoman L. A. Farris, the governor's writer, was sent for from the personnel who were under guard in the plaza. Thereupon, a surrender document was dictated by the Japanese and typed by Chief Farris.

This document was brought to the governor's quarters for his signature. After reading it, he was furious. He sent it back to the Japanese, declaring it unsatisfactory and insisting on the addition of an extremely important paragraph that had been agreed upon but had been omitted. This all-important paragraph stated that the civil rights of all natives on the island would be respected by the Japanese, a stipulation that they disregarded totally during their occupation of Guam. After this addition had been incorporated, the document was signed by the governor and the Japanese commander, a most difficult and disgraceful thing for the governor to have to do.

It was a sad sight to see the good old Stars and Stripes struck from the plaza flagpole and the Rising Sun flag raised in its place. Right then I felt that there were so many misguided Americans who did not respect our country's flag, a flag under which our forefathers had bled and died to keep our country free. Would they be pleased to be in our position? Thank God this was the only time I have seen our colors struck, the flag under which I was born and which I swore to serve and defend for my entire life.

✴ Ensign Leona Jackson, one of the navy nurses captured on Guam, summarized her feelings as follows: "I think the bitterest moment of my life came at sunrise when, standing in the door of the hospital library, I saw the Rising Sun ascend the flagpole where the day before the Stars and Stripes had proudly flown."[7]

Major Donald Spicer was among the many other members of the defeated garrison who shared in the overwhelming depression that morning. He was establishing a defensive position near the marine barracks in Sumay: "As I approached the position with 70 men, we got word of the surrender of the island by the Naval Governor. After destroying rifles and machine guns, we marched to the flagpole and I lowered the colors. Tears rolled down many a suntanned cheek. It was only by a great effort that I was able to steady my hand and keep the tears back."[8] ✳

After the surrender document had been signed, Mr. Shinohara informed the governor and me that we were to remain in Government House along with Chief Yeoman Farris. Because of this, we went without food and drink from early morning until late in the evening, when we were transferred to the Naval Hospital.

Although the battle had not lasted long, we had suffered numerous casualties, some occurring during the brief battle, others being the product of Japanese brutality. Four men who had taken refuge in the palace tried to escape by the rear entrance. Although they could not have planned to do so, as they exited the building they broke into two groups, taking off in slightly different directions. Both groups drew machine-gun fire. As the enemy commenced firing at them, Chief Machinist's Mate Malvern H. Smoot returned their fire with his .45, striking several Japanese as he ran alongside John Kluegel, a civilian in the Public Works Department who had also been inside the palace when the attack commenced. As they approached the plaza wall, they were cut down. Although they were probably dead, a soldier proceeded to bayonet Kluegel; one of the Japanese officers unsheathed his sword and decapitated Smoot.

The other group did not get more than a short distance from the building before they also drew machine-gun fire. Chief Yeoman J. H. Blaha fell to the ground, still alive but badly wounded, having been shot in the pelvis and back. On the other hand, Yeoman First Class Lyle W. Eads was not hit but fell to the ground and feigned death, hoping to get away during a lull in the action. At first the Japanese seemed convinced that Blaha and Eads were both dead and left them lying in the plaza. Subsequently they returned and bayonetted the already grievously wounded Blaha. Although left for dead, he managed to live, was hospitalized, and joined us subsequently as a prisoner of war in Japan.

As Blaha was being bayonetted, Eads started to rise, preferring to take his chances running than to be bayonetted as he lay, and was made prisoner. How he escaped the bayonet is left to conjecture.

After surrendering, the prisoners were herded into the plaza, where they were stripped to their underwear and searched. There could have been an understandable reason for this search—to insure that there were no concealed weapons—but the arrogant manner in which it was accomplished seemed designed more to cause us to lose face before our Japanese captors and in the eyes of the Chamorro. Of course, none of us knew Japanese, and our captors made no concessions regarding our inability to understand their orders. Feeling that a marine named Kauffman was too slow to obey, a soldier bayonetted him, ripping the sharp blade from one side of his belly to the other. Two of his buddies instinctively stepped forward and were decapitated instantly. Shortly thereafter, two Japanese soldiers dragged Kauffman's gutted body from where he had fallen and threw it onto a nearby trash heap.

❋ A similar story of brutality was provided by Quartermaster Andrew Carrillo, USN: "The Japanese formed us in a single line and ordered us to take all our clothes off. One Marine Corps enlisted man, whose name I do not know, was late in getting his underwear off and one of the Japanese, whose name I do not know or description I cannot give, stepped forward and drove a bayonet into his stomach. The Japanese troops then built a bonfire and took this Marine, who was still alive, and threw him on top of the fire and burned him to death."[9]

I am certain that there are many stories associated with the capture of Guam that should be recorded. One is certainly the unique way in which one brave sailor surrendered. At about 0300 Signalman First Class Reginald W. Reed was sent to Agana Heights to line up the water pumps and guard the pumphouse. Shortly before dawn, the water pumps stopped working and communications with Agana went dead. Realizing that Agana must either be under attack or have fallen to the Japanese, Reed secured the pumphouse and shoved off, walking back toward Agana and what he feared might be a rendezvous with death.

As he walked along, alone with his thoughts and fears, Reed encountered no one—no civilians, no soldiers, not even a sentry. Except for periodic aircraft that circled overhead, the sounds of sporadic firing in the distance, and the stirring of an old sow that crashed out of the underbrush in his direction, the island seemed at peace. Walking down the middle of the road so as not to appear surreptitious, Reed proceeded, as he wrote, "past the tubercular isolation ward, past the communication center, and to the wall of the Palace where I turned to the left and saw for the first time the flag of the Rising Sun!

"The worst had transpired. Guam had really fallen. The Japanese soldiers were all intently watching the center of interest by the flagpole. They were a weird looking lot with their fishnet-covered uniforms, foliage bedecked. Literally covered from head to toe by the camouflage of leaves and vines, they must have been indistinguishable during their early morning attack!

"I walked very deliberately, for, needless to say, I was scared almost to immobility. But somehow, mechanically I traveled the last hundred yards that surely could have been no worse than 'the last mile.' Then they spotted me, and with wild gesticulations and aiming of rifles, they sort of escorted me from a distance of twenty-five yards.

"My comrades were seated in several long rows, covered by machine guns, and I signified my intention to join the other prisoners by raising my hands as I walked along. I sat down at one end of the group, but immediately there was a commotion and I was pointed out, much to my dismay. Roughly I was jerked to my feet and, with a half dozen bayonets ready to skewer me, I tried to fathom the wants of these yellow bastards. I was truly on the spot, for I could not figure what they wanted, though I did manage an attitude of willing cooperation, should their wants sink in.

"To my great relief, an interpreter who was obviously from Saipan came to my rescue and told me to strip. Strip I did, to the skin! But that was too much, and there was more jabbering, so I partially dressed my nudity as they he-haw'd over what to me was a most serious matter. Anyway, I grinned a grimace and looked as foolish as I felt, thereby heightening their self-esteem, which is good medicine to those sawed-off, eight-year-olds-in-their-fathers'-pants runts!"[10] ✳

Not long after Reed's unorthodox surrender, personnel who had been captured at the Piti Navy Yard were marched into the plaza under guard, with the naval station beachmaster, Lieutenant Commander Oliver W. Gaines, in the lead, clad only in his undershorts and carrying a white flag.

With our dead and wounded shipmates lying nearby, we were held under heavy guard in the plaza for most of the day. There were no areas of shade, and the sun beat down incessantly, raising the temperature to an almost intolerable level. What an introduction to hell.

✳ According to Reed, "An officer of the Jap army, presumably a doctor, made a quick survey of the wounded, kicking Gwinnup [R. W. Gwinnup, electrician's mate first class, USN] in both feet, which were practically pulverized by machine-gun fire! Gwinnup didn't even mur-

mur, but grinned at the Jap. No one will ever know how hard it was for 'Windy' to force that grin."[11] ✳

In what seemed to be an additional indignity, the clock in the Catholic church tower was set back one hour to Tokyo time, to a time zone in which, we would learn, there were more than twenty-four hours in a day and no bounds to the possibility of human cruelty.

6 ✳ Aftermath of the Attack

That afternoon we were assembled and counted for the first of many times. The Japanese did this repeatedly during the time we were their "guests." The counting was done both by Chief Boatswain's Mate Robert Bruce Lane—whom I had deputized to be our official counter—and by the Japanese, and the resulting counts were different. Again we were counted, and again the results differed. No one agreed on how many of us there were. Although all hands were dead-tired, hungry, and more than slightly depressed, this counting exercise did provide us with a few smiles.

Finally a number was arrived at as being the "official" count. Then came the bad news—not that we shouldn't have expected it. We were told that should anyone attempt to escape, the rest of the prisoners would be shot. We had already witnessed examples of Japanese brutality and had little reason to doubt that they would make good on the threat. What if a mistake in the count had been made? What if some of the younger, hotheaded prisoners decided to head for the hills? The bars in the windows were wooden, and an escape might not be too difficult.

At about 1900, after the count was completed, we were moved to our quarters. During the one month (to a day) that we were held on the island, we were kept in the hospital compound, the Insular Force Guard barracks, or the cathedral and parish house. I was confined in the Naval Hospital with the hospital personnel, Governor McMillin, and some administrative personnel. These were probably the best accommodations, because they had been built to American standards and, being a hospital compound, had an adequate supply of water. The other officers and our enlisted personnel were divided between the Insular Force Guard barracks and the cathedral and parish house.

The Insular Force Guard barracks had once been the public market, located between Government House and the Public Works Building. It had a concrete floor and thick stone walls that kept it comfortably cool on even our hottest tropical afternoons. The inside dimensions of this building were roughly fifty by one hundred feet, and the prisoners slept on cots arranged on the floor.

The cathedral was a lovely old building, but there had never been any thought that it would have to house a large number of people. Under appallingly crowded conditions, prisoners slept on the pews or wherever else they could find an open space. The cathedral had only one toilet, and there were insufficient bathing facilities. There was little water, either for washing or for drinking, and what was available flowed at such low pressure that it came as a mere dribble. Even with the continual repair work of Public Works mechanic J. Fearey, the water shortage became serious.

In addition to their plumbing and water problems, those in the cathedral were on reduced rations from the beginning. They were fed one boiled potato and a thin slice of bologna twice a day. These spartan rations were served grandly, however, on Minton china looted from various quarters. Undoubtedly some had come from our house, having belonged to Bill Lineberry.

The nurses were kept in their own quarters and were allowed to eat their own food. Knowing that the Japanese would not import food and that we would soon be hungry, after a few days the nurses reduced themselves to two meals a day.

Mr. D. Encerti, the power plant foreman, was left at large for several days because he claimed that he was an Italian. This strategy did not work for long, but he was frequently released temporarily to repair machinery at the power plant and in the hospital laundry. The Japanese were unable to keep anything going.

The only Caucasian at large on the island was George Scharff, the dredge captain. Although he had tried for years to become an American citizen, Scharff was still a German national. It was obviously in his interest at this time to claim German citizenship in order to remain on Guam with his family.

While held on Guam we experienced three primary problems: inadequate food, mental and physical abuse by our captors, and uncertainty as to our future. Our four years of starvation began immediately, and we were introduced to forms of inhumanity that are difficult to describe and cannot be comprehended by anyone not schooled in them.

A standard occupation of most enlisted personnel is complaining about their chow. There is not enough (ever); it is not sufficiently varied; it is too hot or too cold. All of these complaints have been heard at one time or another by every commanding officer. However, no one who was a prisoner of the Japanese will ever complain again about food. He has already experienced the worst. While we were held on Guam—and it was no better when we reached Japan—we were served an unvarying menu of moderately warm rice gruel twice a day. Those of us who were kept in the hospital compound also had reduced rations, but they were better than the gruel handed out to the others, primarily because of the convenience of the hospital commissary. However, not knowing how long the food would last, we ate sparingly.

Prisoners were punished severely for the slightest infraction or assumed infraction. Punishment was delivered on the spot, without any thought of due process. Normally it took the form of beatings, bamboo canes being the favorite delivery instruments, although in at least one instance a marine was struck with a wide belt having a large brass buckle. This was followed by a smashing fist to the face. Other favorite instruments used to punish or subdue prisoners were the bayonet, used with alacrity, and the water hose, thrust into a prisoner's mouth to subject him to repeated near-drownings.

In a general sense, those Japanese troops who were better disciplined and were well controlled by their officers treated us with consideration. However, those who were fanatical, overbearing, and bloodthirsty made life miserable. The military discipline of the Japanese apparently paralleled their caste system. Officers were unusually hard on their subordinates, and noncoms would beat their subordinates if they erred. It was a discipline of fear, and no appeal was possible.

Although prisoners were treated severely, the natives suffered as much as we did, if not more. In the surrender document that Governor McMillin signed, he insisted on a key provision calling for protection of the rights of the natives. They were noncombatants in the truest sense of the word. The Japanese forces that occupied Guam made little effort to abide by the terms or spirit of this provision. People were harassed, their homes were looted and burned, and many were killed, usually by the ever-popular bayonet. When approaching a sentry, people were required to bow very low three or four times before being allowed to pass. Food, already in short supply, was stolen frequently from them.

Although many of the natives suffered severely, three of the Japanese citizens of Guam were rewarded handsomely. The contents of our commissary were given to Mr. Shinohara and Mr. Shimizu, who moved it to their stores for sale. Mrs. Sawada was installed with the senior Japanese officers in Government House almost like a local queen. Toward the end of our stay on Guam one of our men was called to Government House to do something for one of the Japanese officers. That evening when we debriefed him he said that Mrs. Sawada's quarters were very plush. In a corner of her living room she even had a green upright piano. The Japanese also gave Mrs. Sawada two buildings in Agana, which she turned into recreation halls and managed at considerable personal profit. Shinohara, Shimizu, and Sawada spent much of their time in meetings with the Japanese officers and were unquestionably the three most important Japanese civilians on the island. We did not know exactly what they had done to merit such special treatment, but rumors abounded.

We wondered again about the purpose of their yearly "buying trips" to Japan. It was alleged that Mr. Shimizu owned a radio that he had used to send secret messages to the Japanese prior to the attack. There had been little need for the Japanese to have help from within Guam to insure a successful assault. But the early and effective destruction of our communications and the precision with which some of the targets had been chosen made it almost certain that there had been a fifth column on Guam. And although we did not know how many people had been involved, we were certain that these three had been prominent members.

Several weeks after the surrender, prisoners from both the cathedral and the hospital compound were brought out of their areas of confinement to witness the armed might of our Japanese captors. The first such occasion was a parade through the streets of Agana. At the head of the parade, a Japanese general rode in Dr. Mack L. Gottlieb's car— a car with swank fittings and chrome, suitable for a commanding general. This was the first time we had seen this officer, who must have arrived after the landings had been accomplished. He was followed by Rear Admiral A. Goto riding in the governor's official vehicle. Although this car was adorned with the seal of Guam on its side, being a government car it was somewhat less grand and had therefore been reserved for the officer of lesser rank.

Undoubtedly the parade was intended to impress both us and the Chamorro with the superiority of the Japanese military machine. Insofar as we were concerned, this was not a difficult task. We had sampled it firsthand. But not having anything like the weapons they displayed, we could only wonder how we had stood up to them for as long as we had.

On another occasion all of the commissioned prisoners were mustered and marched off. Not knowing where we were being taken, when some of the nurses heard shooting, they assumed the worst, their fears being relieved only when we were marched back to Agana several hours later. We had been taken to witness a second demonstration of Japanese armed might on the Officers Club bluff above Agana. This demonstration included maneuvers that were intended to show off their equipment and to demonstrate their proficiency in landing-force operations and in the use of field pieces and horse-drawn equipment. Yes, along with all the other equipment, the Japanese had brought one cavalry troop and any number of horse-drawn field pieces and ammunition carriers. These hand- and horse-drawn field pieces were of a very modern type.

During this demonstration we also had an opportunity to note conditions on the bluff. Although it had not been damaged during the attack, the Officers Club—where Bill Lineberry and I had passed so many pleasant afternoons in what seemed like such a long time ago—was in complete disorder, doubtless the result of extensive partying by Japanese officers. Alongside the club, stables had been jury-rigged to house their horses.

Our captors had a passion for beds, an item of furniture not found in Japanese homes, and these were seized anywhere and everywhere they could be found. The nurses kept their five beds until the last week. Then one day they found some soldiers removing one of the beds and placing two others side by side. The soldiers then adjusted the mattresses on the two beds and indicated that three nurses would be expected to sleep there. The nurses, however, took turns sleeping on the divan in their living room.

Fearing that Japanese soldiers might steal their bicycles, Miss D. Yetter and Miss L. Christiansen had moved them from the laundry under their house up onto the porch. Here, inside the house, the bikes were not touched. But shortly before our evacuation from Guam the American nurses were moved into the native nurses' quarters, leaving their bicycles unattended. Soon thereafter they saw two Japanese soldiers riding the bikes wildly around the porches of their former home, ringing the bells and having a grand time. At least someone was enjoying the occupation.

Finally, during the first week of January, we were told that we were going to be moved from Guam to a place in the south that was much to be preferred and where we would be more comfortable. We were told that because we would be moving to the south, we would not need to bring heavy clothes. This was our first experience with Japanese veracity, and taking them at their word almost proved to be our undoing. Many who were able to contact their old servants managed to have some lightweight clothing brought from their homes, if they hadn't been plundered. A few left Guam with only the clothing in which they had been captured.

❋ Dr. H. J. Van Peenen describes the visit he made to his quarters to obtain some clothing and personal possessions: "Before our forced departure from Guam, I was allowed to visit the house from which my family had been evacuated two months before to secure clothing. I was accompanied by a Japanese guard with a loaded rifle. Since the doors of the house were locked, it was necessary to climb in through a window. This I did, and the guard handed me his rifle to hold while he grunted his short body over the sill. The situation was ludicrous but suggested no mock heroics on my part. . . .

"Once inside the house, I concentrated on what clothing I should take. We were allowed little. . . . Obviously, I should take nothing of a sentimental nature, but I did. I took a briefcase given to me by my wife when I graduated from medical school. The briefcase was to become my dearest possession."[1] ❋

When they heard that we were going to be moved from Guam, the doctors, nurses, and hospital enlisted personnel quietly managed to collect many drugs and medicines from the pharmacy. They were each allowed to bring one seabag of clothes,[2] which they interlined with medical supplies. These were relied upon extensively for many months in the Japanese prison camp and undoubtedly contributed to the saving of many lives. We knew that in Japan medical supplies were limited, and we suspected that they were not as good as those we had.

❋ Dr. Van Peenen continues his story: "The first articles to find their way into that receptacle [his briefcase] were filched drugs and small instruments. In filching, I could depend upon the intuitive and silent cooperation of that ablest of corpsmen, Keck [T. W. Keck, pharmacist's mate first class, USN]. . . . It was well that we laid in this small supply of drugs promptly. Soon the Japanese sealed up our storerooms with strips of rice paper that bore the warning, in Japanese characters, that tampering would be punished by death. And, as usual, the presence of an armed sentry emphasized a Japanese statement."[3] ❋

Our captors enjoyed American food, and what we were able to scrounge become extremely scarce. During our last few days on Guam the Japanese let us prepare our own food—why, we never knew. This permitted us to supplement what we had with other food brought in secretly by friendly natives. Because we didn't know how long our food supply would last, we cut our ration to two very light meals per day. Kindly natives gained access to us through such ruses as claiming that they had a protracted illness, or that their child was in the hospital, or that they wished to worship at the cathedral. This permitted them to bring us news, food, and clothing. If caught doing this, they were rudely slapped or beaten. Somehow the maid who had worked for Bill Lineberry and me managed to bring us a steamer trunk containing tropical clothing that had been removed from our house prior to its being ransacked.

✳ The loyal assistance of native friends is described by Major Donald Spicer: "Had it not been for the amazing loyalty of our Chamorran friends, we would have fared much worse. As long as we were there they brought us food, clothing, soap, tooth paste, cigarettes and tobacco, candy and other things. They gave a demonstration of unswerving loyalty that would be utterly incomprehensible to certain people in the United States."[4] ✳

In addition to witnessing the damage that had been sustained, during this final month on Guam we were able to count noses and bury our dead. We interred our fallen comrades with military honors in a cemetery close to the point where the Japanese had made their initial landing. Those whom we buried were:

Harry E. Anderson, corporal, USMC
William W. Bomar, Jr., private first class, USMC
Graham P. Bright, lieutenant (SC), USN
William A. Burt, private first class, USMC
R. W. Ernst, signalman first class, USN
R. G. Fraser, boatswain's mate first class, USN
S. G. Hurd, signalman third class, USN
John Kauffman, private first class, USMC
John Kluegel, civilian
F. J. O'Neil, boatswain's mate first class, USN
L. J. Pineault, coxswain, USN
J. Schweighart, gunner's mate first class, USN
Malvern H. Smoot, chief machinist's mate, USN
Robert G. White, ensign, USNR

On 9 January we were told that we would be leaving Guam the next day, and again we were told that we would be heading south, where our tropical clothing would serve. The departure date was exactly one month after our surrender.

Early on the tenth we were served an unusually hearty breakfast consisting of a piece of luncheon meat, a cold boiled potato, and a bit of coffee. Then we were formed up and counted. Bishop Olano, the American priests, the nurses, Mrs. Hellmers and her new baby,[5] and the baggage (seabags and suitcases) were loaded onto trucks and driven to the Piti Navy Yard, approximately four miles from Agana.[6] Governor McMillin and the other male prisoners walked. This hike provided us with a further opportunity to observe what damage had been done during the attack.

Several of our automobiles had been run into coconut trees and were all bashed in. Because most of the Japanese soldiers must have known how to operate a car, this damage could have resulted from their not being accustomed to the size and power of our automobiles, or from driving at high speed on the very narrow roads under the influence of too much sake. Their lack of mechanical inclination was indicated also by the number of automobiles we saw abandoned alongside the roads with their hoods up.

I never saw my 1939 Chevy but hoped that somehow it had managed to strike back on my behalf, taking at least one Japanese in the process.

The four-mile march was both difficult and sad. The Japanese seemed overly anxious to get in one more lick before we left. For a month they had weakened us with insufficient food and worn us down by torment and torture. Now they hastened us along under heavy guard in what to some seemed like a death march. It was difficult for any of us to make good the pace they demanded, and it was absolutely impossible for some. We were all poked at and jabbed by the bayonet-wielding guards, and those of us who lagged behind were singled out for special attention.

As the road approached the Piti Navy Yard, we were marched past a line of Chamorro. We believed that these people had been made to line the road in order to witness this final humiliation, a march that was intended to display us in the most degrading light. This was a miscalculation. The natives looked at us with obvious sympathy in their eyes, and we could see in their faces that they wondered what the future held for us as well as for themselves. Some cried openly, and in a few instances those who were more courageous reached out and grabbed our hands as we passed. Also, when the guards were not looking or were too far away, small packages of food and clothing were thrust into our hands.

What did the future hold for these loyal people? Under the best of circumstances they were mistreated by the Japanese. In other instances they were tortured horribly and killed. Although I had counseled against it, several Americans had escaped into the bush to hide out from the Japanese. As I had feared, friendly natives risked their lives repeatedly to feed, hide, and shelter these fugitives, many of the natives making the supreme sacrifice.

Radioman First Class George R. Tweed was the most publicized American who made his escape into the jungle, where Chamorro hid and fed him for the entire time the Japanese occupied Guam. This brought untold hardships upon the natives, several of whom were beheaded for harboring the American, and it culminated in the torture and death of a Catholic priest who refused to reveal Tweed's whereabouts. After the war Radioman Tweed was promoted and decorated by Secretary of the Navy James V. Forrestal.

Finally we arrived at the Piti Navy Yard, where we were formed up, counted again, and herded aboard an ancient lighter. Numerous ships were moored in the harbor. Most of them were rusty transports, but in their midst a beautiful passenger ship lay at anchor. This was the *Argentina Maru,* a Japanese luxury liner that traveled between the Far East and South America.[7] She had been recalled from this service for use as a troop transport and was diverted in her passage to Japan to pick us up.

After boarding the *Argentina Maru* we were taken past the luxurious first-class cabins and herded down into the hold—four decks down, deep in the bowels of the ship. (The five nurses, Mrs. Hellmers, and her infant daughter were quartered in a cabin on the second deck.) Any thoughts anyone might have enjoyed of traveling in style were thoroughly doused.

In the hold we were kept cramped on six-tier shelves, with eight men lying side by side on each shelf. There was little space between one's face and the shelf above, and there was no room to move. Perhaps worse was the total lack of ventilation and the virtual lack of sanitation in the hold. The *Argentina Maru,* as luxurious as she was, had never been intended to transport prisoners. Except for the lack of chains, we were there as galley slaves.

At sundown the ship got under way—bound, we were told, for an unnamed prison camp in the South Pacific. There was much speculation among the prisoners as to whether we would be landed in New Guinea, the Philippines, or someplace else that was under Japanese control. No one could decide which place would be better, or worse. Later that night, after we had left the harbor, buckets of slop were lowered to us on lines from the boat deck above. One of the prisoners commented, almost to himself, "At home we wouldn't even feed this to our hogs." Such were to be our meals during this luxury cruise.

There was no thought of a possible submarine threat. We traveled unescorted and did not zigzag. In not many months, however, American submarines were to drive the Japanese merchant navy from the seas. Perhaps it was fortunate that we were captured early in the war. Had we been transported to prison camp while American submarines were active, we could easily have been killed. There was no way a submarine could know that prisoners of war were being carried as cargo by one of its targets.

Several times a day small groups of prisoners were allowed on deck under guard. These visits topside allowed us to get a breath of fresh air, a tremendous relief from the impossibly crowded conditions and the stifling, rotten air in the hold.

On the second day of our journey there was no question but that the temperature was dropping. Instead of being taken to a prison camp in the southern Pacific, we were heading north. Acting on what we had been told repeatedly by the Japanese, we had brought only warm-weather clothes with us. Why had we been so misled? Had the Japanese officers on Guam not known? Or had we been lied to so that we would not be properly clothed? We were heading for Japan where, as we were to find out, the winter months can be bitter cold.

During this period of congested, uncomfortable confinement, I was approached by several enlisted men with a plan to take over the ship and turn her about toward freedom. I have to say that at first blush this was an intriguing idea. We had on board a wide assortment of line officers and petty officers of all ratings, and they would have been capable of taking over the ship after subduing the guards and ship's personnel. However, there were other things to consider before embarking on such a course of action. All markings on the valves and equipment in the engineering spaces would be in Japanese, as would those on the navigation equipment and any charts that we would require. Moreover, who was to say that the *Argentina Maru* was not being escorted by a combatant ship sailing at some distance from us, or under the observation of a following aircraft? During their infrequent visits topside some of the prisoners had thought that they saw an aircraft in the distance. Reluctantly, after considering all aspects of the matter, I decided that the plan, though tempting, was foolhardy, and that we should not pursue it.

On and on we went toward Japan, every day the weather growing colder and the air in our hold becoming more foul. The only thing that seemed to remain constant was the quality of the "food" they lowered to us twice a day.

7 ✳ Missing in Action

As a result of the initial Japanese bombing, we had been without radio communications. Without radio communications, no word about the fall of Guam reached the United States. Nothing was known at home about what had happened—no word on the loss of life, on the vicious and unwarranted nature of the Japanese attack, on destruction on the island. The catastrophe we had suffered at Pearl Harbor seemed to have eclipsed official interest in our situation. Again, Guam was being written off. Of course, on a personal level what had happened was of vital concern to us and, more important, to our families and loved ones at home. It became more and more difficult to shake off the gloom.

After I was repatriated in 1945, I learned what had transpired at home during the first months of my captivity.

On 13 December 1941, three days after the surrender, the following first information was made public:

> The Navy Department announced that it is unable to communicate with Guam either by radio or cable. The capture of the island is probable. A small force of less than 400 naval personnel and 155 marines were stationed on Guam. According to the latest reports from Guam, the island had been bombed repeatedly and Japanese troops had landed at several points on the island. . . . The above is based on reports until 9 a.m. today.[1]

Not being certain of what had happened or of what casualties had been sustained, the Navy Department declared all Americans stationed on Guam to be missing in action. Because of this, pay allotments for everyone on Guam were stopped. What a demoralizing blow to the dependents! They were uncertain as to our fate; the entire garrison had been declared missing in action; and the navy had cut off their financial support. This was a real concern to those families who were living in rental properties. Without their monthly allotment checks, they could be faced with eviction.

We had been ordered by our government to man a defenseless island outpost surrounded by enemy military bases, an assignment that could result only in our capture or death. And now that we had been captured and were on our way to an uncertain future in a prison camp, our government was exacting an additional price from our families. It was fortunate that we did not hear this devastating news. Otherwise even the most loyal among us might have been further embittered.

Virginia and Don were living with her mother, Mrs. John Basil, in Annapolis, not far from Washington, and she took up the gauntlet on behalf of the Guam dependents, making their case as best she could in the Navy Department and on Capitol Hill. Eventually, after sufficient pressure had been brought to bear from many sources, the decision was reversed and pay allotments were resumed.

On 22 January 1942 the Bureau of Navigation, now called the Bureau of Naval Personnel, sent the following letter to Virginia and to my mother (in Syracuse, New York):

From the latest report which we have received, it appears that your husband (son), Commander Donald T. Giles, United States Navy, was attached to the Naval Station, Guam, at the time of the capture by the Japanese military forces. As his name does not appear on any casualty list thus far received, it is probable that he is now a prisoner of war.

The Secretary of the Navy appreciates your anxiety and directs me to inform you that the Department of State is making every effort to obtain data regarding the location and welfare of prisoners of war. As soon as any information is received, you will be promptly notified.

In the meantime, the Bureau would appreciate being kept advised of your forwarding address and of any information you might receive concerning your husband (son). It is understood that the International Red Cross Committee has delegates who act in a liaison capacity in obtaining information concerning prisoners of war. Inquiries may be addressed to the nearest chapter of the Red Cross or to the headquarters at Washington.

When we were transferred to Japan in early January, and for some time thereafter, the International Red Cross was not prepared to address our needs. Because of this, the Japanese news media were the first to provide any information to the outside world regarding our situation. The Japanese Broadcasting Corporation and various propaganda groups were early visitors to our prison camp—the latter doing an outstanding job of publicizing our fate and the many losses suffered by the imperialistic United States. This propaganda was intended primarily for Japanese consumption.

In late January the following article, provided by the Associated Press, described the esprit de corps among the prisoners from Guam:

GUAM STAND PRAISED: FOE QUOTES GOVERNOR

Prisoner's Message Says Defense "Fought Valiantly to the Last."

Tokyo, January 17 (from Japanese broadcast by the Associated Press). Domei, official Japanese news agency, reported today, that it has interviewed Captain George McMillin, Governor of Guam, at a prison camp on Shikoku Island and quoted him as expressing the wish that President Roosevelt be informed that Guam's defenders fought valiantly to the last. Domei said its correspondent asked Captain McMillin if he had any message and was told: "I want you to tell President Roosevelt we of the American forces fought valiantly and defended our posts until the last!"

Domei said the Governor of Guam was asked if he had been confident that Guam would hold out against the Japanese and replied: "I was not. It is impossible to defend a little island like Guam with a small garrison composed of a group of marines and police against a strong attacking force."

Domei said that in answer to other questions Captain McMillin said he had not underestimated Japan's strength: that the Japanese were well equipped and prepared for their attack, and that his treatment as a prisoner at the hands of the Japanese had been satisfactory.

The Domei correspondent said Captain McMillin seemed "well and chipper" after a 2,000 mile trip to Japan aboard a warship.

The article said the reporter noticed that the American used his left hand to sign his name, and when he commented upon this was told: "I kick with the left foot, too."[2]

In February, through the cooperation of the War Ministry, the War Prisoner Bureau, and Tokyo radio personnel, a Nisei from a Tokyo radio station visited the camp with complete sound-recording equipment. He had been trained in America and spoke excellent English interspersed with American slang. He had been sent to record any messages we would have liked to have broadcast from Japan at a later date. We would be allowed to reveal our names, serial numbers, where we had been captured, and where we were interned. Naturally, nothing that reflected unfavorably upon our treatment by the Japanese would be transmitted. It was through these recordings that our voices were broadcast to the outside world, providing the first information concerning our whereabouts. As we knew would occur, the Japanese also added certain propaganda items to the recordings. However, we felt that this was an excellent way for us to get information to our government, family, and friends, who would certainly be able to sift out the interspersed propaganda.

Later that month Virginia received a letter from a Mrs. Adam Welker of San Francisco. It had been written on 4 February. Mrs. Welker wrote that she and her husband had intercepted the following shortwave-radio broadcast from Tokyo: "I am safe and well as a war prisoner on an island near southern Japan. Left Guam on January 10th; arrived here the 16th. I am safe and well. Readdress mail and save all magazines for me. Anticipate exchange of prisoners soon. Love to all, Donald."

On 18 April Mr. Welker intercepted another message from Japan. This time he was able to record the message, and he sent Virginia a copy of the recording on 17 May:

I am Donald T. Giles, commander, U.S. Navy, former aide for civil administration to the governor of Guam. I hope that this message will reach my wife and mother or may be [forwarded to] them by anyone listening in. My wife's home is on Prince George Street, Annapolis, Maryland, my mother's Woodbine Avenue, Syracuse, New York. I have been a prisoner of war in Zentsuji Prison Camp on Shikoku Island in the southern part of Japan since January 16. Treatment in prison camp is good as could be expected and could be . . . [garbled] . . . before I came to Guam will be saved for me as U.S. war news is scant here. It is hoped that the United States and Japan will soon arrange for an exchange of prisoners of war as it has been almost a year since I last saw my family. In this part of the world . . . [garbled] . . . the ability to carry out. I find that my time is up. I send all my love to my wife, son, and mother, and, with regards to all my friends in America, I say goodbye.[3]

After receiving Adam Welker's recording, Virginia and Don took it to the Navy Department, where it was listened to with interest. Virginia said there could be no doubt that it was my voice. This was the first

Map of Japan showing locations of Zentsuji and Roku Roshi prisoner-of-war camps

bit of information that had been received concerning the whereabouts of the missing garrison from Guam.

On 19 May Virginia received the following letter from the Navy Department:

> Information has just been received from official Japanese sources, via Geneva, to the effect that your husband, Commander Donald T. Giles, United States Navy, is a prisoner of war at Zentsuji, Shikoku Island, Japan. This confirms our previous letter to you indicating that he was probably a prisoner of war, as he was at the Naval Station, Guam at the time of the capture by the Japanese military forces.

A Prisoner of War Information Bureau has been established in the offices of the Provost Marshal General at the War Department to assist families in obtaining data. . . .

We share in your anxiety concerning the welfare of your husband and hope that his good health will continue. We trust that the day is not far distant when he may be returned to our country.

In addition to other information, the following announcement was received in the United States and forwarded to Virginia in Annapolis:

Dr. Fritz Paravincini, International Red Cross delegate in Tokyo, cabled Geneva on February 17 that he had received a letter dated January 25th from Captain McMillin, ex-Governor of Guam reporting the disposition of 355 war prisoners, 134 civilians, 13 Catholic priests and a Bishop removed from Guam. The Red Cross said it had received information to show how many American civilians are interned in Japan. The Japanese Government cabled the Red Cross on February 15 that for the entire duration of the present war, the Japanese Government will apply the articles of the 1929 Geneva Convention on Prisoners of War, also on non-combatants, internees of enemy countries on the condition that the belligerent countries do not submit them to physical labor against their will.

The War and Navy Departments announced that a Prisoner of War Information Bureau and an Alien Enemy Information Bureau have been established in the Office of the Provost Marshal General in the War Department to collect and disseminate information from enemy nations concerning Americans, either military or civilian status, who have been captured or interned by the enemy.

As might be expected, family members of the prisoners communicated with one another extensively, exchanging news items and newspaper clippings, many of which seem to have been generated by the press on the basis of the little information actually available. Later, when we were permitted to write infrequently, an active information-sharing network came into being among our dependents.

In addition to these sources of information, Virginia was touched deeply by the many letters from past acquaintances and thoughtful strangers who wanted to add what words of support they could. One such instance will always be remembered. In the late 1920s I was a young officer attached to the USS *Utah,* a Norfolk-based battleship. Like many of the ships, the *Utah* ran boats to a small landing in Stockley Gardens, an attractive residential area of Norfolk. Every afternoon young children would play there, and there was always a lady in attendance, probably paid a small salary by local residents or by the city of Norfolk. Each afternoon Virginia and Don would wait there for me, and she developed a passing acquaintance with this lady. Now, in 1942, among the letters of support Virginia received was one signed by someone who identified herself simply as "The Park Lady."

8 ✳ Prisoners of War

Early on the morning of 15 January, the fifth day after we had left Guam, the *Argentina Maru* arrived in the Inland Sea, the large body of water that separates the main Japanese home island of Honshu from the island of Shikoku. At 0530 breakfast was lowered to us: two slices of bread per man. Several hours later we anchored off Tadotsu, a port on the northwest coast of Shikoku. Because Tadotsu did not have docking facilities for a ship of our size, the *Argentina Maru* had to anchor out. To unload 420 prisoners of war from a ship at anchor would present any dockmaster with a bit of a problem, and the Japanese had not coordinated their plans for our arrival. Transportation from the ship to Tadotsu had not been arranged, and some scurrying around was required to locate a lighter in which to ferry us ashore.

While this was taking place we were kept below, where an additional burden was levied upon us. With the ship being at anchor, the boilers had been secured. There was no heat, and the hatch covers had been removed. Having come so recently from a warm climate, we thought we would freeze. There must have been a real shortage of boats in Tadotsu, because as the sun set and the temperature in our foul-smelling hole became colder, we were still aboard the *Argentina Maru*.

Although our hold was almost like solitary confinement, we did not lack for sources of rumor. Much to our dismay, we heard that the dockmaster was proposing that we remain aboard ship until the following morning. This ran counter to the desires of the local authorities in

70

M/S *Argentina Maru,* the Japanese passenger ship diverted to transport prisoners from Guam to Japan. *(Steamship Historical Society Collection, University of Baltimore Library)*

Tadotsu, who knew that it would be less complicated to move a large number of prisoners through town after dark. Siding with the local authorities, the captain of the *Argentina Maru* was not anxious to delay offloading us until the following day. He was less than overjoyed to be carrying a cargo of prisoners in his hold and wanted very much to be rid of us. As if to emphasize his desire, he had us hustled up on deck at around 1900.

It was bitter cold. A light snow was falling, and there was no place on deck where we could find protection from the strong offshore wind that drove its icy fingers through our scant tropical clothing. We huddled together shivering, like pawns in a game of will between competing authorities.

At about 2000 a small wooden coastal trawler with a one-lung engine and an open hold came alongside. Many such vessels ply the coastal waters of Japan, and though disreputable looking, they are quite seaworthy. A gangplank was laid across to the top of the trawler's pilothouse for the nurses, Mrs. Hellmers, and our sick and wounded. The rest of us shinnied down several greasy lines. With so many prisoners crowded together on deck, the vessel was not as stable as we would have liked it to be, and we shared a few terrifying moments as we cleared the side of the *Argentina Maru* while the wind and tide threatened to capsize us.

We placed the nurses, Mrs. Hellmers with her two-month-old baby, and our wounded in the lee of the pilothouse, a very poor shelter. The rest of us stood or sat on the badly crowded deck, huddled together to protect ourselves from the cold wind and to share some human warmth.

Our teeth were chattering so much that none of us could speak. The enlisted men, many of whom were wearing only shorts, suffered acutely during the ride to shore and during the night that followed. This was indeed a different climate from what we had been told to expect. What a heartless deception!

When we docked at Tadotsu a small group of newsmen were waiting to record our arrival. We were hastened ashore by a platoon of soldiers armed with the fixed bayonets to which we were becoming so accustomed. There was much yelling that none of us understood and more than a little jostling as we were lined up on the snow-covered pier to be counted. Then we were herded into the building, where we were each given a cup of hot water, a frozen piece of bread, and an orange. The oranges were quickly grabbed from our hands after the newsmen departed to meet their deadlines. Although we never saw the newspapers, we were certain that they highlighted the Japanese kindness of giving us fruit.

At about 2200 we were marched up the street a few blocks and crowded into trolley cars for transportation to our new home, the Zentsuji War Prisoners Camp.[1] The town of Zentsuji is only about five miles to the southeast of Tadotsu, but it took half an hour for us to make the trip by rail. Along the way, although it was dark outside, I could see many small villages. The small villages of rural Japan have a certain charm of their own, a charm I found to be intensified by the falling snow. They appeared so serene, so much in contrast to the treatment we had been receiving. Could the occupants of these small, rough wooden houses know what was transpiring outside? I thought not. I hoped not!

Just before midnight the train stopped with a screeching of worn brake shoes, and we were aroused roughly by curt Japanese guards shoving their way through the train. After piling out of the cars onto a small railroad platform, we were formed up, counted, and herded toward the camp a few miles away, at the eastern edge of town.

As we found out later on, Zentsuji was a market town with a population of about twenty-five thousand. It was situated on a plain, just to the west of the Kanakura Gawa and about five miles from where that river enters the Inland Sea near Tadotsu. Osa Yama, a small mountain rising to a height of two thousand feet, lay about two miles to the south of town.

The camp occupied an area of about five acres surrounded by a high board fence topped with barbed wire. There was only one gate into the camp, and it was well guarded at all times. Somehow the barbed wire

Osa Yama seen through torii at civilian shrine *(Courtesy Mrs. Nancy Cross)*

and the guarded gate seemed ludicrous. It would have been impossible for an occidental prisoner to escape into a society in which he would have stood out dramatically and in which he could not speak, read, or understand the language.

After entering the camp we were directed to several two-story barrack-style wooden buildings, which were to be our home away from home. I was shoved into the building occupied by senior officers, several to a room. The rest of the prisoners were kept in the other barracks under extremely crowded and uncomfortable conditions. An average of fourteen prisoners filled each of the rooms—rooms that were adequate for no more than about eight.

One of my roommates was Lieutenant Commander Orel A. "Skipper" Pierson, USNR. Skipper was a senior captain with the American President Lines. He had been master of the SS *President Harrison* and had been en route to Chinwangtao, China, to evacuate U.S. Marines from Peking when the war started. When attacked by the Japanese, rather than allow his ship to be captured and used by the enemy, Skipper put on more speed, turned smartly toward the beach, and ran her aground on an island at the mouth of the Yangtze River. Another occupant of these senior officers' rooms was Lieutenant Colonel R. R.

"Robin" Petrie, Royal Army. Robin and I became fast friends. Our friendship continued after repatriation and included visits to one another's homes in Annapolis and on the Scottish moors, where he owned a small castle.

Each room measured about twenty feet square and had two transverse shelves mounted eighteen inches above the floor. These served as sleeping platforms on which eight prisoners were expected to stretch out and attempt to sleep, with only a thin tatami mat as a mattress. The hard boards of these sleeping shelves became a great deal harder as the months passed, our body padding becoming thinner and thinner and our bones commencing to protrude. We were also provided with small, hard, cylindrically shaped Japanese-style pillows filled with straw or rice husks. The only other furnishings were a mess table and two benches located in a clear area in the center of each room. Such crowded conditions were not conducive to harmonious relations with bunk- or camp-mates. Sleeping would have been easier with only six men to a shelf. With eight, each man had only about twenty-four inches of space.

Shortly after arriving in the barracks we were given bowls of hot, albeit tasteless, daikon soup—our first food in almost twenty hours. For those who have not lived in the Orient, daikon is a type of Japanese radish that grows to a length of about two feet and a diameter of something like three inches. Whether the giant size attained by daikon is due to some strange property of the species, to the fact that it is grown in more or less pure night soil, or to both, I was never certain. However, daikon soup was made by boiling this giant radish in water—cooking off some of the night soil in the process, one hoped. The result was a thin and tasteless soup, in each bowl of which we were treated to three or four small slices of radish.

I believe that if all of the prisoners who were at Zentsuji could be polled as to what they remember most about their introduction to Japan, they would agree that it was the cold. Coming from a tropical climate and having only tropical uniforms, we suffered horribly. We arrived in mid-January, and words cannot describe how desperately cold we were. In fairness to the Japanese, I must say that no Japanese home had central heating. Indeed, by our standards they had no heating at all. However, we were not accustomed to this environment and found our barracks to be just a few degrees warmer than the outside. They were "well ventilated," and with an outside temperature in the low teens, we almost froze.

In Japanese style, our rooms were heated by hibachis. These braziers were modest-sized ceramic pots in the bottom of which a few pieces of smoldering charcoal were placed to "heat" the room. It became generally accepted practice for a few prisoners at a time to get as close as a few feet from the hibachi, alternately exposing their rear ends and then their torsos to the charcoal. Unfortunately, while giving off what little heat it did, the charcoal also emitted fumes that gave severe headaches to many of the prisoners.

After many protests, additional hibachis were supplied, one more for each room. Of course, it was ridiculous to try to use hibachis to heat large barrack-type rooms of some eight thousand cubic feet of drafty space. Ludicrously, a bucket of water was placed in each room, to extinguish fires. These told us how cold it really was, when the water in the buckets froze into blocks of ice. The few hibachis we had couldn't warm a flea, much less start a fire. Although we had few hibachis, we did have a goodly supply of bedbugs and lice. We wore our overcoats all the time, even in bed. On the day after our arrival we had been issued thin, working topcoats, which we wore nearly twenty-four hours a day, and khaki-colored ersatz blankets. I say ersatz because there was no sign of any wool in them. They consisted of cotton netting that had been impregnated with bits of paper. So at nighttime, still wearing our overcoats, we would roll ourselves up in these paper-filled blankets and try to retain all the body heat we could. If you could get close to the hibachi, you could get a little warm, either on one end or the other, depending upon how you were facing.

We were appalled at the lack of sanitation. The latrines were open troughs and concrete pits that were sometimes emptied while we were eating, a few feet away. The odor was terrible, and flies abounded.

From the start, our nurses posed a problem, both for us and for the Japanese. In Japan a woman occupies a subservient position, and neither the officers who administered the camp nor the enlisted guards could understand our occidental regard for women. The nurses were typical American girls, and they were shocked on the night of our arrival when the Japanese ordered them to bunk with the men. The Japanese were probably shocked also when several of us interceded quickly in the nurses' behalf, making it abundantly clear that these arrangements did not jibe with our sense of propriety. After a short and heated discussion the Japanese relented, assigning the nurses a large room of their own that was separated from the rest of the floor by a swinging door. Before too long we posted a watch to insure privacy for the nurses and to protect them from some of the Japanese sentries, who seemed determined to "inspect" the nurses' quarters.

The unpleasantness continued over the next few days when we demanded a wood-burning stove for the nurses instead of the single hibachi that had been supplied to their room. After much arguing with the Japanese officers—and receiving numerous face slappings as a result—we were able to get a pot-bellied stove for the nurses, which proved better for them. It must be remembered that they had only white tropical uniforms to wear.

A few days after arriving at Zentsuji, our ragged bunch was assembled in company formation along the road adjacent to our barracks. Then the camp commander strutted out and read the following speech, copies of which were given to us to keep so that we could reread it from time to time:

I am Major General Mizuhara, Superintendent of the Zentsuji War Prisoners Camp. Receiving you American Marines here, I should like to give some instructions to you all.

You were faithful to your country; you fought bravely; and you were taken captive, unfortunately. As a warrior belonging to the Imperial Army, I could not help expressing the profoundest sympathy and respect towards you. I hope you will consider how this Greater East Asia War happened. To preserve the peace of the Pacific had always been the guiding principle of Japan's foreign policy, and the Japanese government conducted patiently and prudently for eight long months diplomatic negotiations with the United States, endeavoring toward a peaceful settlement, while America and Britain increased military preparations on all sides of the Japanese Empire to challenge us. The very existence of our nation being in danger, we took up resolutely with a unity of will strong as iron under our Sovereign to eliminate the sources of evil in East Asia. The rise or fall of our Empire that has a glorious history of 3,000 years and the progress or decline of East Asia depend upon the present war. Firm and unshakable is our National resolve that we should crush our enemy, the United States of America and British Empire.

Heaven is always on the side of justice. Within three days after the War Declaration our Navy annihilated both the American Pacific Fleet and the British Far Eastern Fleet. Within one month, our army captured Hong Kong and the Philippine Islands; and now the greatest part of the British Malaya have already been occupied by our army. Singapore being on the verge of capitulation and the Dutch East Indies too, having been suffering several surprise attacks by our landing forces since the 11th of the month. In the Pacific arena there is left not a single battleship belonging to allied powers. Above our land there has appeared not a single aircraft belonging to them since the outbreak of the war, their air forces having been entirely crushed elsewhere. Who can doubt this is the most brilliant success that has been recorded in the world history of war?

About the significance of the present war, I hope you will reconsider deeply with clairvoyant calmness of mind that you must have acquired after the life and death struggle.

What I would like to explain [are] some principles as to how we shall treat you and how you should behave yourselves:

1. Though treating you strictly in accordance with the regulations of our army we will make every effort to maintain your honor of being warriors and your persons shall be fully under fair protection.

2. You should behave yourselves strictly in accordance with the discipline of the Japanese Imperial Army. Otherwise you will be severely punished according to Martial Law.

3. As far as Japan is concerned, you must do away with the false superiority complex idea that you seem to have been entertaining towards the Asiatic peoples. You should obey me and other officers of the Japanese Army.

4. Prejudice against labor and grumbling over food, clothing and housing are strictly prohibited. Because we are now launching death-defying attacks on the Anglo-American military preparations in East Asia, all the nation with a unity of will, strong as iron. There is not a single man or woman who is idling about in this country; everyone is working as hard as possible in order to attain the aim of the present campaign. Therefore you must regard it as natural that you should not be allowed to be loose and reckless in your living. You ought to work as hard as the people of this country do.

5. Don't be demoralized and do take good care of yourselves. As long as the war continues, your present mode of living will remain as it is. In order to endure this mode of living you should encourage each other in avoiding demoralization and taking good care of yourselves. Don't fail to hold the hope that peace will be recovered in the future and you will be allowed to return to your homes. I have ordered our medical officers to offer enough medical treatments to you in case you should be taken ill.

6. Among you officers and men of the American Marines you must attain discipline. Be obedient to your seniors; be graceful to your juniors. None of you must bring disgrace upon the American Navy's glory.

7. If you should have any troubles in your personal affairs don't refrain from telling our officers of them.

With the deepest sympathy with you as captives, I and our officers will be pleased to be consulted with and will make every effort to alleviate your pain. Trust me and our officers.

Closing my instructions, I advise you all to study the Japanese language. I wish you to master it in the degree that you will not feel much difficulty in understanding instructions and I hope you will be able to establish friendly relations between Japan and America when peace is restored in the future.

During our years in prison camp we heard the good general's advice "Take care of yourselves," or the equally ludicrous "Take care of your health," so often that it was disgusting.

The Zentsuji POW camp was the first such camp established in Japan. It was administered by Japanese army reserve personnel under the command of Major General Mizuhara, who had given us the stirring address quoted above and was rarely seen thereafter. In his absence, administration was handled by a reserve captain named Yuhei Hosotani, who in civilian life had worked in a bank. There were also three other officers: a Lieutenant Nakajima, whom we referred to as Sake Pete; Dr. Saito, a lieutenant aptly dubbed Dr. Sade; and a supply officer. All contacts pertaining to the running of the camp were made by me or by two others among the senior officers.

That ours was the first POW camp in Japan, and that it was administered by reserve personnel, worked to our favor. Early on we stood firm on our rights under the Geneva Convention, and to our surprise, at least some of those rights were respected. From what information we could obtain, it appeared that prisoners at other camps that had been established soon after ours were treated much more cruelly than we at Zentsuji. I don't mean by this that life at the Zentsuji camp was a bed of roses. We starved like the rest, and we were treated brutally from time to time. After their repatriation several of my fellow prisoners bore scars on their bodies to attest to the harsh treatment they had received. Some died in the camp, and many more died soon after their return.

Because few of us had any degree of fluency in the language, we persuaded Captain Hosotani to provide an English-speaking Japanese as an interpreter. This was a tremendous help in our getting settled, in becoming accustomed to their customs and procedures, and in conducting our day-to-day business with the camp authorities. Our interpreter was named Asabuki. He had been educated at Cambridge and could speak almost perfect English. He came, we heard, from the aristocracy of Japan and was quite courteous to the prisoners. One could not say as much for the other interpreters assigned to the camp from time to time.

✻ Major Joseph D. Kwiatkowski, an army officer captured in the Philippines and interned at Zentsuji, provided the following information regarding one of the interpreters: "Prisoners were subjected to severe mass punishment, mostly at the request and insistence of one Kobiashi, a Japanese civilian interpreter. If, for example, one prisoner was late for formation, all of the prisoners were required to stand at attention for 1 hour and often in cold inclement weather. In addition, Kobiashi called us pigs, sinister minded people and hurled other profane epithets at us. He also told us we were weak from practicing masturbation. He would enter our barracks quite suddenly and if he did not care for the way one of the men was standing, he would kick them and beat them with his fist. All the other prisoners were also forced to stand at attention for other violations of regulations by any one American prisoner—such as smoking where smoking was not permitted."[2] ✳

After several weeks we were able to organize ourselves somewhat. Without organization it would have been difficult, if not impossible, to maintain discipline, and morale would have suffered dramatically. An officer or enlisted man was placed in charge of each room in the barracks, and senior petty officers were assigned specific responsibilities within the camp.

I assigned Chief Boatswain's Mate Robert Bruce Lane to assist me in supervising the prisoners and to help straighten out problems that arose (periodically) among the prisoners themselves and (frequently) between the prisoners and the Japanese camp authorities. Lane had served directly under my command during the attack on Guam and had conducted himself gallantly while he and I were under fire. In this new assignment in prison camp Lane served again as my right-hand man and did a commendable job. Unfortunately, some of the enlisted men felt that he catered to the Japanese and tended to wave his authority about the camp. For one reason or another that I could never sort out, many of those who were critical of Lane had also disliked him on Guam.

Chief Boatswain's Mate R. W. O'Brien was placed in charge of the galley (under a Japanese mess sergeant, of course). Because there was never enough food, and because of the questionable quality of the ingredients, O'Brien had a thankless job that could have earned him more than his share of gripes. However, as I will detail subsequently, O'Brien did indeed feed the multitude with a little bread (or rice, in our case) and just a few fish (or bits of seaweed).

Chief Boatswain's Mate Homer L. Townsend was in charge of buildings and grounds, and he promptly set about alleviating many of the unsanitary conditions that abounded in the camp.

Chief Boatswain's Mates P. E. Sanders and W. H. Fisher were responsible for organizing working parties, of which three or four were always "working for the glory of Nippon." Sanders and Fisher were also responsible for organizing cleanup details, the most pressing use of which was to dress up the camp prior to the arrival of Japanese officials, propaganda teams, or Red Cross inspectors.

Zentsuji had been singled out by the Japanese for use in publicizing their "fair treatment" of prisoners of war, and because of this, many still and moving pictures of the camp and its occupants were released by the Japanese for international consumption. Naturally, these were accompanied by captions or text that described how well we were being treated. Such a vacation spot we were in! Some of this good-treatment news was seen in the United States, having been provided by the Japanese to the International Red Cross.

Prior to visits by propaganda teams or Red Cross officials, we were worked extremely hard to make what was actually a lousy camp appear presentable. As the visitor arrived, we were lined up on the road alongside the barracks and inspected.

One of these early visitors was Fritz Paravincini, a Swiss representative of the International Red Cross. His report described us as being well cared for and in good spirits. The report also included references to how efficiently our barracks were heated. As it turned out, Paravincini was married to a Japanese. I wonder if the objectivity of his report was ever questioned outside of Japan. Regardless of objectivity, we never had an opportunity to talk with him and tell him our story.

Prisoners at Zentsuji being inspected by Japanese officials. Commander Giles is in front of prisoners, wearing cap and overcoat. *(Courtesy Mrs. Nancy Cross)*

On 15 January our first new prisoners began to arrive, commencing with Radioman First Class Arthur H. Griffith, USN, who had been captured at the American Consulate in Tsingtao, China, and H. C. R. Fulford-Williams, the governor of Butaritari.[3] They both rated diplomatic immunity, a nicety the Japanese were not anxious to recognize. Then on 29 January there arrived thirteen prisoners who had been captured on Wake. Until this time we had no idea of what had happened there, and these men provided us with another unfortunate data point on how the war in the Pacific was going.

Those of us who had hoped that the war would soon be over were beginning to reconsider their position. It was going to be a long haul.

9 ✳ Our Early Months in Camp

The Japanese must have worked hard thinking of ways to make us more miserable. They punished us for anything at all, without rhyme or reason. During our first week at Zentsuji they used one of our officers to demonstrate what we might expect as retribution for an infraction of regulations. They made him remove his shirt, tied his hands, and ordered him to kneel. Then a soldier beat him around the head with a bamboo pole and slapped his bare back with the bottom of a rubber-soled tabi until his back was raw and bleeding. As the first blows began to fall, several of the men surged forward in outrage. They were promptly restrained by soldiers and thrown into the brig to think about the error of their ways.

✳ Major Donald Spicer reported that "the worst treatment was given to people who were put into the brig. They were deprived of all liquids (on one occasion four enlisted men were given nothing to drink for 60 hours), their rice ration was cut in half, and salt was added to it—the only time rice was ever salted."[1] ✳

If anyone broke a dish, he was required to write a letter to the Japanese authorities giving a full account of the circumstances and begging forgiveness. Then he had to stand at attention, holding the broken pieces at arm's length, for an hour or two—in 12-degree weather, and without coat or gloves—before receiving a replacement from the supply office. Of course, as time passed and we became progressively weaker, we were unable to stand at attention for very long before our knees would buckle and we would collapse. Then it was to the brig for further instruction.

✳ None of the punishment was funny, but there were some humorous aspects. Major Spicer related the following episode to the Oakland *Tribune*. Spicer was unable to understand some rapid-fire orders given in Japanese by a "little squirt of a Jap sergeant" who proceeded to slap him around a bit. "So twice, the first time in the barracks, I stood and took it while the Jap soldier leaped up to slap my face. After knocking me about a bit in the barracks," Spicer related, "he took me over to the officers' headquarters where he apparently complained that I was not obeying his orders. Orders that I couldn't understand. And the little guy worked himself up into another frenzy about it and started in again. But I stood up straight and about all he could reach was my neck—so my face didn't suffer much. I had the greatest difficulty to keep from laughing."[2] ✳

In late February I started a diary to record my experiences and the many atrocities we suffered in Japan. I knew that others were doing this also and hoped that someday we would be able to combine what we had individually recorded into one comprehensive indictment of the Japanese. To keep such a record was difficult. I was always afraid that a guard would find my diary and punish me severely. Others shared my fears, and at least one who also kept a diary falsified some entries, changing them after repatriation.[3] In spite of the fear of being found out, however, I knew a record had to be kept. I wrote short entries every week and kept the diary sewn into the lining of my clothes.

Surviving the bitter cold was our primary concern when we first arrived. In the months that followed, avoiding starvation was certainly not far behind.

Because of the disorganization of the Japanese authorities, on our first full day in camp we received no food. By the following morning, however, the enlisted men I had assigned to the galley detail had obtained some rice and made a rice gruel for all hands. I can't say it was good, but it was warm and sort of took the edge off. These men knew little about cooking, even less when using Japanese equipment and methods. One can be certain, however, that when there is anything unusual to be done, our enlisted men can do it.

As time passed we were provided with three "meals" a day. Breakfast usually consisted of hot green tea and a small portion of *lugao,* a watery gruel made from rice. Other meals consisted primarily of rice, pick-led or steamed seaweed, daikon, and the inescapable hot green tea. Occasionally we were served a thin, meatless soup made by boiling fish heads with sweet potato vines, lily leaves, *gobo* (our common burdock), or other greens—a concoction some of the men referred to as *benjo* soup.[4] Meat was never seen, nor was any form of seafood, except for the occasional fish head that found its way into the *benjo* soup. Without any salt or other seasoning, the meals were bland.

The Japanese prefer long-grain white, polished rice to the gray-colored, unpolished variety, which they consider to be suitable only for coolies. Of course, as prisoners we were looked down upon and so were always given what they considered to be the less desirable unpol-ished rice. I am certain that they were unaware of it, but they were doing us a great favor, for the unpolished rice was a boon to our health. It contained all of the rice germ, minerals, and vitamins that the more attractive polished variety lacked.

However, this rice was bagged with sweepings from the dock and contained straw, small stones, dirt, and rat droppings. At the begin-ning these foreign particles were a problem to our galley crew, who worked hard to remove them by hand. But soon a solution presented itself. A group of newly arrived prisoners, officers who had been captured in the Philippines, included several mining engineers who knew what to do, even though they had never before had to remove unwanted ingredients from rice. When they heard of the problem they constructed several primitive sluices similar to those used in the sluic-ing of gold. Using these crude devices they washed the rice down the sluiceway, leaving pebbles, stones, and other heavy matter trapped by ridges in the sluice. Straw and dirt were skimmed off the top either while being sluiced or during the cooking. Although the galley crew was not sluicing gold per se, rice was our most important food item, and it really was gold to us. And as another important by-product of the sluicing, there were fewer chipped or broken teeth among the prisoners.

Because of the efforts of our galley crew, there was little beriberi in the camp. They would not even throw away the water used to wash the rice. After a degree of clarification, it was used for cooking the rice, thus preserving all of the food elements that might have remained in the wash water. The galley crew's interest in our well-being was most important for all in the camp and will never be forgotten.

Our cooks were always looking for things to incorporate with the rice so as to extend it, to make it more tasty, and to improve its nutri-tional value. Sometimes they were provided with tofu (a white, cus-tardlike soybean cake), which they would stir in with the rice. Because the Japanese did not relish soybeans, these were given to us as well, almost like a throwaway. Our self-taught cooks had learned that soybeans were high in protein, and they stirred them in with our rice whenever possible. Later, millet, wheat, or oats became available and were also mixed into the rice.

During the entire time we were interned, the enlisted men who were assigned to the galley were always fair in the handling and distribution of the food that was given to them to cook, even to the distribution of any small amounts of fish or meat that were infrequently allotted by the Japanese mess sergeant. Minute particles of these items were mixed into the rice so that everyone in the camp received his fair portion of the scarce protein available.

As mentioned above, vegetables were usually boiled and made into a meatless soup. Sometimes, however, they were cooked and stirred into the rice. This made us all feel that the rice was more of a meal than it was, and it also allowed a more equitable distribution of the scant vegetables that were available.

The Japanese mess sergeant watched our enlisted cooks like a hawk, overseeing everything they did and measuring out each item of the food they were using. Particular attention was paid to the amount of unpolished rice that was used. Initially we were allotted a cup of rice per man per day. But as time dragged slowly (and hungrily) by, our rice ration was reduced drastically, as was the quantity of all the other foods provided.

It took us some time after our arrival to become familiar with the Japanese way of life and to become somewhat accustomed to the bare conditions under which we were to live. During our meetings with the Japanese camp administrators we referred constantly to the terms of the Geneva Convention. Most of our early discussions with them centered around our treatment as military prisoners and their abiding by the precepts of international law that we had studied as midshipmen at the Naval Academy.

By cajoling and with some argument, we obtained a partial assurance that they would consider abiding by the Geneva Convention in their treatment of us. Although the Japanese had not ratified the convention, we convinced them that as military representatives of a humane nation, they should treat their prisoners humanely. I do not believe that this agreement could have been reached had they been regular officers of the Japanese army. Generally speaking, they agreed to the following conditions:

1. We would be treated humanely (you could interpret this broadly).
2. We would be allowed to keep our clothing and a few personal items (very little).

3. Enlisted men would be required to work and would receive commensurate (though minimal) pay.

4. Officers would be allowed to work or not, as they desired.

5. Officers would be paid wages commensurate to those paid to the corresponding rank in the Japanese army.

6. Accommodations and food would be similar to those supplied to the Japanese army.

7. Prisoners would be subject to the laws, customs, and orders of the Japanese.

Having succeeded in convincing the Japanese of their capacity for humane behavior, we found our other discussions with them to be less difficult. We were quite positive about our wishes regarding some things and were able to get many requests granted that would otherwise have been denied. All of our meetings with the Japanese were very delicate, because they did not like any display of superiority on our part.

Most contacts with the Japanese officer-in-charge were made by me and a few other senior officers. These meetings were difficult under the best of circumstances, and if we were there to register a complaint or to request something, the meeting frequently resulted in immediate punishment. It was reminiscent of an unusually violent Plebe Year at the Naval Academy. The routine never varied. Arriving at his office, one would stand at attention for a long time before being acknowledged. Then one was expected to bow deeply from the waist—something that I found psychologically very difficult to do. As the discussion progressed, one could expect to be slapped across the face or to be hit with a split bamboo stick as punishment for being "too arrogant"—say, for looking the officer in the eye instead of looking at his chest, as we were supposed to do. On those occasions when I was the subject of the officer's wrath, it was all I could do to keep from throttling the little Japanese bastard.

Because I was one of the more senior officers in camp, I had many contacts with the Japanese officers. I was frequently punished and was the target of many face slappings. *Slapping* does not adequately describe the experience. It was much more violent than that word can encompass. I lost several teeth as a result of these slappings. My family and I were patients of an outstanding oral surgeon in Baltimore, and after my repatriation Dr. Bock spent many hours repairing the damage that had been done to my mouth by sadistic Japanese fists.

When a request was made, in many instances the Japanese would not give a direct reply. As time went by we came to realize that this was an aspect of their culture, all tied up in the matters of "saving face" and "status." Frequently a request would be held in abeyance, an assent being given some time later, along with a Japanese interpretation of the answer. Frequently a vague assent to a request would be included in a written order promulgated by the Japanese, making it seem as though it had been their idea in the first place.

Of course, it was not possible to "negotiate" with the Japanese on the basis of Western standards. This is a problem that is inherent today in both our commercial and governmental negotiations with Asian societies. Our cultures and histories are so vastly different that there is little common ground for understanding.

Senior officers attempting to discuss problems within the camp often found that negotiating with the Japanese was virtually impossible. After many such meetings they were forced to return to their campmates totally frustrated, frequently having suffered a considerable lowering of personal dignity in the process. A hard slap or a kick in the shins was the painful answer to many items taken up with the prison-camp authorities.

Although they had agreed to treat us in accordance with the Geneva Convention, the Japanese held that there were no distinctions of rank among prisoners of war. In their eyes we were all the equivalent of coolies. During our years as prisoners the Japanese made many attempts to degrade the officers and to lower our prestige. They did this by such mechanisms as giving the enlisted men additional privileges, more food, and sometimes small gifts or favors. It was to the credit of our men that these ruses did not succeed. Whatever favors they were given they frequently shared with the officers. The loyalty of our men was outstanding, and I am unable to praise them too highly. Their conduct was magnificent.

Because almost all of the prisoners were from the U.S. Navy or Marine Corps, it was not long before the Japanese guards became fluent in navy terminology. Soon they were referring to the cookhouse as the "galley," the *benjo* became the "head," the walls were "bulkheads," and so forth.

In late January one of the guards was seen peeking through the window at some of the nurses, and another painful trip to see the officer-in-charge was made. After inflicting the usual humiliations, he agreed to provide a cotton sheet to hang across a corner of the nurses' room for privacy. No thought was ever given to reprimanding the guard. At another time a guard entered the nurses' room and awakened one of them. The nurse, seeing the Japanese face hovering over her, screamed bloody murder, awakening all in the vicinity. The guard was only tucking the ersatz blanket around her neck, but—another trip to the office.

We knew that many of the Japanese officers understood English. However, all of our dealings with them were done through the interpreter. We always felt that this worked to their advantage when we were asking for something, in that it gave them additional time to decide on a response. It also gave both them and us an opportunity to observe each other's facial expressions, although on most occasions we couldn't interpret their usually blank expressions.

There was little doubt that the Japanese officers hated our feeling of superiority toward them—an emotion not one of us could deny. Whether or not this feeling was displayed, however, we were the losers in whatever we did. In contacts with the camp authorities, if a prisoner was too servile, he was liable to be picked on and beaten. If he was too straightforward, his actions were regarded as insulting, and he risked being berated or beaten. Each meeting had to be planned in advance, and we had to be prepared to alter our behavior as the meeting progressed. Who could understand these people?

There was one sergeant who would search the barracks hoping to find something to raise hell about that would provide him with an excuse to beat someone—not that he ever seemed to need much encouragement. There was also a particularly sadistic corporal with a shrunken hand and forearm. Because of his deformed limb and the alacrity with which he used it to beat the prisoners, we dubbed him Club Fist.

✳ Chief Boatswain's Mate H. L. Townsend, USN, provided the following assessment of two guards, one of whom was probably the Club Fist referred to here: "There were two guards at this camp who I feel were probably the worst Japs in the place. They were returned wounded soldiers, whose wounds had incapacitated them for any further service in the Army. One had the nickname 'Nub Fist' inasmuch as his left hand had been injured. The other's nickname was 'Yellow Glasses' due to the fact that he wore glasses with heavy yellow lenses because of an eye injury. Both had served with the Jap Army in the Philippines and had been wounded there."[5] ✳

Sunday, 25 January, was a red-letter date at Zentsuji. It was our first bath day since arriving in Japan, and our first experience with a Japanese-style bath. It had been fourteen days since our departure from Guam, and longer still since our last bath. "Cleanliness is next to godliness," and sometimes we felt far removed from both. We were a pretty raunchy bunch.

The weekly bath was accomplished Japanese-style, using a concrete tub that measured about eight by ten by three feet deep. The nurses went first, then the officers, the chief petty officers, and the enlisted men. Using buckets of cold water, a group of bathers would soap themselves and rinse off beside the tub. Then they would climb into the tub for a final rinse in very hot water. Periodically the men detailed to take care of the bathhouse would use wooden buckets or ladles to skim off the heavy layer of scum that collected atop the hot water.

Bathing was usually accomplished after church on Sunday, church service being conducted by Guam's chaplain, Lieutenant (Junior Grade) James E. Davis (ChC), USN, and by other chaplains who had been captured elsewhere. The service was always well attended, proving the old saying that "there are no atheists in foxholes."

After church we also washed our clothes. This was not easy to do with cold water and our limited supply of poor-quality Japanese soap. Then we called on the nurses, who had the only iron in camp. The electricity was on for only one hour each night, but the nurses ironed what shirts they could before lights out.

Some interesting beards of all types were grown by the prisoners, and long hair was prevalent. This was more or less forced on us, our razors, clippers, and shears being dull. It was painful to fight the pull of dull tonsorial supplies.

In February our enlisted men were assigned to one of two working parties. One was engaged in laying drain tiles in the camp. Although this was the easier of the two jobs, by all accounts it was rather boring and seemed to be a job of which you could make a career. Also, it did not require the workers to venture outside the camp. The second job was kicked off by what was billed as a "recreational hike up a nearby mountain." The job was to clear rocks and roots from the soil and to terrace the mountainside for planting. The Japanese had organized the hike to find out how early to make reveille, to get the men to the mountain in time for work. This was a backbreaking job that also seemed to go on and on. The men who were assigned to this working party were out of the camp for almost the entire day every weekday, however. I believe that many of them looked upon this as a bonus.

Not all of the enlisted men were forced to do manual labor. Those who were assigned to the galley force were excused—after all, they had a full-time job trying to make something out of nothing—and those on the sick list were exempt. The Japanese restricted the number of men allowed on the sick list, an insidious technique on their part. No prisoner wanted to take a place on the list that should be filled by an even sicker shipmate, and on many occasions the working parties included men who were actually too sick to work.

Little medical care was given by the Japanese to the many sick prisoners. Without our own doctors and corpsmen, we wouldn't have been able to "take care of our health." As noted earlier, the doctors and corpsmen had loaded their baggage with drugs and medical supplies from our Naval Hospital on Guam. Had they not done this, many of

Prisoners being marched to work on slopes of Osa Yama near Zentsuji
(Courtesy Mrs. Nancy Cross)

us would not have survived. It is true that we were able to get minimal care from the Japanese camp doctor, but he was not interested in maintaining the health of coolies. Many of us owed our lives to Doctors William T. Lineberry, H. J. Van Peenen, and Tilden I. Moe, and to the hospital corpsmen who kept us going, and we thanked God for their presence. Our doctors constantly fought the Japanese for medicines and better treatment of sick prisoners. In this they were stymied by Dr. Saito, the camp doctor—a vindictive man who was particularly sadistic toward our officers. (After the war Dr. Saito was sentenced in the Japanese War Crimes Trials to a long prison term.)

✻ Dr. Van Peenen describes the task that faced him: "Malnutrition and dysentery were already beginning to pave the way for disease and death. In a rough, lined child's copybook, I kept case histories, wills, death records. . . . This book was kept in my briefcase, now broken and shabby reflecting the universal POW look. . . .

"The care of the sick became daily more difficult, and my briefcase was opened more and more to receive the small keepsakes of the gravely ill, often apologetically, 'In case I don't make it, doctor. . . .'

"There were not enough blankets. Those we had were steeped in filth of patients too weak from dysentery to aspire to cleanliness. We [Dr. Van Peenen and Corpsman T. W. Keck] washed the blankets in inadequate buckets of cold water and held them between us before the miserably small charcoal stoves. It was not encouraging to know that our own blankets, wrapped around the sick, were becoming as useless to us as the ones we held. . . .

"Keck, by training and endurance, was of inestimable value. His hands were gentle in caring for patients; his manner was reassuringly jaunty. He was adept at drawing the wrath of the guards to himself and away from sick men less able to cope with any new form of misery."[6] ✻

I have always marveled at the ingenuity of enlisted men in obtaining things through the complexities of "midnight requisitioning," and those at Zentsuji were unusually adept at obtaining the unobtainable. Somehow members of the working parties managed to obtain drugs when they were outside camp. Then they would smuggle them in to Dr. Van Peenen, who cached them in an unknown hiding place for future use.

By February we were becoming accustomed to our daily camp routine. Each morning after a predawn reveille we fell in along the roadway in front of the barracks. Then Lieutenant Commander Samuel A.

Newman led us in calisthenics. These calisthenics and frequent walks along the roadway were about the only physical exercise received by those who were not in one of the work details. Furthermore, by doing these calisthenics we were able to warm up a little and to relieve some of the stiffness from the cold and from the previous night's attempt at sleeping on the boards.

After calisthenics, we had breakfast. Frequently this consisted of some bread, thin *benjo* soup, and tea. Those on the sick list received additional bread, plus an occasional egg and a little milk. Even so, their recovery was slow and wounds that should have cleared up quickly seemed not to heal for some time. There was such an insufficient amount of protein in the diet.

Following breakfast, the working parties were mustered and marched off to work, those going to work on the mountainside carrying their picks, sledges, shovels, and noonday meals with them. Depending on the point of view, those who worked on the mountainside could be considered fortunate. Although they truly performed coolie work in its most rugged form, they experienced a bit of freedom from the camp and were rewarded with better chow. Whereas we in camp would typically have a slice of bread and some variety of thin soup for lunch, those working on the mountainside might have rice or bread and a couple of ounces of dried fish or some seaweed.

✳ Reginald W. Reed recorded this detail: "Since the fish heads were so salty, and were likely to be somewhat spoiled (they stank), they were boiled in the canteens which each man had carried up. We ate as soon as the fish heads were cooked. I had a fish head which was quite vile tasting (putrid, if I couldn't eat it), but being famished by then, I struggled and gulped until the filthy thing was devoured. It is quite disconcerting to try eating a fish head which has an eye staring fixedly, almost reproachfully, at one while one sinks his teeth in it."[7] ✳

Dinnertime was geared to the arrival back in camp of the mountainside working party. The Japanese wanted to extract from them every possible ounce of labor, so they seldom stopped work until late in the afternoon, returning to camp around dusk. This was our big meal of the day. On one occasion of note, in addition to *benjo* soup we each had a sparse ration of rice with a bit of soy sauce and nearly two ounces of ancient fish. Another meal that I remember consisted of noodle soup and rice in which there were microscopic bits of pork with just the barest suspicion of fat.

During our first months at Zentsuji groups of us were occasionally taken under guard on hikes in the area around the camp and through the nearby hills. Why this was done, we never knew. Sometimes these walks went through the town of Zentsuji.

In addition to being a farming community, Zentsuji was the birth-place of the Buddhist priest Kobo Daishi and the location of the Zentsuji Temple, the most famous temple on Shikoku, and of an army shrine. The army shrine was located just on the other side of the high board fence that imprisoned us. The Japanese have an aversion to anyone looking down from a height upon their shrines or their dignitaries. Because of this, whenever a ceremony was held at the shrine, blackout curtains had to be drawn on that side of the barracks, and we were or-dered not to look out the windows. Sometimes the second floor of the barracks was vacated.

Once when a ceremony was under way at the shrine, someone noted that a fellow prisoner was bowing. This piqued his curiosity, and the following conversation took place:

"What are you bowing for?"

"To greet His Imperial Majesty."

"You're bowing in the wrong direction!"

"No, I'm not! Check the direction of my rear."

Ceremonies were held at this shrine quite often, and small gifts of food were left as offerings to the spirit of a dead family member. With so many hungry prisoners of war next door, this food never remained at the shrine very long. I never knew how the men managed to get the food, but some things are better left unexplained. At other times little white boxes holding the cremated remains of a lost one were placed at the shrine. As the war progressed, the sight of these white boxes be-came increasingly common.

We were taken past the army shrine one day on one of our hikes. We halted in front of the *torii,* faced the shrine, uncovered, and bowed. Then, proceeding another fifty yards or so, we came to a civilian shrine. Here we halted again and repeated the same honors. The Japanese were very exacting in their observance of customs and honors.

My first glimpse of the town of Zentsuji came shortly after leaving the shrine area that day. The side streets were literally teeming with life. Numerous small shops lined the way. Odors of dried fish and bak-ing mingled with other odors that were distinctly oriental.

As we passed through town, people stopped and stared at us, and bowed ceremoniously to our guards. As they stared at us there was no hint of malice in their eyes, just intense curiosity. I wondered what they had been told about us—certainly nothing good.

The parasols and bright kimonos of the women formed a striking contrast to the somber clothing worn by the men. Most of the men wore dark, long, loose-sleeved shirtlike garments called *hakama* and

Zentsuji seen through gate of civilian shrine *(Courtesy Mrs. Nancy Cross)*

lightweight coats called *haori*.[8] Many of the people wore *geta,* wooden clogs that raised their feet about an inch and a half above the dusty street.

In town I was surprised to see several people wearing gauze face masks. They completely covered the nose and mouth, being secured by ties over the ears. The people wearing them looked like operating-room personnel. When we returned to camp Asabuki-san, the interpreter, said that people with colds wore these masks so as not to spread germs. Not a bad idea. For all this concern with sanitation, however, we were stunned to watch how night soil was gathered.

Throughout the town, people (irrespective of sex) pulled heavy two-wheeled carts carrying half a dozen large wooden barrels. The person pulling the cart would sidle up to the rear of a house or privy, remove a small window, and, using a long-handled dipper, scoop out the human excrement and pour it into the barrels. The abundant use of this

Prisoners being marched through Zentsuji *(Courtesy Mrs. Nancy Cross)*

night soil contributed to the prodigious size of the vegetables we were (occasionally) given. This was also the reason why those vegetables had to be boiled.

Gasoline was at a premium. Most of the vehicles I saw were fueled by fumes created by burning charcoal or wood chips in cumbersome stoves, with the combustible fumes being fed to the engine by a specially designed carburetor. In passenger cars and small trucks, these stoves were located in back of the driver. In cargo-carrying trucks, they were located in front. The drivers had to stop frequently, refill the firebox, and crank the blower that fed the combustible gases to the engine. These engines were very inefficient and created clouds of heavy black smoke. Except for those used by a few senior army officers, not many automobiles were seen.

All of the houses were made primarily of shoji screens, tatami mats, bamboo, and wood. Because of this, before Pearl Harbor many in the U.S. military felt that a war with Japan could end quickly. The rationale was that a few well-placed bombs would cause the entire island to go up in an all-encompassing blaze. No one had considered the difficulty of getting *to* Japan to drop those well-placed bombs, or that Japanese industrial buildings were of more substantial construction.

Firefighting was a farce. Firefighters used long bamboo poles that had rope or jute wound around the ends. These were dipped in water and used to beat out the fire. In camp, buckets and barrels of water were placed at strategic locations so that a bucket brigade could be formed. This might have worked moderately well during most of the year, but during the winter months these containers of water froze solid. We also had a manually pulled and operated fire wagon. The whole exercise reminded me of the Keystone Kops.

✳ Fortunately, while engulfed with misery the prisoners were sometimes able to relax for just a few moments and see some beauty. The following observations were recorded by Signalman Reed on 22 May 1942: "The morning was splendid. Toward noon it became pretty warm up there on O-Asayama hill, as it is called. The entire lowlands and lower hills shimmered in the sunlight, looking very much like a mosaic of green-brown tones, with the sapphire blue of the sea beyond. Yet in the foreground of the mainland of the island of Honshu, several ships appeared scarcely to move, crossing ever so slowly the smooth expanse of the blue Inland Sea. Everywhere down in the pine woods the cicadas set up a mighty symphony as the breeze sounded ever so gently in accompaniment. Far off below ran the toy-like train, leaving in its wake plumed feathers of steam as it silently whistled for the crossings. From the distance the dull swoosh of coast defense guns is felt, rather than heard, while the occasional staccato of machine guns on the ranges beats a tattoo to punctuate the rhythm of the East. Overhead sailed a hawk in search of lesser animals. Just below us in the forecourt of the panorama lay the barren ground we'd been filling and the partially completed stone walls of the terraces.

"A huge cauldron steamed and gurgled on a stone fireplace, preparing the noon tea, while close by a rivulet from the spring trickled with a musical tinkle. The metallic ring of the picks on the rocks rolled like the beat of a drum, echoed across the dell."[9] ✳

In February and March the Japanese began to separate the civilian, diplomatic, and military prisoners. First, the Catholic priests and civilian construction workers[10] who had been captured with us were transferred to internment camps near Kobe, on the main island of Honshu.[11] Then, in March, the nurses and Mrs. Hellmers and her baby were transferred to Kobe for further transfer home, along with the American ambassador, Joseph C. Grew, in exchange for Japanese diplomatic personnel interned in the United States.

The nurses earned our highest praise. Prior to leaving the camp they each wrote down the names and addresses of all the prisoners, along

Photograph taken at Zentsuji. Chief Boatswain's Mate Lane, Chief Yeoman Farris, and Commander Giles (wearing cap). Two unidentified interpreters are shown kneeling. This photograph was brought from Zentsuji by Nurse Leona Jackson when she visited Mrs. Giles in Annapolis in 1943 after being repatriated aboard the S/S *Gripsholm*. (Collection of Donald T. Giles, Jr.)

with any message a prisoner wanted to send home. After arriving in the United States the nurses visited, wrote, or telephoned the prisoners' families, passed on the messages, and permitted themselves to be debriefed by these worried loved ones at home. This was a long and difficult but heartwarming task. Nurse Leona Jackson spent half a day with my family in Annapolis, providing them with details on camp life and on my health and well-being. Truly, our nurses were wonderful Americans.

The nurses were still in Kobe when General James Doolittle led the surprise bombing raid on Tokyo in April. After returning home, Nurse Marion B. Olds said, "The sound of those bombs exploding sounded so good to us we forgot to be afraid one might hit us."[12] When we heard of this daring raid against Tokyo, our spirits soared.

✳ Major Paul A. Putnam, one of the marine officers from Wake, was so moved that he "warned the Japs after the Doolittle raid to 'pull in your necks, there's plenty more coming' without receiving their usual reprisals."[13] The Japanese must have been so flabbergasted by his audacity that for once they did not punish him. ✳

In May Radioman First Class Arthur H. Griffith left to join the nurses, Ambassador Grew, and others with diplomatic status who were to leave Japan.[14] Those leaving Japan sailed aboard the S/S *Gripsholm* via Portuguese East Africa, arriving in the United States in August 1942.[15]

✳ Events associated with Griffith's departure from Zentsuji exemplified the dichotomy in the Japanese personality that was so difficult for the prisoners to fathom. The following information was recorded by Reginald Reed: "My opinion of the Japanese wanes and waxes according to what I observe or hear about them. This time they've grown in my opinion. When Griffith took his departure yesterday a Jap officer gave him 10 yen as a token of his esteem and bid Griffith bon voyage. Matsumoto, our regulation sergeant, who accompanied Griffith to the train, bowed and saluted continuously in the most touching fashion until the train was out of sight."[16] ✳

Before leaving Japan Ambassador Grew arranged for books from the embassy library to be sent to Zentsuji. I do not know if other camps received any of these books, but we read and reread ours countless times. They did much to bolster our morale during the years ahead.

After the nurses and Griffith left, conditions at Zentsuji deteriorated quickly. Possibly the Japanese knew that no one else would be leaving to carry back news of what was taking place. Our only objective was to exist. Reality for us was the lack of food, the lack of medical care, the physical labor, the increasingly frequent beatings, and the gradual loss of hope.

10 ✳ Sources of Information

When Guam was attacked, one of the first targets that was destroyed was our high-power radio station, cutting us off from the outside world. We knew that Pearl Harbor had been attacked, but we had no idea of the extent of damage. We knew that Wake and Corregidor had been attacked, but again, that was all we knew.

Many of us had hoped that, in Hollywood style, the U.S. fleet would come barreling over the horizon with guns blazing and relieve us. When this did not happen, we rationalized that the fleet had been engaged elsewhere, perhaps insuring the safety of Wake or the Philippines. We knew that our military might would prevail. The war could not last very long. With 20/20 hindsight, I can say that there was merit in the old saying, "Ignorance is bliss." Had we known the extent of our losses, I am not certain that we could have hung on at Zentsuji. Perhaps it was better to be able to fool ourselves, and to receive the bad news in dribs and drabs.

Two sources of information were the newspapers and the English-language publications to which we were able to subscribe using the meager yen we were paid. The daily newspapers we received were the Osaka *Mainichi* and the Tokyo *Nichi-Nichi Shimbun,* which were printed in English. We knew that the Japanese press was controlled and therefore not objective. Furthermore, such English-language editions would be intended solely to publish propaganda for foreign consumption. Nevertheless, we read these newspapers carefully, trying to sift some small grains of truth from the chaff. But how to assess what was true and what was not?

We supplemented this information with that contained in English-language publications such as the *Japan Times Weekly* (similar to *Time*), *Contemporary Japan* (a monthly magazine), and *Sakura* (a monthly picture publication similar to *Life*).

Other war information was obtained by members of our working party on the docks at Takamatsu, where they worked as stevedores. En route to and from Takamatsu, although they were normally herded into boxcars, on some occasions they were crowded into passenger cars with civilians. During these trips, when no one was watching, they were able to retrieve the Japanese-language newspapers that the other passengers dropped. Also, being in such extremely close quarters with the Japanese civilians, they were able to jostle about and pick their pockets, obtaining pocket change and other small items of interest and potential value. This was a dangerous activity, but it did permit the men to supplement their meager pay, and remarkably, no one was caught.

When these Japanese-language newspapers were brought back to camp, they were passed on to a member of our translating squad—officers and men who had been Japanese-language students. Some of them had been attached to our embassy in Tokyo or had served in COMINT (Communications Intelligence) billets.[1] At night, after the newspapers had been translated, a small group of translators would visit each room. Lookouts would be posted at windows and doors, and the visiting translators would brief us on the news. This activity was never discovered by the camp authorities.

We found little pleasure in reading these publications. At first the news was so bad that we tended to discount much of it. Although we could not understand how it had occurred, we began to realize that our losses at Pearl Harbor had been significant. The Imperial Army and Navy were riding high, and the newspapers continuously reported their most minute successes. As might be expected, individual prisoners reacted differently to these glowing reports. Whereas some believed every word that was published, others thought that some of the Japanese claims were exaggerated.

As time went on we came to realize that the American ship sinkings that were reported in the Japanese press were grossly exaggerated. Following major engagements between units of the American and Japanese fleets, the press would describe heavy losses to the U.S. units and only minor losses or damage to the Japanese. If these newspaper reports were correct, so many of our ships had been sunk that our navy would have been wiped out. Furthermore, we knew the capacity of our shipyards and realized that even if they worked around the clock they couldn't possibly be replenishing the losses that were being reported in the Japanese press. After several months of this we began to study these reports carefully and to keep score. We noted that some ships that had been reported, by name or class, as having been sunk were subsequently named as participating in later battles—in which they were usually damaged or sunk again.

The Japanese also gave us a variety of books, many of them written in English. If anything, however, these were even less objective than the newspapers and magazines. They described the Japanese version of how the war had started, and the beginnings and rationale of the Greater East Asia Co-prosperity Sphere.[2]

Another, surprising, source of news was some of the friendly Korean guards at the camp. There is a longstanding animosity between the Japanese and the Koreans. At Zentsuji the Japanese looked down on the Koreans and treated them, at best, as second-class citizens. These guards had been pressed into service and, to put it mildly, were not happy in their work. Whereas Japanese guards were assigned to secure the barracks, the Koreans were relegated to patrolling the wall that surrounded the camp. Because of their disaffection, some of the Korean guards were friendly to us and were inclined to provide us with certain favors, one being periodic tidbits of news.

The *Japan Times Weekly* of 25 December 1941—which we received much later—contained an imperial rescript from the emperor to the Diet, in which he laid at the Allies' feet the causes of the Pacific War: "It is Our great solicitude to contribute to the world peace by ensuring stabilization of East Asia. Notwithstanding, both the United States and Britain dared cause disturbance in East Asia, contrary to the desire of the Empire. Thus the Empire has been forced to take up arms against them. We regret this deeply." Of course, no reference was made to Japanese atrocities in China, or to Japan's annexation of Manchuria.

The Comments section of the *Japan Times Weekly* of 25 December 1941 gave the following assessment of the situation in the United States:

The confusion of American popular mind caused by the series of blitz attacks on Hawaii by the Japanese force, and reports of continuous war reverses on land and sea has finally driven the United States to unleash random radio news throughout the country. Apparently with the object of hoodwinking the American citizens, who are dazed by the air attacks on Hawaii, the Philippines and other key points one of the most absurd and laughable rumors that can be imagined was broadcast.

Apparently news reports transmitted from the United States had been received in Japan, and those responsible for generating Japanese propaganda wanted to squelch the reports as "laughable rumors." This helped bolster our morale at Zentsuji. It appeared that everything wasn't entirely to their liking. Could it be that the capture of Wake had not been as successful as we had been led to believe? The only news we could find was in the *Japan Times Weekly* of 25 December 1941: "The Imperial Navy shelled Wake Island on December 11 by warships and dealt heavy losses to the enemy. Our side suffered some damage, too." If the truth had been told, on 11 December the Japanese amphibious landing on Wake was beaten off by coastal defense guns; the Japanese lost two destroyers and at least five hundred men, compared with minor losses to the American defenders.[3]

Undoubtedly our best and only objective source of information was newly arrived prisoners. Having been captured later than we had been, they could update us on what was taking place. The first new prisoner to join our ranks was Radioman First Class Arthur H. Griffith, USN (captured at Tsingtao, China), who arrived in late January 1942. Two weeks later Griffith was followed by Commander Campbell Keene, USN, and twelve of his shipmates from Wake.[4] Until their arrival we did not know what had happened at Wake Island, which had fallen to the Japanese on 23 December. The effect on our morale was significant. We had hoped that before long we would be either picked up or exchanged for Japanese prisoners. Apparently this was not to be the case, at least not for some time to come.

On 18 February 1942 another group of prisoners from Wake arrived, an ensign and three sailors. Although they had been captured at the same time as the rest of that garrison, their arrival had been delayed. They were in terrible shape—emaciated and looking as if they had been through hell. Because they were communications personnel, they had been routed through what we called "questioning camps." Although we knew of their existence through information provided to us by prisoners who had been there, the existence of these camps was never revealed by the Japanese. It was at these camps that the Japanese practiced their skills in extracting information from selected prisoners.

Early on the Japanese insisted that we have maps of the Far East posted on the barrack walls. They even helped keep them current as their forces advanced to the south. Of course, this was not for our edification, but served as a means of lowering our morale. Our morale continued to sink as we read reports in *Contemporary Japan* and the *Japan Times Weekly* describing Japanese successes in the Philippines:

"The encirclement moves of the Japanese forces compelled the American-Filipino troops to make a general retreat to Manila. Another glorious chapter has been written into the pages of history by our valiant Army and Navy when Manila, the last outpost of American Imperialism, was occupied by our forces on the afternoon of January 2."

The April issue of *Contemporary Japan* contained a devastating report that worried us greatly:

> Bold and free activity of Japanese submarines in the waters off the American Pacific coast has struck terror into the hearts of Americans. Since the opening of hostilities on December 8, 1941, these submarines have daringly operated over the vast expanse of the Pacific. It was on the night of February 24 that a Japanese submarine made its appearance off the California coast and bombarded military establishments at Santa Barbara, inflicting heavy damage to enemy property.

What a horrible thought! Could Japanese submarines be ravaging the United States with impunity, as the article suggested? Somehow we did not think so, but we had little on which to hang our hopes. Many depressing articles followed on what seemed to be an almost daily schedule: the Japanese Malayan campaign; the fall of Hong Kong and of Singapore; the loss of the British cruiser *Exeter;* the occupation of lower Burma, the Netherlands East Indies, and New Guinea.

It was claimed that Japan, through its rapid acquisitions in Southeast Asia, had secured almost inexhaustible material resources to prosecute the war. We knew that Japan depended heavily on imports of practically all basic materials, including rice and many other items of food. Where were our submarines to interdict the shipment of such items?

In the April 1942 issue of *Contemporary Japan,* the effectiveness of the Japanese navy in attacking anti-Axis shipping through February was assessed as 128 vessels sunk (aggregate of 680,000 tons) and 92 vessels seriously damaged (aggregate of 300,000 tons). Articles continued to praise the advancing Japanese forces and the formation of the Greater East Asia Co-prosperity Sphere, through which they were obtaining many of the materials needed to continue the war. All of the news was so bad. We felt as though we were being slowly but surely pounded into the ground. Would things ever get better?

In early May the *Japan Times* referred to a naval battle in the Coral Sea, that large body of water bounded by Australia, New Guinea, the Solomon Islands, the New Hebrides, and New Caledonia. At first the press described it almost as if it were a nonbattle, hardly a skirmish. It was obvious that a battle was taking place, but few details were forthcoming.

✳ The following diary entry by Reginald W. Reed describes how the prisoners felt regarding the general lack of news and the obvious inaccuracies they noted in the Japanese press regarding the Battle of the Coral Sea: "This day, Mother's Day, begins with a certain amount of conjecture on the progress of the battle in the Coral Sea. This could break Japanese sea power, without which she will undoubtedly be helpless to conduct military operations outside Japan proper. It appears that the Allies are making a determined effort to regain the lost tin and rubber supply and vital bases in the Southwest Pacific. According to today's paper, America is taking a shellacking in the Coral Sea. However, I'm a bit inclined to doubt the veracity of these statements. We shall wait and see. At any rate, there's a good-sized naval engagement going on down there which should about decide the outcome of the war in this part of the globe. It is unthinkable that Nippon and her allies could win this war, especially Nippon. In fact, the hint was dropped in one of the papers that before the war ended the Japs would be in Washington, D.C., and would eventually enslave the world."[5] ✳

On 9 May the *Japan Times* began to publish details of Japan's victory by identifying the many U.S. and British ships that had been sunk or severely damaged. The Japanese claimed to have lost only one small aircraft carrier. What was not reported—and what we did not know at the time—was that although the Japanese had scored a tactical success in terms of the number of ships sunk, our forces had won a strategic victory. We had checked their advance through the Coral Sea to dominate the approaches to Australia. For the first time, we had stopped the Japanese.

✳ In late May 1942 Major Donald Spicer recorded the following observations regarding some of the news being reported in Japan: "This is a sample of the kind of stuff we read. General MacArthur and General Brett fled from the Philippines because they were cowards. The same is said of General Stilwell in Burma. General Wainwright is alleged to have cried and pleaded with the Japanese while he was returning to Corregidor under a flag of truce, escorted by Japanese, to have the Japanese artillery cease firing because he was afraid of being killed. . . .

"Another time we read that whenever the U.S. Navy went on extended maneuvers they had to take the wives along in transports because they could divorce their husbands if they stayed away more than three months. It looks as though you [Mrs. Spicer] missed a chance to get rid of me when I was in Nicaragua for fourteen months. Now you have another chance."[6] ✳

On 25 May two out-of-the-ordinary events occurred. First, we spent several hours having our pictures taken by Japanese army photographers. No explanation was given for this, and we had learned from past, frequently painful, experience to ask few questions. We were posed in groups of three to six, sitting on long wooden two by eights in front of the barracks. The first group included Captain George J. McMillin, Bill Lineberry, Alvin H. "Doc" Cecha, Campbell Keene, and Don Spicer. Orel Pierson and I were in the second group, with four army officers captured in the Philippines.

The second unusual event occurred late in the afternoon. We were each issued a pencil, a razor blade, and a toothbrush. To us such things, which are taken for granted at home, seemed luxurious.

✳ On 8 June 140 of the enlisted men were moved from Zentsuji to a camp in Osaka, where they were forced to do back-breaking work at the docks.[7] ✳

It was not until late in June that our spirits began to climb. The *Japan Times Weekly* of 18 June 1942 reported that the Japanese had attacked the Aleutians and Midway:

> Japanese Navy Units, in close collaboration with Japanese Army Units, attacked and occupied a number of important points on the Aleutian Islands last week in the first military invasion experienced by the Western Hemisphere in more than one hundred years. At the same time, a Japanese fleet attacked Midway Island, sank two American aircraft carriers and inflicted other damage on the American Fleet which it drew into action.
>
> In the attack on Midway on June 5, Japanese aircraft subjected the enemy stronghold to severe blasting, and shot down 100 enemy planes, while the Japanese fleet drew out the American fleet into action. An American aircraft carrier of the *Enterprise* class and another of the *Hornet* class were sunk. Japanese losses were stated to be one aircraft carrier.

Very little news ever appeared regarding the Battle of Midway, and after reading the above brief announcement—combined as it was with a report on the attack in the Aleutians—we felt that the Japanese must have taken a beating. In fact, as we were to find out later, it was a turning point in the Pacific war, a disaster from which the Japanese never recovered. No mention was ever made of their loss of four aircraft carriers. Any hint of such a devastating loss to the Japanese was completely squelched, and much was said about the minor action in the Aleutian operation.

Captain George J. McMillin, USN, governor of Guam *(Photograph taken by the Japanese at Zentsuji; courtesy Mrs. Nancy Cross)*

Commander Donald T. Giles, USN, vice governor of Guam *(Photograph taken by the Japanese at Zentsuji; courtesy Mrs. Nancy Cross)*

Commander William T. Lineberry (MC), USN, commanding officer, Naval Hospital on Guam *(Photograph taken by the Japanese at Zentsuji; courtesy Mrs. Nancy Cross)*

Lieutenant Colonel William K. Mac-Nulty, USMC, commanding officer, marine detachment on Guam *(Photograph taken by the Japanese at Zentsuji; courtesy Mrs. Nancy Cross)*

Major Donald Spicer, USMC, executive officer, marine detachment on Guam *(Photograph taken by the Japanese at Zentsuji; courtesy Mrs. Nancy Cross)*

Lieutenant James W. Haviland III, USN, commanding officer, USS *Penguin (Photograph taken by the Japanese at Zentsuji; courtesy Mrs. Nancy Cross)*

On 19 July 1942 a large contingent of prisoners from the Australian army arrived in camp. They had been captured at Rabaul, New Britain, and educated us on what was taking place in that theater. These Australian prisoners were followed on 3 August by four Royal Navy officers from HMS *Exeter* and five U.S. officers from the USS *Houston,* USS *Pope,* and USS *Perch.* On 18 August two more officers of the Royal Navy from HMS *Exeter* arrived, as well as an officer and an enlisted man from HMS *Encounter;* they were followed on 8 September by eleven officers of the Royal Navy (four of whom were from HMS *Exeter,* her commanding officer being among them), six U.S. officers from the USS *Perch,* and two Dutch officers from HNLMS *DeRuyter.*

Because all of these ships had gone down during the Battle of the Java Sea in March, the new prisoners were unable to provide many details regarding Coral Sea or Midway, which had occurred somewhat later. However, during their five- to six-month-long trip to Zentsuji they had encountered other prisoners, and on the basis of what they had heard from these sources, they could reassure us that both Coral Sea and Midway had been Allied victories.

We continued to read and to question what we read, trying to glean elements of the truth and hoping that the truth would be in our favor. Although the Battle of Midway had been an important turning point in the war, there was little doubt from what we read that we were in for a long haul. Though much discouraged, we all had faith that someday, if we lived, we would join our own. But when? Maintaining morale among the men was becoming a primary concern among the senior officers. And how was this to be done, when our own morale was so frequently low?

As time passed, newspaper coverage of the war became less regular, a fact that was not wasted on us. Hope springs eternal. Could it be that the Japanese public had become tired of so much war? A great many of their men had been lost in the long China affair that had preceded the current world war. Or could it be that our forces were turning the tide? We knew from past experience that the Japanese did not highlight news of their own losses. Based on information learned from new prisoners and brought in by our working parties from Takamatsu and Zentsuji, we knew that all was not going well for the Japanese, particularly at home. Food and fuel, among other necessities, were in short supply.

That summer the *Japan Times Weekly* and *Contemporary Japan* carried articles that hurt us deeply. The first described labor strikes in the United States, and was illustrated with photographs of the striking workers and miners. The second was headlined "Race Riots in America." These articles did not help our morale. That fellow Americans were striking and disrupting production was deeply irritating. We had done our bit, had been captured, and now had constant doubts as to whether we would ever see our country or friends and families again. What was wrong at home? Had we lost our continuity of purpose? Had we been forgotten?

After July 1943 we were no longer allowed to obtain newspapers in camp. Although we missed the news they brought, the fact that they were no longer available further strengthened our belief that the tide had turned. We knew that when all of the war news was favorable to the enemy, newspapers had been provided as a means of destroying our morale. Thus, if the tide had turned in our favor, providing us with news would be counterproductive as far as our captors were concerned.

Our nerves were very much on edge. Rising in the morning and seeing the same grim faces was not conducive to good relations. We attempted to set standards of courtesy and friendliness, although I must admit, at times it was easier to frown than to smile. A "good morning" helped a great deal to start the day off on the right foot.

In addition to the bitter cold, the starvation, and the continual harassment, we were fighting depression. I truly believe that in some of the deaths that occurred, the man wanted to die and would not fight to live. An abiding faith and trust in God saved many lives and brought men home.

11 ✳ Under Duress

In the late summer of 1942 we heard that Captain George J. McMillin, the former governor of Guam and the senior officer in camp, was to be transferred to Formosa, where flag officers, governors-general, territorial administrators, and other higher-ranking prisoners were being assembled. Rumor was that General Jonathan Mayhew Wainwright was among this group. Whenever the Japanese suggested that they were going to transfer prisoners to another camp, the buildup for the new camp was tremendous: food would be better, accommodations improved, treatment more humane, and so on. Such promises were never met. As a rule, the new destination was worse than the original camp.

At the end of the war there were twelve prisoner-of-war camps in Japan proper. In addition to ours in Zentsuji, there were camps in Fukuoka, Himeji, Kobe, Yawata, Osaka, Hiraoka, Roku Roshi (Fukui), Yokohama, Kawasaki, Tokyo, and Hakodate. Most of these camps were located at or near shipyards, steel plants, and iron or copper mines, where work was the first order of business. There were eight more camps on mainland China, and five on Formosa. When prisoners were transferred to another camp, we usually did not know to which one they were being taken. Because of this, keeping any sort of record was almost impossible.

On 21 August 1942 Captain McMillin left Zentsuji. With his departure we lost a wonderful and gifted commanding officer. I had been privileged to serve under him both on Guam and at Zentsuji, and I felt his loss deeply. After the war I learned that he had been moved to Karenko Camp on Formosa, and that the governors of Hong Kong, Singapore, and Sumatra, in addition to the governor-general of the Netherlands East Indies, had also been assembled at that camp.

If I seem to dwell on food so much, it is because it was at the root of our greatest problems of health and morale. There was never enough, either to savor or to meet dietary requirements. A continual gnawing in the pit of our stomachs kept food constantly on our minds.

A starvation diet of several years' duration explains why former prisoners of war abhor seeing food wasted or thrown away. At Zentsuji our hunger was so intense that on many occasions prisoners raided the camp garbage dump and ate the uncooked scrapings and peelings they found there. One really has to *want*, not only for food but for other necessities of life, to realize how wasteful Western civilization has become. As time passed I began to realize that the strength of Japan stems in large measure from the austerity of its people. To this day I dread seeing anything wasted, particularly edibles. Material things have little meaning to one who has experienced so much want in captivity. We are so fortunate in the United States. We don't realize how lucky we are.

Our craving for food was so great that at times we would meet around a table and talk about our favorite restaurants, the most popular ones being earmarked for visits after repatriation. One that I recommended heartily was Keene's Old English Chop House in Manhattan. How I savored the memory of their steak and kidney pie! Favorite recipes were also discussed and dutifully written down. As I review some of these recipes today, they appear foolish. Most of them would make a gourmet turn somersaults. We dictated them from memory, and important ingredients were sometimes omitted. But it was a very serious business to us. Whatever an individual hankered for, that item dominated his recipe.

Some of the more clever prisoners found ways to get into the storeroom and galley to steal food—knowing that if caught, they would be severely punished. Of course, this would create a ripple effect: an officer would go to the camp authorities to protest the punishment, and he in turn would almost certainly be punished for his efforts. All for a little rice, a piece of daikon, or a bit of dried fish.

Because our diet included few vegetables, we thought it would be helpful to start a small garden. The Japanese agreed to this, believing, I am certain, that in addition to increasing the food supply it would occupy some of the prisoners who might otherwise get in their hair—the old idle-hands syndrome, although there were few idle hands among us, certainly not among the members of the working parties. The Japanese designated an area within the camp that we could use, and provided us with a few ancient spades and rakes and some seeds. The dirt in our plot was full of small stones and barren of nutrients. The Japanese suggested that we use night soil, but we resisted this adamantly. In spite of the poor soil, however, we were able to raise quite a crop of recognizable vegetables.

When our garden began to yield results, the Japanese reduced the supply of vegetables provided to the galley. The result was that we ended up working not to increase our supply of vegetables, as had been our intent, but to maintain the meager supply we already had. We couldn't win. Then the Japanese began to raid our vegetable plot for their own use. At this point we gave up, terminated our farming, and returned to more productive forms of exercise, such as bridge and acey-deucy (a kind of backgammon).

Seeing how successful we had been at farming, the Japanese gave us some rabbits and suggested we raise them for food. This seemed like a good idea. They would certainly supplement our bland diet and would provide us with some much-needed meat protein, something seldom allowed to prisoners in this or other camps in Japan. Then the Japanese established a quota for us: we were to raise fifty rabbits. No one was certain of the significance of the quota, but it sounded ominous.

We built a hutch by the wooden fence and set about our new avocation with enthusiasm. Navy Pay Clerk R. C. Haun took charge of the project, and groups of prisoners collected clover and other greens so that the rabbits would quickly become suitable additions to our diet.

Initially we thought that the stories about how rapidly rabbits multiply must have been exaggerated. Even with the loving care that Haun and his assistants showered on them, the rabbits seemed to be doing only so-so. Within a month two of them had died, and we began to wonder if we would ever achieve our quota. Perhaps the rabbits didn't like living in captivity any more than we did. Somehow, however, the rabbits must have gotten the word about the birds and the bees, because within another month their population had increased by fourteen. Then a second litter of eleven was born, and like true capitalists, we began to think in terms of enlarging the hutch.

As might be expected, we became attached to them. One little doe came frequently to have her nose scratched. However, attached to them or not, we knew that it was very much a proposition of "live or let live," and during the month of May our diet was supplemented. Our cooks cut the rabbit meat into very small pieces, which they added to our soup or mixed into our rice gruel so that it would be distributed equally.

This activity lasted only a few months. In June the Japanese began stealing the rabbits, whereupon we refused to continue raising them. To raise food for our own use was one thing, but to raise it for the benefit of our captors was something entirely different.

At about this time a stray dog wandered into camp and was seen no more. The life of any animal that strayed into our midst would naturally be quite short. We wanted meat desperately, meat of any kind. Snake meat was a delicacy—not that we had it frequently.

Occasionally the working party brought back a bit of dried fish from Takamatsu. This was a real treat. It had a very salty flavor, which helped pep up our bland, almost tasteless food. The fish was hard as a rock, and one had to work hard carving or scraping off thin slices to eat or to use as seasoning.

We also became familiar with a coarse variety of seaweed that was served frequently. When cut up it resembled watermelon-rind pickle. Although tough and unappetizing, it did serve as a stomach filler and added an agreeable salty flavor to our rice. We were seldom given the shredded variety of seaweed—when marinated in soy sauce, this was a delicacy, something that must have been deemed unsuitable for our occidental palates. Of course, even though we disliked the thought of eating seaweed, it did provide us with minerals, iodine, and vitamins.

As I mentioned earlier, in February four new prisoners arrived who had been captured on Wake. They had been through the Japanese interrogation wringer. They were emaciated and looked more dead than alive. In order to build them up, camp-mates shared their already meager rations so that the new arrivals could have a bit more to eat. Occasionally others arrived in pretty much the same shape, and each time other prisoners stepped forward to share what little they had with these unfortunate men. Although we were a camp of individuals, with different likes and dislikes, with different objectives and different stories, we were a family. It was only this that permitted us to survive.

Almost all of the prisoners made deals with one another for food. Those who could not digest the rice we were given swapped with those who found the frequently moldy bread to be intolerable. Before long, exchange rates were developed: so much of one thing was worth so much of something else. The prisoners bartered with one another, and to my knowledge no one ever complained that he had been taken advantage of. Some of the exchange rates that developed were a half-ration of bread for a bowl of rice, a half-ration of bread for three or four packs of cigarettes, or a half-ration of bread for a ration of dried fish (on those occasions when this delicacy was served). When small bottles of milk were available, some prisoners tried to trade them also.

Their trading value varied greatly, however, and it was difficult to break even on those deals.

By mid-April 1942 our complaints to the Japanese regarding the lack of proper food had become so insistent that the authorities issued a memorandum, the subject of which was "Plans for Improving Methods of Cooking with the Limited Amounts of Material Available without Additional Expense":

> It is believed that with more effort from the cooks assigned to the galley an improvement in the ration can be made.
>
> With the use of the limited amount of materials available, and at moderate expense, the cooks must strive in every possible way to improve the ration by using utmost skill in its preparation. Of course the Japanese Supply Officer and Petty Officers will endeavor to promote the ration, but the prisoners are also expected to exert all effort and study the best manner for preparing such materials available in order that it may be most palatable. . . .
>
> With the above in mind, three officers and ten Petty Officers from the prisoners will be selected to cooperate with the men in working in the galley as a ration improving committee. The committee will make plans and submit them to the Nippon Supply Officer.
>
> The aim of this committee should be the preparation, quantity, etc., of such foods as have been served, i.e.,
>
> 1. Quantity of staple food, especially quantity of staple food for working party.
> 2. Opinions of preparing menu.
> 3. Seasoning to taste.
> 4. Balanced ration.
> 5. Equal distribution of ration.
>
> S. Yoshido
> Supply Officer.

I felt that this provided us with an unequaled opportunity to put our complaints into writing, so on 20 April Sam Newman, Arnie Carlson, and I fired off a response. This put me, as the unofficial leader of the responders, in line for a round of face slappings (or worse). On this occasion, however, I managed to escape their "undivided attention."

Our response to the Japanese prison officials included the following major points and recommendations:

> With the present food provided, little improvement in the ration can be made.

We are each receiving 1,500 calories per day, whereas the requirements of a nonworking man are 3,000 calories and those of a working
man are 4,000 calories per day. Lack of sufficient food is indicated by
the large number of prisoners suffering from beriberi, edema, scurvy,
and exhaustion. In order to prevent the loss of man-hours of productive work by the working parties, we recommend:

—Double the quantity of vegetables issued.
—Serve meat or fish at least once a day.
—Increase the amount of rice served.
—Add fresh or dried fruit at least twice a week.
—Increase the amount of vegetables served.

Salt should be provided to improve the taste of food and to replen-
ish that lost by working.

Additional sugar would increase the energy content and taste of many
foods.

But the interest shown by the authorities in our well-being was a cha-
rade. Instead of showing any improvement in type or quantity, as time
went by our food got steadily worse.

✳ On 16 January 1943, 140 new prisoners arrived. These men had been
captured in the Philippines and had survived the infamous Bataan
Death March to Camp O'Donnell in April 1942. They had then been
moved to prison camps on the Japanese home island of Honshu before
being brought to Zentsuji. Yeoman First Class Lyle W. Eads describes
the arrival and condition of these men in graphic terms:

"The . . . 'Death March' survivors were in the worst physical condition that the prisoners in Zentsuji had ever seen. It made most of them
ashamed to think of having wallowed in self-pity, when here were men
who it was obvious had suffered ten times as badly. Men whose bodies were caked with grime, lice-infested, many hardly able to walk, all
mere skeletons with skin stretched over the bones. Americans all and
Americans . . . whom the hearts of the Zentsuji prisoners went out to,
for whatever was necessary to help these fellow POWs be restored to
human beings.

"The prison doctors prevailed upon the Japanese for hot water with
which to bathe these men and for a change of clothing, any kind of
clean clothing. . . .

"The . . . new officer prisoners were placed in one end of the POW
barracks and quarantined. . . . A dozen of the Zentsuji officer prisoners volunteered to enter the quarantine and assist with getting the new
men bathed and into clean clothes. . . . The prisoners were then picked

up as though they were babies and lifted into the tub where they were soaped and scrubbed. . . . Most, though grown men, weighed less than 100 pounds."[1] ✳

Our most eagerly anticipated morale boosters were the infrequent letters and packages we received from home. *Infrequent* is inadequate to describe their arrival. Although Virginia wrote many letters, I received only a few of them.

Our mail was censored, both at home and in Japan. After reading them, we tried to fill in the blanks where words and sometimes entire sentences had been crossed out with heavy-duty black felt-tipped pens or had been cut out entirely. The Japanese imposed the following restrictions: letters must be less than twenty-five words long; they must be typewritten or legibly printed in block letters; and the subject matter must be strictly personal, including no military or political matters or opinions.[2]

There was a lot of confusion about how to address our mail. Some of the first letters I received from Virginia were addressed c/o International Red Cross, P.O.W. Information Bureau, Geneva, Switzerland. These letters arrived very late: the one postmarked 10 March 1942 arrived on 3 December, after a delay of nine months; the one postmarked 6 July 1942 arrived on 7 April 1943—another nine-month delay; and the one postmarked 4 September 1942 did not arrive until 11 January 1944, a full sixteen months late. Virginia addressed subsequent letters directly to Zentsuji Prison Camp, Shikoku Island, Japan. These letters took an average of six months to arrive—a big improvement.

Factors that contributed to this long delay undoubtedly included the burden of censorship in both the United States and Japan; the long distances, through war zones, over which the letters traveled; and the lack of transportation. Additionally, our camp administrators frequently did not give us mail that we knew had arrived until several weeks later. When they did deliver it, we thought they did so reluctantly.

When mail was withheld, it was my responsibility to ask why. The usual excuse was that censoring the mail took a long time. Of course, we knew otherwise. The man responsible for reading the mail was a Nisei well educated in English. Because the length and content of the letters were limited by the Japanese-imposed restrictions, we knew that he could read them quickly. Nondelivery of mail was just another means of harassing us: mental hazing, mental torture.

Although the content of their letters was restricted, our families developed an uncanny expertise at inserting special words or phrases that carried hidden meanings to the addressee. For example, Virginia included the following phrases in letters dated 21 and 24 November

Envelopes of letters mailed from Zentsuji *(U.S. Naval Academy Museum)*

1943, respectively: "She went off proudly, impressive ceremony. Don so erect, happy. Moving pictures. Ryden, Holzworth and Bill Lineberry at breakfast. Wore orchids." "She is a beauty, very heavy, we named her Guam. Don out today." These two letters told me that Virginia had been present at the launching of a new ship, the heavy cruiser *Guam*.[3] From the names she mentioned I knew that she had been in Philadel-

Sponsors at launching of USS *Guam* on 17 September 1944. Shown left to right: Mrs. Todd (wife of aide to Governor McMillin), Mrs. McMillin, Mrs. Giles, and Donald T. Giles, Jr. *(Collection of Donald T. Giles, Jr.)*

phia, where the ship must have been launched. "Don so erect" and "Don out today" told me that our son was a midshipman at the Naval Academy, and that he had also been present at the launching.

In a subsequent letter, written in June 1944, Virginia included the phrase "Don is a happy youngster." Although this would have meant nothing to a Japanese censor, to me it brought the unmistakable news that our son had been promoted and was entering his Youngster Year (i.e., second year) at Annapolis.

I do not remember the date, but sometime in 1943 some Red Cross packages arrived in camp. During our time at Zentsuji we each received at most only seven or eight packages. Although more were sent, I received only three. None of the packages arrived in good shape. Some had been opened and plundered. Items packaged in tins were satisfactory, but cheese was moldy, crackers were dry, and any cigarettes that had not been stolen were stale. These packages had surely been in storage for a long time.

When packages arrived in camp, instead of giving them to us the Japanese placed them in a warehouse as a matter of course. This, and the withholding of mail that we knew had arrived in camp weeks earlier, affected our morale seriously. Although many of us had been treated brutally for supposed infractions, the most damaging punishment of all was this withholding of food packages from starving prisoners, packages that we knew had arrived in camp and been placed in a warehouse.[4]

On one such occasion I asked the Japanese many times to release packages that we knew had arrived in camp more than a month earlier. Each time, I was turned down on one pretext or another. Finally, before relenting, the authorities showed their true colors. In essence they said that the Japanese had allowed the packages to enter their country and had gotten them to our camp, but they were not responsible for having them distributed. Only someone who had attempted to deal with the Japanese for a long time would recognize this as a typical response.

Pilferage was apparent immediately, because each package was supposed to contain the items listed on an enclosed bill of lading:

Evaporated milk, irradiated, 14$\frac{1}{2}$-oz. can
Hardtack, 8-oz. pkg.
Cheese, 8-oz. pkg.
Instant cocoa, 8-oz. tin
Sardines, 15-oz. tin
Oleomargarine (vitamin A), 1-lb. tin
Corned beef, 12-oz. tin
Sweet chocolate, 2 5$\frac{1}{2}$-oz. bars
Granulated sugar, 2-oz. pkg.
Powdered orange concentrate (vitamin C), 2 3$\frac{1}{2}$-oz. pkg.
Dehydrated soup, 2 2$\frac{1}{2}$-oz. pkg.
Prunes, 1-lb. pkg.
Instant coffee, 1 4-oz. tin
Cigarettes, 1 pkg. of 20
Smoking tobacco, 1 2$\frac{1}{2}$-oz. pkg.

Our doctors cautioned us repeatedly to be careful, advising us to make the contents of the package last for about a week. Our systems might be unable to accept the rich food. Rapid consumption of it might cause edema or beriberi. But we were ravenously hungry, and because we had not had good food for so long, it was difficult to follow the doctors' advice. I witnessed one instance in which a prisoner was unable to do so. Some of the packages contained a tin of milk powder called Klim.

Although several of us tried to stop him, the man took a spoon and consumed practically the entire can. In a short time he swelled up like a toad.

Swapping became routine. Some felt that the moldy cheese was better nutritionally, so they swapped their "good" cheese with other prisoners for cheese that was moldy. Those who didn't smoke swapped cigarettes for food items such as cheese or cocoa. Such swapping continued until the contents of the boxes were consumed.

There were many cooks and bottle washers in camp, and they dreamed up some wild concoctions using items from the food boxes. The rice we were given to eat frequently looked like an unappetizing sticky substance bearing some kinship to wallpaper paste. Some prisoners would save this gluey substance until they had enough to mold into a disklike flat object that resembled a cake (or a discus, depending upon your physical dexterity). Then they would mix some water with milk powder and, using chopsticks, would whip it to the consistency of whipped cream. As you might imagine, this was a time-consuming process, but time was something we had in abundance. Finally, they used the "whipped cream" to decorate the rice cake. Many peculiar designs and decorations were devised, some prisoners even using cocoa and vegetable colors to make their cakes more appealing.

Time hung heavy on our hands, and little jealousies began to crop up. The Japanese were riding high on their wave, and the news brought by new prisoners did not raise our hopes for an early end to the war. Morale was sinking, and I felt that we needed something to think about besides ourselves. I discussed the problem with other senior officers, and we decided to establish a library and open a canteen. After much cajoling and more than a few painful arguments, the Japanese agreed— contrary to their usual behavior. Were they turning soft on us?

In March 1942, when Ambassador Joseph C. Grew closed our embassy in Tokyo and left for the United States, he sent his library, as well as a Victrola with many records, to us at Zentsuji. These books plus those we had brought from Guam formed the basis of the camp library. Including some provided by the Japanese supply officer, we had about five hundred books of all types: novels, histories, foreign-language texts, biographies, technical books and manuals. We selected several men to be librarians, catalogued the books, and opened our doors. I doubt that it is recorded in the *Guinness Book of World Records*, but ours was possibly the first library in a foreign POW camp, certainly the first in Japan. It became extremely popular and did much to elevate morale and bring a renewed sense of unity and spirit to the prisoners.

After several months of constant use, many of the books became worn and in need of repair. Two Australian prisoners who had been printers taught some of us how to repair and bind books. With their guidance we made a crude binding press and started a book-repair shop. Of course, in addition to repairing books, we were getting some occupational therapy.

The Zentsuji canteen was nothing to write home about, but it did provide prisoners with someplace to browse and spend what little extra money they had on the few items available. What was the source of our "extra money"? By the terms of the Geneva Convention, officer prisoners were paid a wage commensurate to their corresponding rank in the Japanese army. For a major, this was 75 yen (or about $38) a month.[5] Contrary to the convention, 20 percent of this pay was set aside in "postal savings"—a misnomer, inasmuch as a large part of it was being diverted by the Japanese to support their war effort.[6] We objected strenuously to this, but to no avail. After these "savings," sufficient money was left that we could still make some small purchases— *very* small purchases.

Our enlisted men were required to work and were supposedly paid the same wage as Japanese laborers. This was minimal, practically nothing. Considering the hard manual labor the men were required to perform, they were really taken advantage of. There was not much in the canteen to be had, but the selections had to be purchased with the few yen they could save from their meager pay.

Stock for the canteen was provided by the Japanese supply officer, who was sure to eliminate anything worthwhile. We couldn't obtain edibles, which was what we wanted more than anything else: crackers, cheese, snacks, candy, pogey-bait. Occasionally there were some Victrola records—Japanese reproductions of British or American classical recordings. These were very popular, and we bought them in a hurry. Most of the stock, however, was sleazy material such as cheap scratch pads, pencils and pencil sharpeners, pens, ink, paper, paste, some art paper, bamboo forks and spoons, cups, straw sandals (which we called go-aheads), straw hats, a powder that when mixed with water tasted like horseradish, and a few varieties of pills. The Japs thrived on pills, thinking that they could cure anything. Because we were always hungry, we bought pills also, hoping they might contain some vitamins that would help us. Among the most popular items in the canteen were bottles of Wakamoto tablets. The label on these bottles claimed that they included vitamins B_1, B_2, and B_6, plus various digestive enzymes. We believed that these tablets helped supplement our vitamin-poor diet.

Although we had little money to spend and there was little of value for sale in the canteen, it proved to be another morale-boosting activity, as we had hoped. Just being able to look at what was there was a tonic for many of us. As our time in prison dragged on, items for the canteen became increasingly scarce, and their quality became even sleazier. The significance of the drop in the quantity and quality of the merchandise was not wasted on us. In some ways, it too served to boost morale: if times were getting tougher for the Japanese, things had to be looking up for us.

The Japanese interrogated us many times during our imprisonment. First we were required to answer extensive questionnaires written on very poor quality paper. Typical questions included the following:

1. What are your impressions of the war?
2. Why did the war start?
3. Who do you think will win the war?
4. What do you think of the Japanese soldier?
5. What do you think of the Japanese artillery?
6. When do you think the war will end?
7. How will world war end?
8. Describe in detail your duties in your service.
9. Do you favor Roosevelt's policy?
10. How great is the Jewish influence in America?
11. What is your opinion of the Co-prosperity Sphere of Greater East Asia?
12. What do you think of England? Of Churchill?
13. Would America annex England?
14. What is your opinion of the Axis Powers?

Other questions were of a more personal nature and covered everything imaginable regarding your life and family, even your hobbies—a complete biography. The information could have formed a valuable biographical-intelligence database, but whether it was retained at Zentsuji or sent to Tokyo, we did not know.

Finally, each prisoner was brought before a group of Japanese officers and questioned in detail about his military activities. We knew that the Japanese had a full library of American publications, including officer directories. In many countries such documents are difficult to obtain, but in the United States they are readily available. Because of this, we knew it would be foolish to lie about any of our duties or assignments. Our answers could be verified easily. The best we could do was color our responses to technical questions so as not to reveal military information that would be of use to the enemy.

When asked about the types of duty I had performed, I enumerated the battleships, cruisers, and destroyers on which I had served during my twenty-year career. When I mentioned my submarine duty, my questioners became extremely interested. However, this duty had been on old boats at the beginning of my career as a commissioned officer, almost twenty years before the war. Because I had not served on our new-type submarines, I was certain I did not have information they would find interesting or didn't already know.

From time to time we were instructed in Japanese subjects, one of which was "The Manner of Rendering the Japanese Salute." The order stated that in rendering the salute we should "stand erect; hold arms and hands straight down the sides; and bow from the waist, holding the back stiff, about thirty degrees from the erect position." We found this manner of saluting by subservient bowing to be extremely degrading. Because of this, on many occasions we did it very sloppily, or exaggerated it so that no one could fail to understand our contempt. For this we were rewarded with severe slaps.

In late September a new Japanese commanding officer arrived for Zentsuji. As was the custom, we were routed from our barracks, made to fall in, mustered, and inspected by the new officer. Then he read a long and pompous speech that presented us with our most difficult problem thus far.

I am Major General Takumi, successor to the post of Major General Mizuhara. I am satisfied to know that, for the sake of your honor as military men of your countries, you will continue to respect the instructions given you by the former Superintendent, also the regulations and orders issued by the Japanese Army. . . .

My principles coincide with those instructions given by the former Superintendent, Major General Mizuhara, and regardless of some repetitions of former instructions, I shall here state a few points with regard to the treatment of you all.

1. The treatment which you will receive will be in accordance with the Regulations of the Japanese Army which you shall respect. . . . You must be well aware of the fact that should you violate them you shall be severely punished by comparing the case with the regulations.

2. You must never escape from this camp or attempt such actions. I wish you fully realize that it is one of the important duties of this camp to let you live the life of war prisoners at ease, first, by having expelled

from your minds any intention of escape, and thus allowing you to pray for early restoration of peace at rest.

3. You shall submit to labor. . . . At present there is not a single idle person in Japan and everybody is enduring hardship and scarcity, and in serving his country to the utmost, within the bounds of his profession. . . . Therefore . . . it is thought to be only natural that there should be no one idle in this camp, and to have you engaged in appropriate labor, and, I wish you all will realize this fact and voluntarily occupy yourselves in assigned labor.

4. Pay good attention to your health. There are many factors in the present war which indicate that it will be a long-termed war. Therefore it is believed that you will be obliged to continue your life as war prisoners. . . . As I am much concerned about your health, I will take further consideration of the necessary provisions regarding the matter in the future.

I will state that especially to those who will obey the Japanese Army regulations and who have taken the oath not to make any attempts to escape, will, it is needless to say, not be treated with hostile feelings, but rather with respect and sympathy.

> Major General H. Takumi
> Imperial Japanese Army.

To take an oath not to attempt escape—this order turned the camp upside down. Discussion was rampant. Of course, we realized that escape was impossible. Even if a prisoner succeeded in escaping from the camp or in breaking away from a working party, he would simply have escaped into another sort of prison: an oriental culture into which he could not blend and whose language he could not speak or understand. At the same time, we all knew that we were expected to make every effort possible to escape and return to our posts. We were on the horns of a dilemma. What could we do?

We told the Japanese that our military doctrine would not permit us to swear to such a document, and we refused to do so. A few days later we were given the oath to sign a second time, and again everyone in the camp refused. We felt that the Japanese were actually surprised by our refusal. Someone had miscalculated, and face was being lost.

Somehow we heard that the camp authorities had passed it up the line to Tokyo for further instructions. Several weeks passed, and we thought we had won our point. Not so—we were the ones who had miscalculated. The senior officers among the prisoners were brought into the camp office and told in no uncertain terms that these papers had to be signed by all. The camp authorities had received orders from Tokyo to get them signed immediately. Again we refused.

Another breathing spell followed, during which the atmosphere in camp was heavy with uncertainty as we waited to see what would occur. What was the significance of the oath? The Japanese knew as well as we did that escape was impossible. If we signed the oath, did they plan to reduce the number of soldiers guarding us so that more men could be sent to combat duty? Perhaps, but we did not think this was likely. We felt that we were caught in the middle of a big face-saving issue, and unfortunately, one of the most important aspects of Japanese culture was face.

After several weeks the period of uncertainty came to an end. Each officer and enlisted man was brought individually into the camp conference room, where all of the Japanese officers were seated around a large, rectangular table. With one notable exception, it reminded me of the setup for a general court martial. The exception was that a long, sharp samurai sword was laid out at each officer's place. Remembering how these swords had been used to behead some of our shipmates on Guam, you might describe the scene as "intimidating." Again, each prisoner was asked, "Will you sign the statement?"—another copy being laid before him.

Again, my response was that it was against our military doctrine to sign such a statement. At this the Japanese officers' tempers rose markedly, and "Sake Pete," one of the more vicious of them, smashed his fist onto the table and shrieked "Banzai!" Hearing this terrifying sound and seeing the samurai swords laid out on the table, I felt that something drastic was afoot. Totally dispirited, I relented and said that I would sign the statement, but under duress. Picking up the cheap Japanese pen that was placed before me, in large, bold letters I wrote, "UNDER DURESS," and signed. In doing so, because of the cheap pen and the poor quality of the tissuelike paper on which the statement was typed—but primarily because I was so upset over my defeat—I tore the paper. This did not seem to concern the Japanese. They had my signature. They had won the battle of face.

After each prisoner had signed the statement, he was taken to a room well removed from those occupied by the prisoners who were yet to be called—this to prevent conversation between the two groups. Some continued to hold out and would not sign the statement. For this they were stripped of their clothes and belts and were literally thrown into cells where they were kept in solitary confinement. There was no light in these cells. They were cold, dank, and lacking in sanitation. After about twenty-four hours of this treatment most of these prisoners also signed. After their release from solitary confinement, they said that it wasn't the lack of food or sanitation that changed their minds, but the mosquitoes that stung them continuously and the many rats that populated the place.

Of course, to sign such an oath, even under duress, was improper, but the conditions of our captivity were beyond the limits of most civilized experience. Each of us responded according to his own capabilities, but to this day I am unsure that my response was sufficient.

From that day on I was compelled to wear a cloth badge on which was written in Japanese, "Person in special need of attention or admonishment."

That September five additional prisoners arrived at Zentsuji. In this group were two of our former shipmates from Guam who had been hospitalized and left there as a result of that action. They were Chief Yeoman J. H. Blaha, USN, and Mr. F. Perry, a former Cable Station employee. We had not expected to see either of these two men again, so their arrival was a real homecoming, if Zentsuji could ever have been thought of as home.

Before long the maple trees that overhung our wall changed color, and the warm autumn winds that blew across the Inland Sea began to chill. Thanksgiving came, then December, and Christmas, and Hanukkah, and New Year's Eve. There was no turkey and no Santa Claus, no champagne or popping corks, and certainly no festivity. Thanksgiving? Yes, we were thankful. We were thankful to be alive, even if only marginally so. We had existed for a year in captivity. For several more Thanksgivings we would have to find things for which to be thankful. Today I am thankful that we did not know this at the time.

12 ✳ I Establish Zentsuji College

"If you don't like the weather, wait. It will get worse!" During the years that followed, at Zentsuji we could replace the word *weather* with almost anything: *food, harassment, living conditions, morale.* You name it, and it became worse.

As the war progressed U.S. submarine attacks on enemy merchant ships became increasingly effective. The Japanese were not self-sufficient. They were importing a large proportion of their wartime materials and food, particularly rice. Throughout Japan belts were being tightened, and news articles indicated that people were being prepared to cinch up even tighter.

Our food got steadily worse. The rice supply became less plentiful and much dirtier. After cleaning and cooking it, we would try, when possible, to fortify it with soybeans, millet, barley, and whatever we could catch: scraps of turtle meat, cut-up frogs, bits of snake. At times it tasted like sawdust, which it might well have contained. Without much relish we would down our cups of seaweed soup, which if we were lucky contained bits of weed or vine. We had forgotten the taste of meat or fish. Such was our gourmet diet.

The enlisted men were allowed more food. This was not because of any special compassion on the part of the Japanese. Without being fed, the men would have been unable to work so hard. Sometimes they were rewarded with additional food—more rice, a pickled plum in a rice ball, sweet buns from the civilian bakery adjacent to camp—and this created some disaffection. Sometimes the men obtained extra buns from friendly Korean guards. Sometimes they even went over the wall and stole food from the bakery.

Our hunger became greater. Occasionally we saved the rice from several meals in order to have at least one that seemed belly-filling. Of course, the hunger pangs returned unabated only a short time after such a "feast." Frequently, if the heat was uneven or too high, when the rice was cooked some of it would stick to the pots and turn brown. Many asked to be served this burned rice when it was scraped off. It seemed to have more flavor.

Every morning one of the working parties was taken under guard to Takamatsu, where they worked as stevedores unloading ships and stocking dockside warehouses. Only a white hat could have accomplished the ruses that these men devised. Ours were among the most imaginative and gutsy men I have ever known.

Prior to leaving camp some of the men would tie their pants legs at the cuff. This was not unusual. It was frequently done to reduce the amount of warehouse dust that got on their legs. Each of these men carried a short, hollow bamboo stick similar to a soda straw, one end of which had been sharpened to a hard point. While working inside the warehouse one of the men would sidle up to a bag of dry cargo such as salt, sugar, or wheat and stick the pointed end of his hollow bamboo stick into the bag. With the other end of the stick inserted into his pants pocket (in the bottom of which a hole had been cut), he would allow some of the cargo to filter down into the tied-off cuff.

From this point on, "Baggy Pants" would be hidden from view—in the squad formation at Takamatsu, on the train to Zentsuji, and marching back into camp for muster. After the camp had quieted down for the night, "Baggy Pants" would untie his cuff, and we would collect the stolen produce. Because the officers were better paid than the enlisted men, we paid a nominal charge for our portion of this bounty. This was money well spent. The working party received very little pay for their hard work on the docks, and they sometimes had an opportunity to visit local stores on the Takamatsu waterfront where they could purchase newspapers, dried or salted fish, cigarettes, and other small items.

These cigarettes were called Kinsees. There were only ten to a pack, and they were poor substitutes for American cigarettes, both in size and in taste. Occasionally some of them appeared in the canteen, where they cost 15 sen a pack, or approximately 8 cents.[1] (This gives an indication of values: members of the working party were paid only 70 sen, or 35 cents, a day for their heavy work.) Because of the poor quality of the Kinsees, many of us soon became nonsmokers.

In the Japanese army, discipline was severe for anyone of lesser rank. For the enlisted man it was both brutal and without recourse. He was indoctrinated to obey swiftly and without question. To him brutality was a way of life. Punishment might be meted out by a fist in the face, by the kick of a heavy boot, or by blows with a kendo stick (a sword-length, two-inch-diameter split bamboo pole).[2] When used to administer punishment, a kendo stick left painful welts that did not heal quickly.

Japanese soldiers were taught to despise Americans who had surrendered. "Do not fall a captive—even if the alternative is death" reads his soldier's manual. "Bear in mind that to be captured not only means disgracing the Army, but your parents and family. . . . You will never be able to hold your head high again, always save the last round for yourself." The suicidal kamikaze attacks on our ships showed how little personal thought was given to death. One died for one's family and emperor, and such a death was regarded as glorious. So to the Japanese soldier, we were weaklings to have surrendered. In their hierarchical system we occupied an extremely low position. As prisoners, we were the ultimate "peckees" in the pecking order.

❋ Reginald W. Reed confirms this characterization of the pecking order: "Soon after our arrival at Zentsuji we chanced to look out of the upstairs window into the compound of the Army Camp. This particular morning the Japanese equivalent of 'Sad Sack,' apparently a raw recruit, dropped his rifle. The noncom in charge whacked 'Sad Sack' in the face several times and then put the platoon through the drill again. But 'Sad Sack' dropped his rifle again, whereupon the noncom directed the whole platoon to work over the unfortunate 'S.S.' with their rifle butts. After which performance 'Sad Sack' was lugged off somewhere, certainly more dead than alive!"[3] ❋

In order to demonstrate their superiority, the Japanese officers and enlisted men both frequently vented their wrath on us. Every Zentsuji prisoner can attest to that. When a prisoner failed to understand an order or to obey swiftly enough and without question, the result would be painful. Toward the end of our captivity, when we were often too weak to carry out orders, the punishments seemed to be that much more violent.

As the fortunes of war began to turn our way, conditions in camp became progressively worse. Under normal circumstances we might have been able to accept the worsening conditions philosophically. We knew it was because our forces were hammering the Japanese, but we had been through so very much. We had been kicked, beaten, and harassed. We had seen friends beheaded and disemboweled. We were suffering the effects of severe malnutrition. Petty jealousies were beginning to surface among us, and arguments were becoming commonplace. Morale was very low.

In an attempt to shore things up, we started a weekly Sunday night smoker, albeit one without cigarettes, and I originated "Zentsuji College."

We found a great variety and depth of talent in camp. There were some excellent vocalists, among whom Major Donald Spicer comes to mind immediately. Major Spicer formed a group called the Bathhouse Gang and entertained us frequently.

✱ Reed describes an evening "singsong" at Zentsuji: "The sing song was pretty good tonight. The 'Bathhouse Gang' really gave out in good style. The men applauded vociferously as they sang *Dolores, Penny Serenade, Tuxedo Junction, In the Mood,* and a couple of others I do not recall. Oh, yes, *Old Man of the Mountain* was in their repertoire. Malloy, Sergeant, USMC, sang the lead in *Dolores,* and the effect was terrific. Carrillo, QM1 [Quartermaster First Class], USN, sang the lead in *Penny Serenade.* His voice is deep and has strong tonal qualities. Malloy's voice is more that of a tenor, and was most suitable for the lead in *Dolores.* I'd still like to hear Carrillo sing *Ave Maria* as he did in Guam. It was a tear jerker."[4] ✱

Spicer's talents and enthusiasm seemed endless. With the help of other prisoners, he got together the words of seventy-six popular songs and several hymns. Then, using paper stolen from the Japanese, he and several other prisoners wrote out additional copies, so there were about a hundred for distribution during the smokers. This was more than just labor-intensive. Spicer's crew had been able to "obtain" only a limited amount of paper, and in order to copy so many lyrics, their writing had to be small. Unfortunately, most of the pencils were so soft that they smeared, making it difficult to write legibly, and the paper was so terrible that it tore easily. Theirs was a real labor of love.

Eventually Spicer's singsongs broadened into full-blown musical productions, variety shows, and full-length "meller-dramas."

✱ Although Major Spicer's efforts were greatly appreciated by his fellow prisoners, they were not entirely approved of by the Japanese camp authorities: "I was called down to the Commandants's office for this but managed to persuade him to permit it. He held me personally responsible for the entire performance and told me that I would be punished if anything in the shows did not meet with his approval. In fact, he told me that if the Nips were insulted I might even be killed. An interpreter was always present at the shows.

"In July . . . he prohibited singing by more than ten people at once except in church. . . . Probably what caused the curtailment of singing was a very lusty rendition of 'God Bless America' on the Fourth of July programs. In February I had organized a choir of ten and a harmony group of eight. Music was continued in this way. Later, Dr. H. B. McInnis, a Navy Dentist, organized a 'swing' group which furnished some excellent music."[5]

Reed reports, "Corporal [G. E.] Nichols delivered two recitations, both of which were of his own writing. The first was a Chicago version of *The Three Bears,* and was fair. The other one was *Horatio at the Bridge—What He Really Thought* and was excellent."[6] ✳

Some of the prisoners were skilled at writing and producing skits that brought laughter from men who had almost forgotten how to laugh. Although there were numerous actors in our midst, production was an area in which the British excelled. They were magnificent. And with a scarcity of materials, it was surprising what the technical-minded could come up with for backdrops, scenery, and makeshift costumes.

Two Dutch officers wrote and recited hilarious risqué poems that had us all roaring with laughter. Because the camp was located at the edge of Zentsuji, I often wondered what the locals must have thought of our uproarious laughter.

Bill Lineberry—nicknamed "Surg," for surgeon—was our best storyteller, his North Carolina drawl and magnificent Southern accent adding much to his witty tales. We enjoyed his stories immensely, although I am sure the Dutch and British must have had a difficult time understanding his drawl. But we were an international camp, and some of the Dutch and British wit was also lost on the Yanks.

Tales were told, many songs sung, pantomimes performed, and poems recited. Thus, for an hour or more each week devotees of the stage whisked fellow prisoners out of the doldrums and into another world. The roars of laughter and sustained applause were medicine for all. The Japanese required that an interpreter be present at our smokers to insure that we did not slander them or their emperor. Of course, at times the performers would do just that, using slang or colloquialisms that we understood and that we hoped would be unfamiliar to the interpreter. Sometimes there were problems, but fortunately they were few.

✳ An example of one such problem is related by Reed: "The program was going along fine until [Boatswain's Mate First Class, G. M.] Maloof was called upon to sing and recite his newest creation, a parody on 'The Ace in the Hole,' entitled 'That Old Rice in the Bowl.' Maloof had gotten half way through and the audience was eating it up, when the Nip interpreter broke in and told him not to go on with the recitation. The parody was screamingly funny to all but the Nip who didn't see it that way at all. Actually, there was nothing in the parody intended to slander, libel, or cast reflection upon anyone or anything. The General was told."[7] ✳

It was at about this time that I proposed the establishment of "Zentsuji College." It would give us something to do besides thinking about ourselves, it would help keep our minds sharp, and it would provide us with knowledge that might be helpful after repatriation.

I guess I could have been called the president of Zentsuji College, or possibly dean of engineering. Because I had a master's degree in mechanical engineering and had spent most of my career in that field, I established and taught the engineering curriculum. Other than those that had come from Ambassador Joseph C. Grew's library, we had few textbooks. Many of the enlisted men were engineers, however, and they were easy to teach, with or without books. They were extraordinarily conscientious and, I like to think, acquired useful information from my courses. Several of my students and I corresponded for many years after repatriation.

If I was dean of engineering, there were many other deans in our college as well. All of our deans and professors were extremely competent in their respective fields. Our curriculum included many subjects. Arnie Carlson, a graduate of the U.S. Naval Academy and the Harvard Business School, taught business administration; Sam Newman, who had been with an oil company before entering the navy, taught petroleum engineering and sales engineering; Don Spicer taught Spanish, and our Dutch and British friends taught a variety of other foreign languages. Courses were also offered in law, psychology, and history, but I do not recall the names of those who taught these subjects. Although textbooks were scarce, our professors were sufficiently skilled in their fields that in most cases books weren't needed.

Although we had extremely competent teachers and managed to conduct classes without many books, we lacked other necessities. Paper, pencils, and notebooks could be purchased in our canteen, but they were all made in Japan and were of such poor quality that they were difficult to use. The paper was akin to onionskin and tore easily.

Enrollment was sizable, and classes were well attended by both officers and men. I believe that some who continued their studies after repatriation did so because of encouragement they received at Zentsuji College. Although we were not licensed to award sheepskins, we did receive "degrees" of a more valuable kind: Master of How to Get along Together under the Most Trying of Circumstances, Master of Consideration for Others, and most important of all, Doctor of Just Staying Alive.

After hours we held discussion groups on such subjects as "What is the strategy of the Allies?" "How is the war progressing?" and "When will Japan be forcibly hit by the Allies?" When these extracurricular seminars were in progress, we would post our own guards so that we would not be interrupted. The lecturer would sit where he could see the guards. If the guard saw a Japanese watchman coming, he would call out "Tallyho," and the discussion would be changed immediately to something more benign. After some time the Japanese began to guess the meaning of *tallyho,* and we were forced to choose other warning signals.

We had several decks of playing cards that had been purchased from the guards. Although usable, they were poor-quality, Japanese-made cards that soon lost much of their stiffness. Although solitaire and poker were frequently played, cribbage was the favored game. Some of the men had made cribbage boards, and we used sticks or stones for poker chips—we had become masters of making do. Using the Vanderbilt System, Commander H. D. Richardson, Royal Navy, taught several of the prisoners how to play bridge. Frequently, while a game was in progress the Japanese guards who roamed the barracks would stop and watch. They knew little of Western card games, and it was interesting to watch their expressions change as they tried to decipher what was taking place.

In addition to making cribbage boards, there were other woodworking projects in camp. One man carved intricate chessmen from cherry wood, and we had an international chess tournament. Someone else carved ornate paperweights. However, possibly the most interesting woodworking activity was Arnie Carlson's pipe shop. Using only the most rudimentary of tools, Arnie fashioned beautiful pipes from pieces of wood that he cut from nearby trees. I have one of his pipes in my collection and treasure it above all others. On the face of the bowl Arnie carved a detailed replica of the navy shield. Several of the pipe smokers in camp recommended Wilke's on Madison Avenue in New York City for pipes, tobacco, and pipe repair. Taking their advice, after repatriation I took Arnie's pipe to Wilke's and had it stemmed. Now, after years of use, in addition to being my most treasured pipe, it also smokes better than most of the rest.

Pipe carved at Zentsuji POW camp for Commander Giles by Lieutenant A. J. Carlson, USN. *(Collection of Donald T. Giles, Jr.)*

Since the end of the war I have read with great interest accounts of how German and Japanese prisoners of war were treated in the United States and in Great Britain. One of the primary concerns at home seems to have been providing adequate recreational facilities for the German and Japanese POWs. We should have been so lucky. At Zentsuji we had no athletic equipment, nor would there have been any place to use it. The best we could do was to improvise and pantomime a game of baseball. One day we organized an entire game on the road beside our barracks. A pitcher would pitch a nonexistent ball, and a batter would pretend to hit it. Bases were run, and a slide was made at home plate: SAFE! The Japanese guards who watched were flabbergasted. *Basu baru* was a popular game in Japan, so they knew it well. They must have believed that we were really off home plate.

During much of our time in camp we were preoccupied with worries about hunger, cold, brutal treatment, and unsanitary living conditions. These concerns occupied our very being, and as these conditions became worse, our worries followed a parallel path and our morale sank lower and lower. We did everything we could to get the men's minds off themselves and off these very real problems. In many cases we were successful and made them think of other things: entertainment, discussion groups, reading, education. Some of the activities we pursued would seem silly today, but I am convinced that they kept us alive.

A few examples come to mind. Like many of us, Group Captain Paul Metzler, Royal Australian Air Force, had studied spherical trigonometry and astronavigation. Sighting through a hollow bamboo tube that was attached to a crude protractor, he measured the altitude of celestial bodies. Using the data provided by these star sights, he was able to calculate our position—placing us at Zentsuji. As he said, this was a perfect example of achieving gratification and depression in the same operation.

In other instances ingenious devices were produced in response to needs, real or perceived. In order to keep whatever heat there was inside the barrack rooms as well as to obtain privacy, prisoners hung weights on the doors, which were constantly being left open by the guards. These weights were suspended by grass ropes so that the doors would automatically close after being opened. This simple contraption intrigued the Japanese.

Having been a prisoner of war, I can understand how some things happen in prisons that stupefy the public. The human mind becomes very active in prison, where life is so institutionalized. Perhaps this is because physical activity is curtailed or channeled. Sometimes this increased mental activity is for good, and unfortunately, sometimes it is for bad. Ingenious schemes are born that might otherwise never be thought up. The "Baggy Pants" method of pilfering that I described earlier in this chapter is a classic example of such a scheme. We delighted in beating Japanese civilians or our jailers at anything, legally or illegally. We relished any opportunity to pull the wool over their eyes, to get away with things under their very noses, to remind ourselves in any way possible that we were not inferior.

Repeatedly, we refused to pay obeisance to the Japanese. Repeatedly, I found it necessary to argue for our rights as prisoners of war, even as human beings. Repeatedly, I complained about our treatment, our food, and our substandard and unsanitary living conditions. Although these conditions only grew worse, my protests and those of others were not without cost, both physical and emotional. All the senior officers came to know too well the pain and indignity of a slap, a hobnailed kick, and the blows of a kendo stick. But to protect ourselves from punishment would have been to knuckle under to the Japanese. This we could never do. There were few days when I did not remind myself with pride that I was an American, that I was an American naval officer, that I had graduated from Annapolis. We would not give in. We would continue to live under whatever conditions were necessary. This was *our* bushido. We could only hope and pray that the war would not last too much longer. We were testing the limits of our endurance.

As Thanksgiving approached, we thought of our loved ones at home, of tables abundant with food, and of the pleasure of being with friends. We had never really appreciated this holiday until now. Virtually out of the woodwork, artists appeared to help lighten our failing spirits during the holidays. Private B. Patrick Ware of the New Zealand army made many drawings of the camp as well as some cartoons. Using crayons, others drew Christmas cards on cheap Japanese paper.

❋ My father liked to make linoleum block prints and line drawings. While at Zentsuji he turned his artistic ability toward helping to build morale—his own, I suspect, as well as that of other prisoners. During his last year at Zentsuji he drew a Christmas card and circulated it to other rooms in the barracks. On the cover of the card he drew three candles and the wish: "Good Health, Good Cheer, Good Fortune for Christmas and the New Year." Inside the card he drew a horn of plenty out of which tumbled the insignia of each military service (foreign as well as U.S.) represented among the prisoners, and the wish: "HAPPY CHRISTMAS from Giles." On the back page he asked: "Room leaders please pass along and return to D. T. Giles." This request was followed by a list of room numbers and the signatures of room leaders indicating that the card with his Christmas and New Year's wishes had been circulated to the other prisoners. One of the rooms was identified simply as "Sick Bay." After his signature, the following words were written from sick bay by D. V. Albertazzi, Pharmacist's Mate First Class, USN: "Thank you, sir. May yours be fulfilled with expectations of the near future." This card is an important part of the record of my father's life at Zentsuji. I do not have the original card, and unfortunately my photo copy is not good enough to be reproduced in this book. ❋

We decorated our rooms with hanging paper chains and bells, with pictures of Santa Claus and sleighs, with wreaths and imitation candles. Major Don Spicer and his vocalists, the Hungry Harmonics, brightened our otherwise colorless days with songs and carols. And our two Dutch submariners and others produced humorous poems, an example of which is quoted below:

'Twas the night before Christmas, time for pleasant surprise,
　But the food buckets brought nothing new to our eyes,
For it's daikons and rice each day of the year,
　And we're lucky to get it with all food so dear.

And all that we heard in that damned Commonwealth
 Was the time worn old adage: "Take care of your health."

'Twas the night before Christmas and all thru the camp
 We lay still and listened to the Benjoe's tramp,
Thru wind and thru snow they got there or bust
 And if shivers don't get them the Chilblains must.
And all that we heard in that damned Commonwealth
 Was the time worn old adage: "Take care of your health."

'Twas the night before Christmas, and all thru Japan
 We all lay here desperate for a white woman's hand.
The Red Cross sent parcels of food and of clothes
 But none of those lovelies who live in silk hose.
And all that we heard in that damned Commonwealth
 Was the time worn old adage: "Take care of your health."

But there'll come a day my friends never fear
 When we shall have bacon and beefsteak and beer.
With a saniflush toilet, and bed to sleep in,
 And the thought in our hearts to make us all grin
That an end has been made to that damned Commonwealth
 Where all that we heard was: "Take care of your health."
(POW author unknown)

13 ✳ Our Last Year at Zentsuji

New Year's Day of 1944 was bitter cold. It had started to snow during the night, and we had nothing left to prevent the cold from penetrating to our bones. None of us had much flesh left to serve as insulation, and the topcoats we had been given upon our arrival were now thin and tattered. Things were definitely not going well for the Japanese. Although we received little news from any source and little propaganda from our captors, there were indications that fate had turned against the Rising Sun.

Occasionally we saw contrails high above us heading in the direction of Honshu. Our prison guards had been replaced by a company composed of boys. Their uniforms were ill fitting, and when they stood at attention, the ends of their rifle barrels came to just about the tops of their heads. We were not the least bit sorry for the Japanese army, but we were sorry for these youngsters. Their lives had scarcely begun.

Perhaps the most telling measure we had of the progress of the war was a negative one: no new prisoners were arriving at Zentsuji. Of course, it could have been that they were being interned at other camps, but we chose to be more positive in our outlook, to believe that there were few, if any, new prisoners to be interned.

We had never realized that we might be prisoners of war this long. That was fortunate. Had we known, we might not have survived. We had miscalculated the strength and economic ability of the Japanese to wage a war this long. We had always hoped that we would be exchanged, or that our fleet would come and release us. Who among us would be able to hold out much longer? However, all the indications we obtained by one means or another were that things were going better for the Allies. It was only this that gave us hope and kept us alive.

Somehow we obtained an issue of the *Japan Times Weekly* from January 1944. It contained the following brief article regarding Tarawa, which helped our morale considerably:

> Having inflicted tremendous damage on about 50,000 enemy troops which had landed and having contributed greatly to the aerial and naval operations of their comrade forces by drawing in a powerful enemy task force, the Imperial Naval Landing Party, of about 3,000 who were garrisoned on Tarawa and Makin Islands of the Gilbert group, made a final charge on the enemy on November 26 and died gloriously, it was revealed in a communique issued by Imperial Headquarters on December 20.
>
> Living up to the traditions of the Imperial Armed Forces, the members of the Japanese garrison commanded by Rear Admiral Keiji Shibasaki, furiously attacked the numerically superior enemy landing forces since November 24 never letting up with their fighting despite the persistent bombing and strafing by the enemy planes and bombardment from the enemy ships, the communique added.

Occasionally one of the Japanese guards who could speak a little English boasted to us of the sinkings of many Allied ships. When we questioned the veracity of this information, the guard would reply, "We believe what His Imperial Majesty tells us, and you must also believe him!" We felt that all Japanese in higher authority knew that they were slowly being defeated. Even so, they kept the propaganda wheels grinding away for the benefit of their people. No one who lives in the United States, where freedom of the press and freedom of speech prevail, could possibly imagine how firmly the news in Japan was suppressed or how heavily slanted it was.

Members of our working parties who visited Takamatsu and the town of Zentsuji were able to observe firsthand what was taking place outside our "controlled environment." They reported that Japanese civilians were also suffering—not as badly as we were, by any means, but they also knew the agony of war. Their food was becoming extremely scarce, priority being given to the army units that had been brought back to defend the home islands. Only pumpkins were plentiful. People had little charcoal with which to heat their homes, and except for army vehicles, no automobiles were to be seen in either city.

Perhaps the most revealing information that our working parties reported was that despite the positive propaganda with which they had been bombarded, people looked sad. Several of our men said that they felt a strange kinship with them. These civilians had not wanted the war that had been thrust upon them, but they were suffering because of it. We had not wanted the war that their military had begun, but we were near starvation because of it.

As spring approached, we noted that the Japanese officers were not to be seen as frequently—not that we missed them—and when we did see them, they seemed quite bitter, both among themselves and in their dealings with us. We were told that our aircraft had inhumanely attacked several civilian targets but that Japanese home defense units had shot them down. We were cautioned to obey orders. The Japanese would protect us.

Our men had constructed an ingenious set of well-concealed trapdoors leading into the crawlspaces beneath the barracks. "Hot" staple items such as salt, hardtack, and extra rice were stashed here. These spaces were never even partially filled, but we guarded them as though they contained the crown jewels. As hunger became a paramount issue, more and more of the prisoners were willing to take a chance and steal food from the Japs (and, I regret to say, from each other, in a few instances). The penalties for stealing were most severe. No one wanted to be thrown into that unsanitary, foul, bug- and rat-infested brig, but we were starving and were frequently willing to take chances. Receiving nothing approaching the minimum 1,500 calories per day that our bodies needed, we were beginning to suffer from beriberi and from severe vitamin deficiencies that caused joint pain and edema.

The high board fence around the camp was normally patrolled by impressed Korean soldiers. They were not very good guards. They were not particularly observant, and better yet, they frequently patrolled in opposite directions, such that there were periods when sections of the fence were not observed by anyone. This made it easier for prisoners to get out and make after-hours visits to the nearby civilian bakeshop. Although the fence had formed a sturdy barrier when we arrived in camp, like us it had suffered from the effects of the war. It had received no maintenance, and some of the boards were loose or rotten. After dark we would watch the patrol and time its motions. Just as the guards would about-face and start to move away from one another, a prisoner would dart across the open space to the wall and clamber under or through the fence. Then he would make his way stealthily to the bakeshop.

Like most stores in rural Japan, the bakeshop was entered through sliding wooden panels. At night these panels were secured by ingenious-looking screw-type locks that would have been the pride of any inventive mechanical engineer. However, ingenious-looking or not, they provided not a modicum of protection against even our most inept break-in artists, who would simply ignore the locks and jimmy the entire panel out of the way.

Inside the bakeshop, the prisoner would find himself surrounded by glass-topped cases of bread, sugar, hardtack, and sweet buns, from which he would pilfer selectively, trying to conceal the fact that anything had been taken. By 1944 the Japanese were also suffering want, and it was not uncommon for them to steal food from one another. This being the case, had the shopkeeper noticed anything missing, he would probably have thought his shop had been robbed by a fellow countryman rather than by a prisoner. However, it would almost certainly have caused him to make his shop more secure, and this was something we did not want to happen.

Returning to the fence, the prisoner would make a prearranged signal to his compatriots inside. Then, when the guards did another about-face in their patrol, one of us would make an answering signal indicating that all was clear for the return dash under or through the fence and across the prison courtyard. This system worked flawlessly on almost every occasion. Had we considered the law of probability, however, we would have known that after numerous trips to the bakeshop a problem had to occur.

One night, after the "all clear, it's safe to return" signal had been made, one of the guards did an about-face and started the return leg of his patrol too soon. He was heading back toward where the prisoner was about to "escape" back into camp. From the barracks we watched in horror, unable to do anything to help, as the guard and the returning prisoner confronted one another. What occurred was something none of us could have anticipated. Stunned at his discovery, the guard paused momentarily, surveying the prisoner for what seemed like an eternity. Then he did an abrupt about-face and returned to his patrol activities, going in the opposite direction, away from the horrified prisoner whom he had surprised. From that time on, few of us wondered about the loyalty of the impressed Korean guards, who must have felt that they were captives also.

To those among us who appeared to be losing hope, we tried hard to provide encouragement. I feel certain that the morale-building programs we had started and our weekly church services helped keep many prisoners from going off their beams. Many who had not believed in the Supreme Being before their capture now most assuredly placed their faith in God and prayed. Unfortunately, there were some whom we were unable to help. As these men lost hope, you could see them go downhill, both physically and emotionally. A few were lost to us as a result of our inability to help them. Although every means imaginable was used to try to shore up their morale and enliven their faith, their will to die was just too strong. Did we fail them? Thank God, they were only a few!

Thanks to the dedication of our doctors, only nine prisoners died at Zentsuji.[1] Each time someone died, the Japanese asked, "What is the procedure in your country?" Our answer was always the same: we would not cremate the body unless this had been requested by the deceased. The result, however, was always the same: cremation.

The Japanese would provide a pine box to serve as a coffin, and we would hold a brief service over the body. Then we would place the coffin on a two-wheeled *benjo* cart and, accompanied by a small cortege of fellow prisoners and a Japanese guard, proceed to the crematory on the other side of town.

Being one of the senior officers, I frequently accompanied the cortege. After leaving camp we would make our way slowly down the dirt road and through Zentsuji to the crematory. As we passed through town, Japanese civilians would appear, face the cortege, and bow. Then, departing from the stoicism so often imputed to the Japanese, many would indicate their sympathy for the deceased.

At the crematory I would witness the cremation, remove the ashes, and place them in an urn. Then we would return through town to a small cemetery outside the camp. Here one of our chaplains would conduct a short service and then bury the urn.

One day, in June or July I believe, we were ordered to run tape across all of our windows in order to minimize the shattering of glass if we were bombed. Why anyone would want to bomb Zentsuji, we did not know. There were no major industrial sites nearby, and the docks at Takamatsu were well beyond the range of concussion damage from even the largest of American bombs. The fact that our captors would even consider the possibility of such an attack, however, confirmed the identity of the contrails we had begun to see and indicated to us that large-scale bombing was under way. Whenever contrails were seen, always to the west of us, we would be hurried into our barracks—"for your own safety," we were told.

Although we were receiving no news per se, the information we could glean from various sources continued to confirm our belief that the unbeatable Japanese forces were not doing well. The following article, headlined "What Has the Greater East Asia War Brought to Asia?" appeared in an issue of *Sakura* magazine (vol. 5, no. 4). Although on the surface it seemed up-beat, to us it indicated that the Japanese were beginning to pull in their overextended horns:

> The Nippon Government has formally relinquished its extra-territorial rights and returned all its exclusive concessions to China. A bold lead has been taken in sundering the fetters that have hindered the development of China as an independent nation for a century since the time of the notorious Opium War.
>
> Moreover, the fact that Nippon has solemnly promised independence to Burma and the Philippines has not only profoundly inspired the peoples of these two islands and the inhabitants of the entire Greater East Asia Co-prosperity Sphere, but has caused a great awakening of all races suffering under the yoke of the aggressor nations, America and Britain.

That summer some of our junior officers and a large number of enlisted men were transferred to other camps, camps that the Japanese identified as "working camps." At first we believed that this was done to make room for more senior officers at Zentsuji. But because no new prisoners arrived to replace them, we began to understand the true meaning of the adjective *working*. The names of the working camps were never specified, but we knew that our former camp-mates must have been taken to locations where something akin to slave labor was required of them for the faltering Japanese war effort.

From time to time we were brought before the Japanese for a "conference." These conferences always opened with the same question being asked, a question that must have been intended to disarm us. One of the Japanese officers would ask, with feigned sincerity, "What do you want?" Of course, this question always elicited the same predictable answer: "Food!" Then there followed a series of questions about U.S. military strategy and tactics, and about our war effort. Considering that we had been out of contact with our military for several years, these questions were ridiculous. Over a period of several months we were called to several identical conferences, in which the same prisoners were asked the same questions. The reason for this eluded us.

A theory I toyed with for some time was that the army and the industrial leaders who were primarily responsible for prosecuting the war could not understand (1) how the United States was able to gear itself up for war after such a late start, and (2) how the United States managed to turn the tide of the war so thoroughly in its favor after the heavy blow it had sustained at Pearl Harbor. To the Japanese it was inconceivable that they could lose the war, but losing it they were. We knew that many of their senior military leaders discounted much of the information that was given to them by their own people. It is possible that they wanted to see if the information we would provide jibed with what their own intelligence people had given them. Of course, this theory does not explain why the Japanese held so many redundant conferences, or why they questioned prisoners who clearly had no current military or industrial intelligence. There was much that we did not understand about the Japanese, and probably never will.

Late in the year we learned via "bamboo radio" that a large naval battle had taken place in the Philippine Sea. Of course, what the Japanese told us differed from the encouraging news that our other, clandestine, source provided. The Japanese told us only of the many successful kamikaze attacks, and of the heavy casualties in men and ships that our side was suffering. To hear them tell it, every kamikaze pilot who took off sank a ship and died gloriously for his emperor in the process. We had heard such reports before and were no longer as susceptible to the propaganda.

Some members of the working parties, our eyes outside of camp, were beginning to see trainloads of soldiers, very young soldiers, moving toward the port of Takamatsu. There was no way of knowing their destination. We did not know where the "front" was. At the same time, trainloads of wounded soldiers and small white boxes were seen returning from Takamatsu. Many of these boxes, which contained the remains of dead Japanese soldiers, were taken to the nearby shrine.

Although rice was the staple of our diet, we were being given much less of it, and it was getting much dirtier. It was apparent that every grain available was being swept up off the floor and used. The rats were becoming bolder, vying with us for what little food we had. They were starving also. We had little stamina left, and prisoners were blacking out with increasing frequency. Once in a great while a few parcels from home would arrive, and the recipients would share the edible items with weaker prisoners.

We fought a continual battle with mosquitoes as well as with hungry bedbugs. The open latrines were causing an insect invasion, and in our run-down condition we were susceptible to every possible disease. Every means at our disposal was used to reduce the insect population, but without much success.

We suffered from a variety of intestinal troubles, and dysentery was becoming a constant problem. Because they were so weak and lethargic, many prisoners skipped the weekly Japanese-type bath, even though soaking in the hot water might have been beneficial. Soap was at a premium and had to be used sparingly.

On one night in November I was awakened by one of the other officers in my room, who called me to look outside. We were allowed to leave the barracks at night only to visit the *benjo,* but on this occasion there was so much excitement in the camp that several of us were able to stand for some time watching in happy amazement. The normally black sky to our north and west was a bright orange. Obviously, our aircraft were having a field day. Although we did not know their exact bearings, large areas in the general vicinities of Yokohama and Kobe were burning furiously. None of us slept much for the rest of that night. Our spirits soared. Our forces were close at hand.

That Thanksgiving I was thankful just to be alive and prayed to remain so. Realistically, we all knew that some of us would never leave Japan. Perhaps it was a selfish prayer, but I prayed that I would not be included in that group. I wanted above all to be buried in my native soil.

14 ✳ A "Better" Camp

"Obey orders; we will protect you!" Why were we given this advice, and given it so frequently, during 1944? Probably it was given in the hope that it would help keep us in line. Other than the impressed Koreans who were not happy in their work, our guards were now mostly young boys in uniform. They had received little training and were totally inexperienced. They needed every bit of help they could get. We sought no protection from the Japanese, nor could they have provided any had they desired to do so.

In late 1944 we began to hear rumors that some of us would be moved. Such rumors were always unsettling. Why was a move being made, and to what new location? According to one widely circulated rumor, we would be moved to a camp near Hiroshima.[1] Although moves were always announced enthusiastically by the Japanese, they were never advantageous to the prisoners. More often than not, moves were made to locations where more "coolies" were required to do heavy work. Moves were frequently made so quickly that we were unable to maintain good records, and many prisoners sort of dropped off the face of the earth.

In early June 1945 the Japanese finally announced that we would be moved to other camps "for our safety." Also, to our deep disappointment, we would be moved by nationalities. We Americans had made close friends with our foreign compatriots, brothers in adversity, and the separation was going to be psychologically difficult. Possibly this was what our captors had planned.

For about ten days we received no more information. Finally a date was set and we psyched ourselves up for the move—not an easy thing to do. The date came, the date passed, and no move was made. This happened several times. Procrastination and uncertainty prevailed. Could it be that the main island was being bombed so frequently that the Japanese could not be assured of a safe date for making the move? Or was it just another example of the uncertainty we had so frequently been made to suffer?

Finally, on the afternoon of 23 June, those of us who were senior officers were called to the camp office, where a huge Japanese officer briefed us. As usual, the briefing was preceded by a flowery speech. We were told that during the past several months the United States had embarked on a deplorable, inhumane strategy of attacking unarmed civilian targets. Of course, these attacks would not be successful, but we were going to be moved to insure our safety from the American bombers.

American prisoners would be going to a camp called Roku Roshi.[2] We would be leaving Zentsuji at 1500 the next day, never to return, and were told to get all our belongings together as quickly as possible. But then the briefer said that we could take only what we could carry. None of us had many belongings, but we hated to leave behind anything worthwhile. We were also cautioned, for our own good, to be careful not to excite Japanese civilians during the move, inasmuch as they didn't like us. This was contrary to what we had observed in the recent past. In many instances we felt a degree of kinship with the Japanese civilians, who were also suffering, and in many instances we felt that this emotion was reciprocated.

In the briefing Roku Roshi was vaguely described as being located on Honshu. But on southern Honshu, where the climate could be warm? Or on northern Honshu, close to the plains of Siberia? This was information we all wanted, but we knew from painful experience that it was unwise to ask questions.

On the afternoon of 24 June we exchanged farewells with our British, Aussie, and Dutch comrades and with our own few remaining enlisted men who were not going with us. Then 335 of us, our belongings in hand, formed in front of the barracks for the unending *bango,* or count-off, to take place. As frequently happened, this took an inordinately long time, because as we counted off, the number would frequently be lost somewhere along the line. The Japanese guards with their one-track minds never seemed able to devise a better system for checking our number, and prisoners, of course, were always ready to help foul up the count and frustrate the guards. Although this little game was played frequently, I don't believe the guards ever caught on.

Why were they so intent on having a precise count? Who among us could possibly escape or get lost in this godforsaken country?

As we were marched out of Zentsuji my dear friends "Briggie" Brigdon and Robin Petrie were standing in front of the barracks to wave final goodbyes. Lieutenant Colonel Lausen "Briggie" Brigdon was a career British army officer who had a very bad limp to show for machine-gun wounds obtained during the First World War. He was a fine officer and friend, and was one of the officers who often helped maintain our spirits. Lieutenant Colonel Robin Petrie, a Scots Highlander in the British army, was one of my roommates and a close personal friend whom I would miss sorely. As we were marched through the gates, we were leaving behind many friends of other nationalities who would soon be transferred to other camps.

Outside the camp several empty army trucks were parked. They could not have carried all of the prisoners to the train, but they could at least have carried our belongings. Obviously this was not in the cards. Not knowing the location of Roku Roshi, we had played it safe and were carrying our winter clothes, which were heavy. Knowing how weak we were, other prisoners who were not being moved from Zentsuji that day offered to help carry our baggage, even though they were weak themselves, but the Japanese would not permit them to do so. The railroad station in Zentsuji was only a mile from camp, but it was more of a march than many could make carrying their meager possessions. Many were forced to leave their belongings in the street.

✳ The prisoners had been through so much, and they were so totally spent, that the short march to the railroad station in Zentsuji was next to impossible for some. The following paragraph was written by Major Donald Spicer: "As we turned the first corner, Bill [Lieutenant Colonel William K. MacNulty], weighing in at 119, dropped his . . . case and staggered wildly about the street, his face an ashen grey and his eyes staring wildly. . . . He came to himself with remarkable speed and insisted on continuing. He rose and insisted that he could 'make it.' Others succeeded in relieving him of his two musette bags and blanket roll."[3] ✳

Arriving at the train station, we were herded into three coaches reserved for our trip to Takamatsu—335 officers and 12 guards packed into cars whose capacity was 150. It was a very bumpy ride, and although it was daylight, there was little war damage to be seen. Apparently our bombers had overflown the area between Zentsuji and Takamatsu en route to other areas that were more rich in targets.

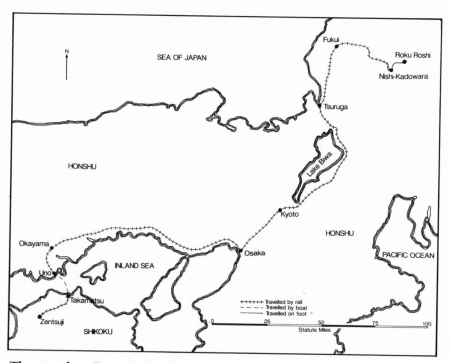

The route from Zentsuji to Roku Roshi

In Takamatsu we were hurried off the train, made to fall in, and marched a short distance to the harbor, where we stood in the rain and waited for a boat to carry us across the Inland Sea. We were too weak and tired to display emotion as we stood there being pelted by rain that ran in rivulets down our faces and soaked our tattered clothes. Finally a small coastal ferry arrived, and we were rushed down into the hold so as to be well clear of the civilian passengers, who watched us intently but with little animation. They hadn't wanted this war any more than we had, and they were suffering too. In addition to suffering from want, many had lost loved ones during the past three years.

The hold was pitch-black, and we hardly had room to lie down even in a cramped position. Once a hugh rat ran through the hold, causing quite an uproar as it scurried across men who were trying to get a little shuteye.

Our trip across the Inland Sea to Honshu lasted several hours. At one point we were taken out of the hold in small groups to visit the head, which to our embarrassment we found was also being used by women passengers. During our imprisonment at Zentsuji we had not been exposed to this Japanese custom, and I must say it was a bit of a shock to attend to the calls of nature while practically every female on board paraded through.

It was after dark when we reached Honshu and disembarked at Uno. After being remustered, we were forced along to a nearby railroad station where we entrained for Okayama, about 350 miles west-southwest of Tokyo, arriving there at 2230.

Rail was the usual manner of travel in Japan, and the Okayama station was crowded with people. Some were well dressed, the men wearing business suits and carrying small briefcases, the women dressed in kimonos and wearing geta. Others appeared to be farm-class people, the men wearing knee-high rubber boots and many of the women carrying tremendous loads on their backs. Although representing different strata, all of the people shared one attribute: they all looked sadly apathetic.

As we entered the station our guards yelled brusquely at the crowds of civilians and elbowed them aside so that we could be herded through and into a small waiting room nearby. It had not been an extremely long day, but we were physically and emotionally exhausted. There were few benches in the room on which we could lie down, so we took turns, some reclining on the benches while the remainder sacked out on the concrete floor in an attempt to get some rest.

At 0600 the following morning we boarded the train for Osaka. Here we were thrown wooden *o-bento* boxes containing a small rice ball, a bit of salt fish, and some dark, bitter seaweed. This was the first food we had eaten in many hours. As we sat on our baggage in the dirt outside the railroad station, the view more than compensated for the rigors of our trip thus far. Osaka was a large industrial city on the Inland Sea. To be correct, I should say that Osaka *had been* a large industrial city. We had seen the contrails of American B-29s overflying Zentsuji en route to Honshu. Now we were witnessing the damage they had wrought. The industrial city of Osaka was almost completely in ruins. (Later we heard that a day or so after we were there the station was blown to bits by American bombers. When we heard this, we thanked God that we had gotten on our way before it happened.)

Finally we boarded a passenger train to be taken to our new camp. During this trip we realized again how small the Japanese people are. The train was overcrowded, and the space between seats was so limited that when we sat down we had to hold our knees up in order not to get leg cramps. As the trip progressed, we took turns changing seats and standing from time to time.

All of the windows on the train had shutterlike shades. As soon as we boarded, these shades were pulled down by the guards, who warned us severely that we were not to raise them. Then they posted themselves at each end of the car. What was it that we were not supposed to see? We could hardly have been considered spies. Our curiosity was overwhelming. As we clacked along, occasionally a prisoner sitting toward the center of the car would quietly turn up the bottom of his shade and peek out. Then he would quietly pass the word from man to man on what he had seen. As we bumped along, several such peeks were made, fortunately unobserved by the sometimes dozing guards.

What our observers reported was spectacularly interesting. Whereas the primarily rural area around Zentsuji had been relatively untouched by the war, the portion of Honshu through which we were traveling was industrialized, or had been, and it had been visited by our bombers on more than one occasion. In some places along the right-of-way whole areas had been devastated or were a smoldering mess, while other areas had been left untouched.

From Osaka we traveled in a northerly direction, passing through the ancient capital city of Kyoto, which had been spared from bombing because of its historical and emotional significance to the Japanese.

During the trip several men, attempting to make the best of our discomfort and anxiety, remarked that we had graduated from Zentsuji College and this trip was our graduation present. Someone said that he had his Bachelor of Tolerance degree from Zentsuji, another had received his Bachelor of Resourcefulness, and another his Bachelor of Abstinence. Now we were going to another "college," to obtain graduate degrees. But would we be studying at the master's level, or at that of the doctorate?

From Kyoto we passed along the side of Lake Biwa and through Tsuruga, on the Sea of Japan. Finally we arrived at our train destination, where the cars were pulled off onto a siding at the city of Fukui. It was late at night when we detrained at Fukui and were herded into streetcars.

❋ The ride is described by Dr. H. J. Van Peenen: "From this point began the strangest and wildest of streetcar rides. For 23 miles up and down mountain precipices, with drops of hundreds of feet, we travelled at top speed."[4] ❋

At midnight we disembarked from the streetcars, were mustered, and started a tough trek up the side of a mountain.[5] For approximately ten kilometers we clawed out way upward along a winding path that was peppered with boulders and ridged here and there with shallow ravines. It was raining hard, and making our way up this path was a tremendous task. Along the way I could hear a nearby stream rushing down the mountain, and through the dark night our way was illuminated periodically by flashes of lightning. It would not have been an easy hike had we been in the best of shape, which of course we were not. Some men blacked out from weakness and had to be helped along. Those of us who could had to carry the sick and wounded. There was no dropping out. No rest stops were allowed. Though short, this was our "death march."

✳ Dr. Van Peenen with his ever-present briefcase full of medicines was among the battered prisoners who fought valiantly to survive that long and rainy night: "Although I had tossed aside excess impediments with the rest, I had stubbornly held to my briefcase. The handle was broken, and I had sacrificed a ragged shirt to make a sling to suspend the case from my shoulder. . . . As I climbed, my foot sometimes struck the abandoned possessions of another. . . . [How] many more steps forward before one's own last possessions joined the discards?"[6] ✳

At about 0300 we reached the top and stumbled onto a small plain between two mountain ridges. In the center of this plain was located an army cantonment: our new home, Roku Roshi.[7] We were truly in a remote spot, so well hidden in the mountains that no one would ever find us. The Japanese had said that they would protect us. Was it their intent to protect us from ever being found?

Roku Roshi was miles from anywhere. It was in an extremely remote spot in the foothills of the Japanese Alps, toward the western side of Honshu and not far from the Sea of Japan. As far as we could determine, the nearest civilization of any sort was Fukui, where we had debarked from our train. The surrounding countryside was wild. As we had edged our way slowly up the mountainside toward the camp, we had cursed and wondered what god would have made terrain like this. But we had seen nothing until we arrived at the plain. Eons ago a glacier must have passed there, making the area all but uninhabitable. The entire area was covered with chaff, and with rocks and boulders of every size and description.

The camp consisted of several one-story frame buildings similar in some respects to those at Zentsuji. I was happy that the barracks were low. In our condition, few of us could have climbed stairs. Whereas the buildings at Zentsuji had been fairly solidly constructed, at Roku Roshi the sides of the barracks were formed of sliding wooden panels similar to those found in Japanese farmhouses. In addition to the barracks that we would occupy, there was one for the Japanese officers, one for their noncommissioned officers, one for their enlisted men, and an office complex. There was also the usual *benjo* for each building.

After entering the camp compound we literally collapsed in the rain onto the rocky ground, unable to summon enough strength even to stand in formation. After we had been allowed to rest here briefly, we were assigned spaces in the barracks and ordered to unpack our belongings and get settled in. Apparently the Nips had some sympathy after all, because we were not made to work until the second day after our arrival.

At Roku Roshi no pretense was made of abiding by the Geneva Convention. The camp was occupied entirely by American officers, and we were expected to work. Roku Roshi had been advertised as a "working camp," and that was what it was. Early every morning we were marched to rock piles in the nearby hills, where we learned all about rocks: big rocks, little rocks, and many of them.

Our chore was to turn the Roku Roshi moonscape into a garden. First we removed the rocks and boulders from a large area. Then we dug and dug and dug until we found soil that could be tilled by hand. Finally we learned about *benjo* dipping and the spreading of liquid human excrement on the newly cleared fields. Like the tools our men had used at Zentsuji, ours were cheap and primitive. With the heavy work we were doing, they wore out rapidly. In more ways than one we were truly between a rock and a hard place. If we used our tools sparingly, we were accused of working slowly and were punished. On the other hand, if we worked industriously and our tools broke or became dull, we were accused of misusing them and were punished.

From what we had seen on our trip to Roku Roshi, we knew that things were really going badly for the Japanese. In our isolated location, however, it was impossible to obtain any news about the progress of the war. There were no newspapers, no contact through working parties with the outside world, and no friendly Korean guards. Both the Japanese officers and the guards were extremely unfriendly and very rough on us. We had no comforts, day or night. We worked on the hill from dawn to dusk and often fell out from weakness.

Our food was even more scant and lacking in nutrition than it had been at Zentsuji.[8] We were all losing weight steadily, and prisoners were blacking out with increasing frequency even as the guards beat us to work harder.

✳ Dr. Van Peenen was acutely aware of both the medical and the psychological problems faced by his fellow prisoners: "We knew from the erratic behavior of the guards that the tides of war were somehow turning and felt that, however they turned, the disadvantages of the captured would be multiplied. As physical men, none of us was worth saving. Tuberculosis and dangerous heart murmurs were in our ranks. We were fetid with dysentery and skeletal in appearance, and as prisoners of war, we had the contempt of the Japanese. It was logical to believe that machine-gunning in a mountain retreat was the most sensible means of extermination.

"The next three months did little to lift our spirits, except that each morning found us alive. These months were a nightmare of brutality, mass punishments, and constant beatings."[9] ✳

At this point even the Japanese military was suffering. Although their army had been receiving plenty of food, they were now beginning to have to scratch to find enough to eat. Stealing was becoming a way of life. Everyone was starving. Those who grabbed whatever food they could were praised for their initiative rather than censured by those in authority.

We now understood another possible nuance to the frequent advice, "Take care of your health." To survive, you had to grab whatever food you could find, by hook or by crook. We were desperate for anything to keep us alive. Anything that crawled contained some of the protein that we so greatly lacked, and we convinced ourselves that many low forms of life were delicious.

There were many prayerful pleas to the Almighty for continued hope and for the strength to return to our families and friends. We feared that we would not survive winter. Winter at Roku Roshi would be harsh, much more so than at Zentsuji. Here in the mountains firewood wouldn't be a problem, and possibly there would be sufficient charcoal. But in the wintertime this area of Japan was chilled by snow and winds blowing out of Siberia, and our meager braziers could not possibly throw out enough heat to warm these drafty barracks with their sliding exterior walls. We knew that we were in for it, and I could visualize being snowed in at this remote spot without adequate heat or food.

Our forced labor was becoming unbearable. We had become so weakened that we just couldn't work. Men fell out and had to be carried back to the barracks by other prisoners who were barely able to walk themselves. Our doctors were now busier than ever taking care of those who just didn't have the strength to take it any longer. We could only keep our faith in God and pray.

One hot day in late July, as I was digging in the rocky soil, my hands uncovered a rusty, dirt-encrusted horseshoe. I had never been one to believe in such things, but I accepted this as an omen. Perhaps my spirits had sunk so low that I was grasping at straws, but to me this horse-shoe had not been merely cast off. It had been placed there for me to find.

On our mostly liquid diet of rice, tea, and soup, we all made frequent trips to the *benjo*. One night in August, after returning to the barracks from a *benjo* outing, one of the prisoners passed the word that something was going on outside that we should all see. A bright-orange glow seemed to cover the sky to our south, in the general direction of Fukui.[10] The entire city must have been ablaze. Now we had seen proof that our bombers were getting close, that our forces were near at hand. Everyone wanted to see the glowing sky and commence dreaming of release, so there was a constant parade to the *benjo* until the guards came and herded us all back to the barracks. There was no doubt in our minds now that the Nips were getting a severe pasting.

We knew that our bombers would not attack indiscriminately, that their attacks would be made in accordance with some priorities. Fukui could not have been a very important target. If it had arrived at the top of the target list, most of the military targets and industrial areas of Japan must have been devastated. Much to our elation, the fires raged for several nights, bringing a glow to us all. Doubtless the war would end soon. Our spirits perked up, hope flourished.

Suddenly the camp authorities became more vindictive, and our work on the hillside rock pile became pure hell. Unquestionably, something was taking place that affected our keepers. Several of us drafted a memorandum to the camp commander protesting this severe treatment, and delivered it to him in person. Although we expected to be punished for this brash act, we did it out of a sense of honor. We simply could not let them treat us so cruelly without protest.

Surprisingly, we were not punished, and for several days our memorandum was not even acknowledged. Then we were told that our captors' harshness had been in retaliation for the United States' use of an inhumane weapon. Of course, we knew nothing about atomic bombs and were unable to imagine what sort of inhumane weapon might have been used. This was followed shortly by another, even more surprising, announcement: there would be no more work on the hill until further notice.

Although we were not receiving any news per se, we had developed an effective underground at Roku Roshi. Through this source we heard that the camp commander had received a telephone call from Osaka ordering him to report there. There was tension in the air. What was going on?

While the camp commander was in Osaka we observed that, except for the guards at the gate, the Japanese were keeping more or less out of sight. We were also allowed more freedom to move about the camp, and it seemed as though we were being given a bit more food—the same food, but a bit more of it. Were we imagining things? Could the war be over, or were we too optimistic?

One day soon after the camp commander returned, an interpreter commented that the Japanese were sad in their great victory.[11] Although no announcement had been made, so many strange things were taking place that we felt sure the war must be over. Cigarettes were issued; more rice was provided; some fruit, which we hadn't seen for a long time, appeared. Then we were given some wheat and a scanty ration of meat.

Even toward the end, the Japanese people were never told that their country was losing the war. Rather, as I have noted before, the news media attempted to cover up the losses of their armed forces and tried to make people believe that they were winning. To admit defeat would be to lose face, a concept many Americans find difficult to understand. To my knowledge the word *surrender* was never spoken.[12]

Finally the camp commander requested—not ordered—the American senior officers to meet him in his office. Here we were informed that the war was terminated. No mention was made of surrender. During the meeting we were asked what we would like, and without too much discussion among ourselves we made the following initial requests, with which the commander complied:

Provide a sizable increase in our rice supply, along with more meat and more fish.
Relinquish the administration of the camp to us.
Replace all of the Japanese guards with our own guards.
Give us more blankets and some cigarettes.

To our surprise, Commander Wilson Hempfield Harrington, USNR, had an American flag. This flag had quite a history. It had been owned by an American woman missionary who, in order to keep it from falling into Japanese hands, had given it to a British soldier as he crossed the causeway, returning into Singapore. The soldier was being taken to a POW camp aboard the *Lisbon Maru* when that vessel was torpedoed.[13] The flag was in the water for forty-eight hours but was saved by members of the British Middlesex Regiment, who laundered it and gave it to Commander Harrington. When Commander Harrington was captured, he concealed the flag and managed somehow to carry it about his person throughout the entire period of his captivity.

Through our years of imprisonment Major Donald Spicer, USMC, and I had carried two terrible personal burdens. I carried the burden of having signaled the surrender of Guam to the Japanese and of our having let the natives down. Major Spicer carried the burden of having struck our colors to the Japanese at the marine barracks on Guam.

✳ Major Spicer described his feelings: "I naturally had a burning passion to avenge myself. I pictured many ways of doing this, such as escaping and coming back in command of a battalion. I never dreamed that there was a flag in camp all the time."[14] ✳

Major Spicer requested that he be permitted to raise our flag at Roku Roshi, a request that was granted without question. Three officers participated in the ceremony, one from each service: Commander William J. Galbraith, USN; Major Donald Spicer, USMC; and Captain Jack K. Boyer, USA.

✳ Although the following words were spoken by Major Spicer, the sentiments they expressed were shared by every other American at Roku Roshi:

"And there, 45 months after I tasted the bitter dregs of humiliation— almost 4 years after I became the first U.S. Marine to strike our colors to an enemy—I was to raise the first American flag over the Japanese homeland."[15]

"My feelings, therefore, as I reverently held the flag in my hands and proudly marched up the hill to the flagpole on September 2, 1945, are not difficult to imagine. With a final caress, I let that Grand Old Flag slip through my fingers, to flutter proudly over the Japanese homeland. As I gazed upward and saluted the Stars and Stripes, I swallowed hard, restraining my tears. After we were dismissed, I let them flow freely, laughing and crying at the same time as we milled about wringing each other's hands."[16]

"Every man . . . was filled with the same surging emotions. Every man was holding on with his last ounce of strength, determined to prove that he came from fighting stock which could not be beaten."[17] ✳

That evening a special prayer service of thanksgiving was held outside the barracks. Only those who were too sick or too weak to attend were not present. We had so much to be thankful for. We had been saved.

Food became a little more plentiful, such as it was. The Japanese supply sergeant had been ordered to issue us some meat, but what we received was full of maggots, and our doctors condemned most of it. And because we had been on a starvation diet for so long, even the lit-

Prisoners in front of barracks at Roku Roshi following repatriation *(National Archives)*

tle additional food that we were given was too much for some of the prisoners, whose stomachs became very swollen after eating it.

On the following morning we were asked again to meet with the Japanese officer who had been the camp commander. He had received instructions from headquarters to proceed to Kyoto accompanied by two prisoners. Those selected for the trip should be a supply officer and someone who knew shorthand. Although there were several supply officers among us, it was difficult to find anyone who had more than a cursory knowledge of shorthand. However, the group was formed and they left by truck, bouncing down the rocky road toward the ancient capital.

In Kyoto these officers met with some of our own forces and found out that B-29s had been dropping food and supplies to POW camps all over Japan for several days. But, "Roku Roshi? Where the hell is that?"

Our camp was tucked away on the western slope of a mountain range, miles from any habitation, and the surrounding countryside was wild and wooded. When the Japanese moved us there, they promised they would look out for our safety. As promised, we had been well protected in our remote location. Because the building roofs had not been marked to indicate that they were POW barracks, our camp had not been identified by the reconnaissance aircraft that had been searching for prisoners.

Having pinpointed the location of Roku Roshi on a map, our officers climbed back into the truck and started back to camp. Someplace between Kyoto and Fukui the truck stopped briefly at an enlisted men's camp to update them on what was happening. When these men, who had already had food dropped to them, heard that we had not yet received anything, they quickly rounded up some of what they had left to share with those at Roku Roshi.

Like an old racehorse, the Japanese army truck was forced up the mountainside with all the power that could be squeezed out of it. Our officers wanted to arrive in camp before morning, when the planes would arrive to make their parachute drops to us.

The race was won! Just before dawn, in rolled the panting truck, its headlights cutting through the September fog. What wonderful news our officers brought: we would soon be visited by aircraft dropping us food—real food! And what a glorious time was had by all, as the food sent from the enlisted men's camp was offloaded and shared! The only ones among us who might have been less than overjoyed were the doctors. They warned us time and time again to eat sparingly. Our systems could not handle large amounts of rich food. "Take it easy. Make it last. It'll still be here tomorrow," they cautioned us repeatedly.

Things began to happen fast that morning. Looking into the sky at about 0800, we spotted a flight of three B-29s to the south. They were the biggest planes we had ever seen. The first pass was a dummy run at an altitude of about two thousand feet. On their second approach, their bomb bay doors were open, and soon we witnessed the most beautiful sight any of us had ever seen. Out came a flock of brightly colored cargo-carrying parachutes, which reminded me for a moment of a bunch of balloons whipping around in the breeze at a country fair. Suddenly the sky was filled with spots of red, green, blue, yellow, and white as the parachutes and their cargo drifted down to the ground in the vicinity of our camp. One of the parachutes did not open properly, and its drum of food plummeted to the ground, burst open, and spewed its contents of peaches and catsup over the landscape.

Immediately after their first pass was completed, the aircraft climbed in a slow turn to the right and circled back to repeat the performance before departing. As soon as the engine noises receded, hungry prisoners dispersed about the camp retrieving and opening the many crates, barrels, drums, and boxes of food and supplies that lay scattered about.

Again our doctors warned us not to make pigs of ourselves. "Don't eat such rich food too ravenously! Take it easy!" This was difficult to do after having starved for such a long time. Tinned meats, especially the corned beef, and coffee were the most popular items. Now we had good old American food, and under the watchful eyes of our doctors we made the most of it for the next three days. Then some very welcome visitors arrived who started us on our long and happy trip home. At long last, we were to be repatriated.

Unfortunately, we had several pessimists in camp, and I am sorry to have to say that the worst of these was a graduate of the Naval Academy. On one of our last days at Roku Roshi, as we were celebrating the end of the war, I found that he had drifted far back into the shadows. When I asked why he wasn't joining in the celebrations, he replied sadly, "Captain, I guess I'm the man who will never smile again."[18] Thus it was with a few of the POWs. Those of us who could smile again were fortunate. After all, four years in hell is a long, long time.

15 ✳ Repatriation

Our visitors came chugging up the mountainside toward midday in Japanese trucks that had been commandeered for their trip. They were a platoon of combat-equipped American infantrymen from the Eighth Army and a contingent of doctors and nurses. This was the first time we had seen any of our post-1941 combat-equipped soldiers. How different they looked from those we had seen prior to our capture! They appeared much more businesslike than either their American precursors or the Japanese with whom we had been associated for so long. From the looks on their faces and their expressions of disbelief, we knew that this must have been a first for them also. We were all horribly malnourished, and many bore the scars of gross mistreatment.

The relief group went about their work with an efficiency such as we had not known during our captivity. First they noted vital statistics: full name, rank, service number, date of birth, home address, religious affiliation, and name and address of next of kin. Then we were given initial physical examinations[1] and were questioned at some length about our capture and our prison experiences. Strangely, these last questions were difficult to answer. We had buried some experiences, repressed some memories. There were some things we wanted above all to forget.

Those judged to be in the worst shape were given immediate medical treatment. Then we were made ready for our trip down the mountainside and back to civilization. Because of the train schedule between

Commander Giles in truck at Yokohama railroad station following repatriation *(National Archives)*

Fukui and Yokohama, we would not be leaving Roku Roshi until the next day. We would have one last night in camp. Although we were all anxious to leave and to start our journey home, somehow this delay was acceptable. That night we continued our celebration and bombarded our visitors with questions. We had been out of circulation for a long time. There was so much we did not know.

The next morning there was no need for reveille. Few had been able to sleep. After waiting so very long, the day had finally come when we would be leaving. We were terribly excited, and happy beyond belief.

Our relief unit had commandeered enough trucks that we could all be transported in reasonable comfort, and at about 0900 we climbed or were helped into the trucks and headed down the bumpy, narrow road to Fukui. Shortly after leaving camp, our truck convoy passed the area where I had learned more than I ever wanted to know about rocks, about hand-tilling rocky soil, and about the spreading of *benjo* juice. This was a very bumpy stretch of road, and we were all holding on to whatever protrusions were offered by the truck. As I was looking for something to hold on to, I happened to glance down at my hands: gnarled, rough, calloused, and torn. Then I turned my Naval Academy class ring around so that once again its sapphire stone faced outboard.

When we had first passed through Fukui en route to Roku Roshi, it had been a city. It had been bombed, but it was a city. Now, as we passed through again, several months later, there was little left. Fukui had been practically wiped out. What havoc our bombers had wrought! After debarking from the trucks we had an opportunity to inspect the city we had seen burning in the distance a few days before. It appeared just as the history books describe the condition of Atlanta after General William Sherman passed through it in 1864. Not much of the city had survived except for the burned remains of Japanese-style buildings and a few burned-out Western-style concrete office buildings. The old railway station was gone, and a temporary one of rough boards had been erected hurriedly in its place. Here we were met by a group of young Japanese Red Cross girls who were handing out rice balls, stick candy, and some fruit with what we thought were gratuitous smirks on their faces. Those who wandered a bit in the area around the station picked up some slightly burned samurai swords as souvenirs. Looking back on it now, I see that I should have done likewise. At the time, however, I wanted nothing more to do with Japan or with anything Japanese.

Our stay in Fukui was short. Before an hour had elapsed the train arrived, and we were urged to get aboard. On the trip through Kyoto to Yokohama we were not herded together as on the trip from Osaka to Fukui three months earlier. No one had to stand, and we were not crammed into the tiny seats. If desired, one could have an entire seat to himself. Such luxury. Even though we were much more comfortable than before, I found it hard to sleep. I was so excited to be heading home, and my thoughts kept tumbling out, one after the other.

Early the next morning our train pulled into Yokohama, and what a welcome we received! The railroad platform was lined with an honor guard of soldiers in combat dress waiting for our arrival, and as the train stopped before them they were called smartly to attention. An army band struck up "California, Here I Come," and General Robert L. Eichelberger, USA, was striding up and down the platform, hugging us, shaking hands, and grinning from ear to ear.

As soon as the trackside welcoming activities were over, we were transported to dockside warehouses, where we were welcomed again. Then we were checked over and led to a group of improvised shower stalls. Here, after placing our clothes on nearby mess tables, we were each given a clean towel and a bar of U.S. Army soap with which to wash. This was a real treat after having bathed Japanese-fashion for almost four years. No more soaping off and dunking in a tub of hot, scummy water. Such little things that we take for granted at home were luxuries to us.

We had hoped to be issued new uniforms, because in many instances the clothes we were wearing were those in which we had been captured. We were a seedy lot, at best. However, our saviors had landed in Japan only a couple of weeks before, and there was no issue of clothing available. For the time being we would have to be accepted as we were: seedy but clean.

After our showers we noted that a change had taken place: our clothes and shoes were white. They had been sprayed with DDT, a chemical with which we were not familiar, because we had been infested with body lice. We had grown accustomed to scratching ourselves incessantly. Now there was no more scratching.

After about an hour the mess tables and benches had been washed, wiped, and rearranged, and we were served some good old army chow. And what a meal it was: griddle cakes with syrup, delicious pork sausage, orange juice, and a seemingly endless supply of coffee. Except for the few Red Cross packages that we had received at Zentsuji a long time ago and the food that had been parachuted to us at Roku Roshi a few days earlier, this was the only American food we had eaten since our capture, and it was hot, tasty, and abundant. Those army mess cooks could not possibly have known how much their efforts meant to us that day.

After this hearty breakfast we were led to the nearby docks, where we were welcomed again, this time by officers and men of the various landing craft moored there. Tokyo Bay was a mass of battleships, cruisers, and destroyers, several of which we had read had been sunk during the war—some as many as two or three times. We were to be billeted aboard these ships for the night, and it was my luck to be assigned to bunk aboard the USS *Indiana,* which was commanded by Captain Francis P. "François" Old, USN, a contemporary of mine at the Naval Academy.[2]

As we passed the ships at anchor en route to our homes for the night, they all looked beautiful. The small boat in which I was riding approached the *Indiana,* and suddenly I felt totally out of place. I knew that after climbing the accommodation ladder and stepping onto her quarterdeck I would be greeted by the officer of the deck. Then, after facing aft and saluting the colors, I would be expected to salute him also, and to request permission to come aboard. Were I that officer, I asked myself, would I allow anyone who looked so disreputable to come aboard? I soon found that my fears were groundless.

USS *Indiana (Naval Institute Collection)*

The waters of Tokyo Bay were a bit choppy, and as I stepped from the boat onto the bottom of the *Indiana*'s accommodation ladder, I was assisted by a young seaman in an immaculately white uniform that contrasted sharply with my own tattered appearance. At the top of the ladder I was greeted by both the commanding officer and the officer of the deck, who were waiting to welcome me aboard. Although not yet home in Annapolis, I knew that I was among my own.

Again we had a warm welcome, followed by questions from both our navy hosts and the former prisoners. We were brought up to date by the ship's officers on naval operations in the Pacific and were able to confirm what we had suspected, that many of the reports of battle losses so flagrantly published in the Japanese press were untrue.

The ship's store was opened, and we were issued whatever we needed. In instances where items of clothing were not available in the ship's store, officers and members of the ship's company gave us some of their own. All hands were most generous. One of the junior officers who gave me some of his clothes had known Don at the Naval Academy. He confirmed what I had deduced from the cryptic messages in Virginia's letters: that Don was a midshipman.

After changing out of our prison garb we all felt much more civilized, and I pinned on the new eagles that were provided by Captain Old.

That night a sumptuous dinner was served in the wardroom, followed by cigars and movies on the quarterdeck. As the movies were being shown, sitting in the dark alone with my thoughts I drifted back many years, to when I was a junior officer on the battleship *Utah*. On nights when I had the duty, Virginia and Don frequently came on board for dinner and stayed to watch movies on deck, just as I was doing that night. Those were more formal times, when an officer's uniform included a sword, cocked hat, and boat cloak. Don was quite young, and on cool evenings he would wrap himself in my boat cloak and fall fast asleep.

Many of the ship's officers vacated their bunks that night for us to use. What a welcome change from the wooden shelf and tatami mat that had been my bed for the last fourteen hundred nights! After so much activity during the last three or four days, and still feeling very shaky, I found it a blessing to enjoy a good, undisturbed sleep in a comfortable bunk.

The next morning, after a hearty breakfast, we thanked the ship's company profusely for their grand hospitality and exchanged goodbyes with them. Then we were taken ashore in landing boats to Chiba, where we would board aircraft and leave Japan. Although we were homeward bound, our happiness was tinged with thoughts of comrades who would not be going home, but would remain buried in Japanese soil. We could only remind ourselves that those whom we were leaving behind had been buried properly and with our love.

16 ✳ Homeward Bound!

For the last three years U.S. forces had been island-hopping toward Japan. Now it was our turn to island-hop, back toward the United States. There were too many prisoners for us all to fly back in the same aircraft. Because of this, we were divided into groups according to our routings home. Some were flown via the Philippines, others were sent back by surface ship. Commander Campbell Keene and I were flown home via Guam with a small group of other ex-prisoners. Then we island-hopped to Baker Island and Hawaii on our way to the West Coast. Although I was most anxious to get home, I was happy to be included in the group that returned via Guam. This would give me an opportunity to see what my old home looked like and to renew acquaintances with a few of my native friends.

When it was attacked in 1941, Guam had no airfield. Now there were several large fields from which U.S. planes had taken off for their attacks on Japan. When our aircraft landed at one of these new fields, Campbell and I were met by a jeep and driven to one of the Fleet Hospitals near Agana.

If I were to say that we former POWs were babied, it would be an understatement. This was true not just on Guam, but at each stop along our way back to the United States. At each stopover we reported to the Naval Hospital for checkups and observation. We were constantly under the supervision of doctors, nurses, and corpsmen, all of whom kept a very close watch on us. This was our armed forces' first experience with prisoners returning from an oriental country, and we were handled with great care.

The food we had eaten in prison camp had changed our metabolism drastically. We had been essentially on an all-rice diet for over three years and could not now assimilate too much protein or adapt our shrunken stomachs to anything like a full meal. We had to be fed sparingly. Instead of having three full meals a day, we were fed five small meals plus snacks. We were told that too heavy a diet could cause edema. In prison camp we had called this beriberi, and we had seen its effect on prisoners who consumed the rich food from Red Cross packages too quickly. Unfortunately, food tasted so good. It was difficult to avoid gluttony after such a long period of hunger. In addition to having our food intake controlled, we were given vitamins, which we consumed like chickens pecking corn.

Soon after we arrived and were settled in our quarters at the Fleet Hospital, I received a great surprise. Leona Jackson, now a lieutenant commander in the Navy Nurse Corps, entered my room.[1] The last time I had seen her was when she and the other nurses from Guam left Zentsuji to join Ambassador Joseph C. Grew and be repatriated aboard the S/S *Gripsholm* in the spring of 1942. After returning to the United States, Nurse Jackson and the other nurses had contacted the families of all the Zentsuji prisoners. She told me in considerable detail how she had spent the better part of a day in Annapolis visiting Virginia and Don. She had given them a sanitized version of the capture of Guam, told them of life at Zentsuji, and reassured them that I was well. It was not until after the nurses left that things got really bad. It was just as well that she had been unable to report on these later conditions.

Like all of us, Nurse Jackson had great sympathy for the natives whom we had left in the hands of the Japanese when we surrendered the island. After Guam was liberated from the Japanese, Nurse Jackson requested to be returned there for duty. During the Japanese occupation the natives had lived under the cruelest of conditions. Many had been killed, and all had lost family members as well as property. Obtaining enough to eat had been a terrible problem for them. Everything edible had been eaten or destroyed by the enemy, and no attempt had been made to continue agricultural production. Many farms had been laid waste and the livestock killed for food. Then, when U.S. forces recaptured the island, much additional havoc was wrought by naval gunfire, air attacks, and ground forces coming ashore in large numbers. When I returned to Guam the natives were just beginning to recover from their nightmare. Many were afraid to return to their devastated farms because Japanese snipers were still at large in the jungles.[2]

Agana, the old capital, was in ruins. Little was left of Government House except for a small section of the old Spanish wall that had formed part of its foundation. This historic building, in which our offices had been located, in front of which we had made our stand against the attacking Japanese and where we had surrendered, had already been replaced by temporary buildings. I could hardly recognize the main street. Most of the stores, movie houses, and residences were gone, and improvised barracks had been erected for the homeless.

The house Bill Lineberry and I had occupied as forced bachelors had been in a target area for preinvasion naval gunfire. It had been destroyed completely. The spot where it had stood was now covered by a wide military highway. Any thoughts I might have entertained of recovering the family flat silver that Sus had buried were pointless.

On the day after our arrival Campbell and I decided to pay a courtesy call on Fleet Admiral Chester Nimitz. The admiral had established his headquarters in temporary frame buildings on the heights above Agana, just in back of where Government House had once stood. It was in this area that Lieutenant (Junior Grade) Graham P. Bright had been dragged from his car and bayonetted during the Japanese attack.

This was a pleasant and informal call on one of the most respected gentlemen in our navy. Admiral Nimitz was extremely interested in the treatment we had received in prison camp and was greatly concerned about our lack of proper medical attention. After about an hour with the admiral we returned to the hospital for afternoon tea, one of our planned mini-meals.

The next morning the admiral's aide came to return our call. In addition to paying the admiral's respects, he said that his call had another purpose. Admiral Nimitz wanted to know if we would be willing to lay over on Guam for a few days before flying on to Honolulu and San Francisco. An elaborate welcome ceremony was being planned in San Francisco, and the mayor had asked Admiral Nimitz to select representative POWs from each place of capture to be welcomed home. Although we were both anxious to return home, we agreed to the request. This would also permit us to explore the island, examine the damage, talk with a few of the local people, build up our strength, and improve our general appearance before arriving home.

Our layover on Guam lasted for ten days. During this time we were driven through much of the island that was accessible, and I managed to locate many of my native friends. Sadly, I was unable to find Sus. Some said that he had disappeared into the brush shortly after we were taken captive. Others seemed to think that he had been caught and killed by the Japanese.

On Friday, 21 September, accompanied by aides provided by Admiral Nimitz, we left Guam on the next leg of our trip home. Although we were still wearing the khaki uniforms we had been given on board the *Indiana,* during the couple of weeks that had passed since our repatriation we had put on a little weight and didn't look quite so haggard.

After making one refueling stop en route, we landed in Honolulu and received another fantastic, heartwarming welcome such as only Hawaii can bestow. After our aircraft had rolled to a stop along the parking apron, beautiful Hawaiian hula girls welcomed us with kisses and placed leis over our heads as the Fourteenth Naval District Band played. Then we were greeted by Vice Admiral Sherwoode Taffinder, USN, commandant of the Fourteenth Naval District. He was accompanied by his staff, their families, and a number of civilian guests from Honolulu. After many handshakes and welcoming speeches, we were led to banner-decorated cars and driven to Aiea Naval Hospital.

At the hospital we were told to place telephone calls to our homes, calls that would be paid for by the city of Honolulu. As the calls were being placed I stood by with the greatest anticipation imaginable. I had not spoken with Virginia for some four and a half years. How would she sound? What would I say? It did not take long for the connection to be made, and suddenly the years fell away. We had an extremely clear connection, and she sounded just as she had when we said good-bye in Oakland in the summer of 1941. I told her that I expected to arrive in San Francisco on Tuesday morning, 25 September, and asked her to meet me. She said that Don was on a midshipman cruise to Panama, and I asked that he order me a cap with scrambled eggs from Peddicord's on Maryland Avenue so that I would have it when I returned to Annapolis.[3]

Although we spoke for several minutes, it was impossible to exchange all the thoughts and emotions that had been unexpressed for such a long period of time. That would have to wait until San Francisco.

During the few days we remained in Hawaii I visited with many of my Naval Academy classmates and their wives, enjoyed the fragrance that is uniquely Hawaiian, and toured Pearl Harbor to see what might be left of ships on which I had once served. The saddest thing I ever saw was the USS *Utah,* on which I had served as a junior officer, canted on her side on the beach. What a horrible sight.

Finally the time arrived for the last leg of our trip to San Francisco. Hawaii had always been one of my favorite spots on earth, but I was itching to leave. Our brief respite had been welcome, but I had sampled the frangipani long enough. Why had I agreed to participate in this damned welcoming ceremony? Admiral Nimitz or not, I wanted to get home. The admiral had chosen about eighty prisoners to participate in the ceremony, and four aircraft were required for the flight.

As we approached the West Coast of the United States, the sun was rising, an event that had added significance for us all. This time it was not the Rising Sun of Japan that greeted us, but a bright sun rising over the United States. I am certain that I was not alone in my feelings of pride and patriotism as we approached our homeland. Anyone entering the United States for the first time should do so through San Francisco. As we flew over the Golden Gate and hovered over the bay area awaiting orders to land, I marveled at what lay below: so clean, well ordered, and full of promise. The good old United States looked so beautiful that morning. It was grand to be home.

Our planes landed at Hamilton Field at fifteen-minute intervals, with the final plane setting down at 10:00 A.M. Those families who could afford to make the trip to San Francisco had been bused from their hotels to the Air Tactical Command Terminal and were at the field to greet us. This was a heartwarming and touching reunion in which many tears of happiness were shed and many kisses exchanged after so many years of separation. This was indeed a glad moment for which we had all prayed for a long time.

Brunch was served at the terminal building, after which we were reluctantly separated again. Our families were driven to a reviewing stand at the San Francisco Civic Center, and we were taken to the Embarcadero, where a parade was being formed. At the Embarcadero we were transferred to individual command cars for the parade up Market Street. In the parade we were escorted by thirteen hundred members of the 104th "Timberwolf" Infantry Division, commanded by Lieutenant General Terry Allen, USA, who led the way.

Because each command car carried only one POW, the parade was long. As each car arrived at the reviewing stand, its POW occupant jumped out and joined his family in the stand to view the remainder of the parade. Among those in the reviewing stand were the mayor of San Francisco, the governor of California, and the lieutenant governor of New Mexico, who had been invited because of the large number of POWs who were from his state.

The following statements from the Welcoming Home Program express the warmth with which we were greeted in San Francisco:

The Golden Gate over which you have just flown is symbolic of San Francisco's open arms of welcome and the people of this city are proud it is here that you first set foot on your own land and breathe the pure air of God's Country.

We feel that our reception to you is indicative of the national feeling towards all liberated prisoners of war.

The privilege is ours of rejoicing with your loved ones on your liberation and safe return. The privations and suffering which you have so heroically endured, the humiliation to which you have been subjected, are over. While we hope the thought of them will be speedily erased from your memories, these sacrifices of yours will not be forgotten by us.

The city that "sitteth at the Western Gate" bids you a hearty welcome home.

After the parade we were driven to the St. Francis Hotel, where a gigantic civic reception was planned. The streets along which we were driven to the St. Francis were lined with San Franciscans who were anxious to participate in welcoming us, but Virginia and I did not notice them. We were much too busy studying each other, getting reacquainted, and attempting to bring one another up to date on four years of news.

As soon as we arrived at the St. Francis, I was handed the following telegram, which Don had sent when his ship moored in New York City:

To: Commander Donald T. Giles, USN, Former Prisoner of War, San Francisco, California.
 Welcome home!
 Your loving son, Don.

At the St. Francis we were faced with another mouth-watering temptation. Such an elaborate buffet I had never seen. Of course, we had all been drilled to eat sparingly, and no one wanted anything to delay his return home. It was difficult to explain to our hosts why we could not partake adequately of their hospitality.

After a brief visit to the Oak Knoll Naval Hospital for a final intransit physical checkup, I was detached with orders to report to the commanding officer of the Naval Hospital in Annapolis for further recuperation. With all of the excitement finally over, Virginia and I headed home on 28 September. What a delightful, leisurely trip we enjoyed across the good old U.S.A. via the Union Pacific and B&O railroads!

After so many years of confinement, I found the sudden reentry into civilization to be confusing. It is difficult to describe my feelings and reactions upon reentering the hurly-burly of life in America in the mid-1940s. It was wonderful to be back home with my family, friends, and neighbors, but the whirl of activity really bothered me. The pace of everyday life was so much faster than when I had left the United States four years earlier. So many changes had occurred during those years that I found it difficult to relate.

Much of the 1945 lifestyle I found unattractive. However, I would not have exchanged the hubbub and turmoil for one additional day of the rice diet, the hell, and all the bad experiences of those past years. Although I had lost all my material possessions, I still had those things that were truly important: my life, my wife, and my family. I was so lucky, and I looked forward enthusiastically to restarting my life.

Upon returning home I found many things still rationed. This was something to which I could relate with ease. In prison camp everything was rationed—totally. But one thing not rationed in America was the friendship of so many people. People whom I knew only in passing stepped forward to welcome me home in so many different ways. The manager of the local A&P knew I hadn't had bacon for years and set some aside for me. Fruit vendors around Market Square insisted on giving me bags of fruit. Oystermen at the City Dock climbed out of their boats to shake my hand and welcome me home. The Chevrolet dealer who had sold me the car the Japs had stolen on Guam put me high on the waiting list for a new car. He added jokingly that he hoped I would take better care of this one. So did I. There were so many people whom I did not know who introduced themselves and welcomed me home.

My treatment at the Naval Hospital continued until the following March, at which time, after a final physical examination, I was returned to active duty in Washington. Although I was highly nervous and my eyesight was somewhat impaired, it appeared that I was as healthy as could be expected after such an ordeal. The human body is designed to take only so much. There would be no more sea duty, which, of course, had been the reason for all my training as a line officer—just shore duty until my retirement.

Many people have said I will probably never again want to eat anything that incorporates rice. This is not so. Although I do not want to go back to the rice diet that was imposed at Zentsuji, I have not lost my taste for it, provided that it is prepared properly. Rice kept us alive, and we thanked God for it. Above all, however, I abhor waste. We did without for so very long.

When I reported for duty to the Office of the Secretary of the Navy on 4 March 1946, I was sworn in as a captain, U.S. Navy, at which time my pay as a captain commenced. Although I had been selected for promotion to that rank in 1942, my promotion did not become effective until I was sworn in, and the back pay I received was that of a commander—a considerable loss of pay.

Captain and Mrs. Giles with Donald T. Giles, Jr., in Annapolis, spring 1946
(Collection of Donald T. Giles, Jr.)

The next six years before my retirement I spent in the Office of the Assistant Secretary of the Navy. I was awarded the Bronze Star with the following citation signed by the secretary of the navy, Mr. James V. Forrestal, and presented to me by Mr. W. John Kenney, assistant secretary of the navy:

For meritorious service as Aide for Civil Affairs and Executive Officer of the Naval Station at Guam during the invasion of that island by the Japanese and while interned as a Prisoner of War from December 19, 1941, until the cessation of hostilities. When the Japanese invaded this small garrison in overwhelming force, Captain (then Commander) Giles remained calm and courageous in the face of the enemy's devastating shellfire, expertly performing his duties and inspiring his men to heroic effort despite the tremendous odds. Concerned only for the welfare of others during his long period of internment under rigorous Japanese rule, he rendered every possible assistance to all men in the camp, organizing classes of study, the library and numerous other activities to sustain the morale of his fellow prisoners. His outstanding fortitude, initiative and indomitable spirit throughout reflect the highest credit upon Captain Giles and the United States Naval Service.

17 ✳ Damage Assessment

How can one assess the damage from our loss of Guam, from our failure to fortify the island for whatever reason? What of the damage to those who were sacrificed there? Careers were wasted, health was squandered, and lives were lost.

Over fifty years have passed since the small garrison on Guam was captured by the Japanese. No one who had been at Zentsuji wanted to look back, and most had no desire to go to Japan ever again. Their memories of Japanese hospitality were too tainted with horror for that to be possible. Rather than return to Japan and testify at the war crimes trials, I chose to provide my testimony in the form of a sworn deposition made in the United States. Many of my former camp-mates chose to do likewise.

For many of the former POWs, much of their time during the postwar years was spent undergoing treatment in various military hospitals. In my opinion, although we were all provided with excellent and careful medical treatment after our return home, the body of knowledge regarding the special medical problems of prisoners of war is not complete. There are both physical and psychological problems that result from confinement, malnutrition, harassment, and torture regarding which little is known.

After I returned home, the results of my annual physical examinations were always satisfactory. Having said that, within ten to fifteen years I lost almost all of my teeth. As I recorded earlier, my front teeth

177

had been knocked out by the Japanese during "discussions" in camp. The loss of the rest of them probably resulted from dietary deficiencies while I was a prisoner. The most significant health problems that I trace to my experiences in Japan are extreme nervousness and a tendency to be very self-conscious. Both of these problems cause me to avoid large groups of people whenever possible.

I believe that anyone who suffered as we did for almost four years would show signs of physical and psychological damage. In discussions I have had with other former prisoners of war, many described a tendency to withdraw from people, a tendency that is difficult to correct. We have all found readjustment to be both disconcerting and difficult.

In 1946 or 1947 a brief questionnaire was sent by U.S. military authorities to former prisoners in an attempt to assess the effects of their captivity.[1] I do not know how many former prisoners were included in the survey, but some 207 responses were received from prisoners who had been held in various camps throughout Japan. The following replies are representative of the answers that were received. It should be pointed out that some of the former prisoners whose responses are quoted below were in their twenties.

1. *Have you any physical impairment or disability incurred in the course of your imprisonment? Does this impairment preclude you from engaging in a gainful endeavor and to what extent does it handicap you, if gainfully employed?*

"I have several physical and mental disabilities that were incurred in the course of my imprisonment. Briefly I cite the findings of the U.S. Army Retiring Board: 'Captain ——— is permanently incapacitated for any type of military service. Psychotic depressive reaction manifested by recurrent depressive moods during which there are compulsive acts of aggressiveness, ruminations about experiences as a Japanese POW; severe incapacity; permanently impaired vision; residual effects of beri beri.' There are a few other things but these are the main ones that the Army found in the 18 months that they kept me in hospitals following my return from prison camp at Roku Roshi. They retired me to the care of my wife who was appointed guardian for me."

"The Veterans Administration has given me a 60% disability due to nervousness, duodenal ulcer and residuals of avitaminosis. These disabilities are coupled with a lack of strength and stamina, and loss of appetite. Also suffer rather frequent attacks of nausea."

"Upon physical examination immediately after my release from imprisonment in Japan it was ascertained that I had contracted tuberculosis as a result of the extremely low standard of living to which I was subjected as a POW. As a result, after treatment over a period of 11 months at naval hospitals I was retired from active duty. I am not gainfully employed by reason of this disability."

"I have had to accept a minor, less responsible position than I had before the war because of anxiety state, poor memory, lack of concentration and general mental step-back."

"Have experienced some physical problems with my legs from knees down which is probably due to beri beri and freezing of my feet. My eyesight has been impaired considerably and I am now unable to do much reading. I lack the stamina and endurance which I enjoyed before the war."

"I appear to have lost my power of concentration. I lack endurance to stay at anything long."

"I am a total wreck. I received a pretty bad beating in the back during winter of '42 when nearly 99% of the fellows were sick. I got it across the back with a pick handle. Another time I was injured while unloading a coal ship. A Jap let go of a plank on purpose while we were down in the hold of the ship and it struck me between the leg and knee. In the winter of '43 I got beri beri real bad."

"My physical impairment as a result of imprisonment includes loss of all my teeth and a diseased mouth which keeps me in constant pain. Other disabilities I incurred can best be described by the following results of a mental examination by a Veterans Administration doctor: 'Subjective findings: constant worry over everything in reality, difficulty in eating, blurring of vision, easy fatigue, irritability, periodic depression, fear, uncertainty, insomnia, nightmares and combat dreams.'"

2. *Do you experience or did you experience any psychological impediments which delayed your readjustment? Do you feel that you have regained the mental and physical condition that you enjoyed prior to capture?*

"There still remains a definite lack of interest in everyday affairs, as everything appears to be relatively unimportant. There is a lack of patience and understanding in regards to other people's point of view, and there is a feeling of bitterness which is hard to control. I am not the same either mentally or physically as I was prior to capture."

"Have a marked feeling of inferiority to others since the time in prison was so unproductive and useless. Am occasionally despondent."

"The mental and physical condition which I enjoyed prior to capture have not been regained. I suffer from a general mental sluggishness, and I find that an ordinary day's work fatigues me far more than it should for my age."

"Occasionally I feel that I am still confined. To a slight degree, I have an anti-social attitude. By this, I mean that at times I feel a dread of attending functions where a lot of people are assembled. I doubt if I shall ever regain the stamina I enjoyed previously."

"I had quite a time to readjust myself. Everything was all new and so far advanced. I can never gain back physically what the Japs took from me."

"I have been extremely nervous since my liberation and this has hindered my readjustment materially."

"I definitely feel that I have not regained the mental and physical condition that I enjoyed prior to capture and I don't feel as if it will ever be possible to do so."

"I am reluctant to go out with a crowd of people. My stamina is considerably below what it should be."

"Constant harassment during imprisonment resulted in loss of force and self-confidence. I have not regained either the mental ability or the physical vigor which I enjoyed prior to capture. I seriously doubt that I shall ever regain the physical health and stamina which I possessed prior to capture."

"I have noticed a definite psychological maladjustment in my relation with other people since my release. I have lost some of the snap and drive that I formerly had."

"Memories of my physical torture are impossible to erase. Whenever I am criticized I know that I am in no danger of physical punishment. But my stomach has never been able to realize this and, as a result, I invariably have extreme nausea."

3. *Have you satisfactorily passed a complete physical examination since your return? Are you satisfied that the examination indicates your true physical and mental condition?*

"I have passed a physical examination but am not satisfied that it indicated my true condition. They have dismissed my general lethargic feeling too easily."

"While I satisfactorily passed a complete Army physical examination when I was separated from the service in 1947, I do not think that the examination was truly indicative of my physical and mental condition."

"I have passed numerous physical examinations since my return. I do not believe they indicated my true physical and mental condition due to the fact that they are limited in scope."

4. *Have you experienced any difficulties of a business, domestic or material nature upon your return, which you consider to be the result of your detention?*

"My married life was broken up by the war because of the Japanese refusing to notify my family that I had been captured for over a year."

"The breaking up of my home was directly caused by my period of detention."

"I have experienced great difficulties in adjusting to business conditions due to the slowing of my mental processes. I feel that the continuous humiliation, repression and mental anguish that I was subjected to while a prisoner of the Japanese have reduced my mental faculties drastically."

"As a result of my being gone so long, my ex-wife sued me for divorce before I arrived back in the States. The first time I saw my four year old son was in a lawyer's office in November of 1945. Although I saw him once more, about a week later, I have not been able to see him since then."

"I have an inferiority complex that is very difficult to overcome. This has proved to be a hindrance in business."

"I get upset easily and can't do the type of work that I should like to do. I don't think it would be possible to go through $3\frac{1}{2}$ years of starvation and mental strife without it having some effect on your productive ability."

"Divorced on my return to the States. Was told on my first night home. Part of the divorce complaint was the separation for four and a half years, of which three years and nine months I was a POW."

"My physical condition and mental attitude are considerably inferior to what they were. This was caused by the terrible strain placed upon both mind and body during my imprisonment in Japan with both the living and the dead. I am suffering from a possibly irreparable cynicism and fatalism due to my experiences in Japan."

"The strain and worry on my wife have made her psychotic. She was unable to hear from me more than six times in three years and eight months, and heard nothing from me during 1944–1945 when she knew I was in the heart of the heavily-bombed area of Japan."

"I have been obliged to resign from two positions since return to civilian life, because of my inability to be confined in an office, and because of extreme restlessness, fatigue and an inability to concentrate on one subject for any length of time."

"A definite tendency to vacillate and uncertainty in making decisions have affected my ability to succeed in the business world."

5. Do you predict that your experiences will result in any shortening of your life span?

"This was one of the many questions that I asked numerous medical doctors who attended me during a year and a half of hospitalization in Army hospitals. The consensus of their opinion was that the mental psychosis and malnutrition I suffered at the hands of the Japanese would shorten my life 10 to 20 years. They all seemed to agree that I would be an old man at 40."

"At least 10 years, probably a good deal more."

"From 50 on I believe I will be living on borrowed time."

"I believe my experiences in Japan and the beatings they gave me have cut at least 10 years off my life."

6. Please relate any additional viewpoints you may have on this subject matter.

"I live in a low melancholy state of mind. My outlook is a combination of dull hopelessness and detached disinterest. I simply don't care much about anything anymore."

"I believe it is impossible to know what the effects of prison life will be on our future. Whether some of us have latent 'bugs' in our systems or mental quirks that haven't surfaced yet, is unanswerable."

"I believe the anxiety that my imprisonment caused my mother killed her. I suffered severe malnutrition and maltreatment. I was beat over the face and head by Japanese guards and choked until I almost turned purple. I was forced to witness my fellow prisoners going through the same unmerciful beatings and various forms of barbaric punishment as I did. I was forced to work as a slave under the most adverse conditions and without any provisions made whatsoever for my health or welfare. There was no sanitation in camp and as a result many men died from diarrhea and dysentery. I had diarrhea continuously for four months but was forced to work every day in spite of my weakened condition."

"I consider myself lucky to be back home. I am incapacitated occasionally as a result of beri beri or some other malfunction caused by malnutrition in camp. I consider it all a result of our unpreparedness and have written it off as a bad deal."

"I believe that it is not possible for the widows and families of POWs who died as a result of the deliberate neglect and mistreatment by the Nips to ever be repaid for their loss. The widows and children deserve full compensation from a barbaric nation that subjected honorable prisoners to inhumane conditions for a long period of time. The abject humiliation suffered by all the prisoners was a deliberate and planned policy by the higher command of the Japanese government."

The following paragraphs contain an analysis made by U.S. military authorities of the 207 responses to the questionnaire:

About 50% report various degrees of physical disability. Some have been retired from the service for obvious organic defects suffered as prisoners of war. Impairment of the functional level is extremely difficult to measure by the present rather crude standards, and an organic basis for many marked functional disorders so commonly complained of is impossible to determine at the present time. The striking lack of stamina, and the extreme fatiguability that characterizes so many ex-POWs is a very definite but unmeasurable impairment. These subjective symptoms, while they remain an enigma to the medical profession, are nevertheless real to the individual. While no studies have been performed, it is inconceivable that POWs would suffer extreme degrees of physical and nutritional privation for nearly four years without permanent sequela.

The psychological and emotional trauma to which prisoners were subjected, as well as the physical brutalities inflicted by the enemy, have adversely altered the personality of many prisoners. Behavior patterns have been acquired which make adjustment to normal life in a community extremely difficult. Aside from marked degrees of "nervousness," many have a defeatist attitude which they are unable to overcome. Hopes and normal aspirations have been replaced by a feeling of morbid futility. Prominent among the complaints of ex-POWs is a marked feeling of insecurity, even though there has been no loss whatever of the material security the armed forces give.

A few people have been surveyed from the Service for physical disabilities resulting directly from maltreatment in prison camps in Japan. Most correspondents feel that the physical exams they have passed gave a true picture of their physical and mental condition. A small minority feel that they have regained their normal physical and mental conditions but most believe they will never regain the well being they would have enjoyed had they not suffered the ordeal of Jap Prison Camps.

About 65% find difficulty in performing the duties required of them. They are unable to carry the work load they would normally be expected to carry. While all recognize that the mere attrition of age is a factor, it is definitely not a major one, for many are in the age group where a space of five years should increase rather than decrease their capabilities in every respect except purely physical endeavor.

About 50% believe their normal life span has been shortened by at least ten years.

✳ Epilogue

The preceding chapters have told a horror story: the story of how my father and his shipmates from Guam were treated by the Japanese during the capture of that island and while they were prisoners of war. They witnessed friends beheaded and disemboweled; they were harassed, beaten, starved, and treated without reference to human kindness. To them the Japanese were vindictive, sadistic, and brutal. When they returned home many had permanent physical and mental scars from their experience. In many cases their lives were shortened by the treatment they had received.

In 1956, as a young naval officer, I was ordered to duty as assistant U.S. naval attaché to Japan. Eleven years had passed since my father's repatriation, and the next generation of his family was being ordered to go live with his defeated captors as diplomats.

During briefings in Washington before we left for Japan I was advised not to discuss his war record or to reveal that he had been a prisoner of war; I was to say only that he was a Naval Academy graduate and a rear admiral. I followed this advice, and during the three years we lived in Japan no one ever asked about his career. Curious? Perhaps, but not unlike the Japanese. I do not believe they knew, but to ask about him would have been out of keeping with their customs. They do not inquire into things that do not concern them, things that might be considered personal.

185

My father gave me only one piece of advice regarding my new assignment: "Don't be taken in." I do not believe we were, although I doubt we could have convinced him otherwise. Our experiences in Japan were vastly different from his. During the years we spent there we lived in a lovely Japanese house in suburban Tokyo with a staff of servants. We tried to learn about Japan and to appreciate its culture. I studied Japanese with a private tutor whom I came to look upon as a friend. My wife, Kathy, taught English to the wives of several very senior officers of the Japanese Maritime Self Defense Force and developed a close friendship with several of them.

We found the Japanese, at least those whom we knew well, to be warm and caring and as curious about us as we were about them. Contrary to the picture that is frequently painted, those whom we knew were not the least bit stoic, and on some occasions they displayed emotions that could not have been anything but genuine.

I believe the viciousness with which my father and other prisoners were treated was primarily owing to the fact that the prison camps were run by the Imperial Japanese Army. The army was in complete control of the country, was incredibly arrogant, and ran the prison camps as it saw fit. Japan's army was, and possibly still is, less familiar with foreign cultures than its navy, which because of the mobility inherent in ship-borne forces had been more exposed to the West. Because of their lack of contact with Western values, members of the Japanese army were more ready to accept and implement a caste system in which prisoners were thought of as very low forms of life.

During the war the Japanese people were bombarded with anti-American propaganda (as we were with anti-Japanese propaganda). Although this might have been very effective, the brief contacts my father and members of the Zentsuji working parties had with the Japanese people seemed to indicate that they were sympathetic to the prisoners' plight.

Many years after we had lived in Japan, on a brief trip to China, Kathy and I stopped en route for a few days in Tokyo to renew old friendships and revisit some of our old haunts. On the day after our arrival some of our old friends entertained us at a luncheon. It was a grand affair, complete with welcoming speeches and reminiscences. Our hosts had also invited one of our American friends, Jean Pierce, a writer who lives in Tokyo.

After the luncheon Jean drove us back to where we were staying in Azabu, taking a circuitous route through areas we used to roam but no longer recognized. As we drove through the impossibly crowded streets, I said I had considered mentioning that my father had been a prisoner of war in Japan. I thought it would have been interesting to observe the reaction to this long-kept secret. But because it would have been a gauche thing to do, especially in Japan, I did not bring it up.

Jean said that it would have made little difference. They would have replied either that my father's experiences were the fault of the Japanese army or that those were events of which they had no cognizance.

Then Jean said something very telling. She said that the Japanese were trying to rewrite history. Instead of teaching their young people about the events of the Second World War in the Pacific, they were trying to avoid the issue or to recast it completely. As my father had observed in prison camp, they did not use the word *surrender*, choosing instead to describe what happened in a different way, a way less damaging to their sense of face. So sorry, please. It never happened.

Unfortunately, there are many who bear scars on their bodies and minds, scars that refute the text of these altered history books. But when they die, who will refute the books then?

✳ Appendix A
Personnel Who Died or Were Captured on Guam

Those Americans killed during the Japanese assault on Guam were buried on Guam. Subsequently the remains of Corporal Harry Anderson, USMC, and of Coxswain L. J. Pineault, USN, were interred in the National Memorial Cemetery of the Pacific (the Punchbowl), and the remains of Private First Class L. R. Bustamente, USMC, and of Corporal R. E. Van Horn, USMC, were interred in the Manila Cemetery.

With the exception of John Van R. Kluegel (who is buried on Guam), I assume that the remains of the others killed on Guam were returned for interment in the United States, although I have been unable to document this.

Those Americans who died in prison camp were buried in Japan. I have been unable to determine if their bodies were returned home after the war.

Military Personnel

Albertazzi, D. V., Pharmacist's Mate First Class, USN
Allain, J. A., Machinist's Mate First Class, USN
Allen, D. M., Gunner's Mate Third Class, USN
Anderson, F. R., Private First Class, USMC; Marine Barracks, Sumay
Anderson, H. E., Corporal, USMC; Marine Barracks, Sumay (*Killed on Guam; buried in National Memorial Cemetery of the Pacific*)
Ankrom, M. W., Private First Class, USMC; Insular Patrol

Arnett, L. A., Seaman First Class, USN
Arnold, J. J., Pharmacist's Mate First Class, USN
Ashton, H. J., Boatswain's Mate Second Class, USN
Atwood, C. W., Pharmacist's Mate Second Class, USN
Babb, J. W., Private First Class, USMC; Marine Barracks, Sumay
Baggett, R. N., Private First Class, USMC; Insular Patrol
Bah, W. R., Private First Class, USMC; Insular Patrol
Bairey, V. M., Machinist's Mate First Class, USN
Baker, F. C., Pharmacist's Mate First Class, USN
Ballinger, R. W., Private First Class, USMC; Insular Patrol
Barnett, C. D., Private First Class, USMC; Marine Barracks, Sumay
Barnum, D. W., Chief Radioman, USN
Bearden, I. C., Private First Class, USMC; Marine Barracks, Sumay
Bell, L. W., Construction Mechanic First Class, USN
Bender, E., Private First Class, USMC; Marine Barracks, Sumay
Benedict, D. A., Pharmacist's Mate Third Class, USN (*Transferred from Zentsuji to Umeda Bunsho Camp, Osaka; died May 1944*)
Benson, A. W., Baker Second Class, USN
Berry, B. W., Pharmacist's Mate Third Class, USN
Binns, D. A., Coxswain, USN
Bircher, N. D., Aerographer Second Class, USN
Blaha, J. H., Chief Yeoman, USN (*Arrived at Zentsuji 8 September 1942*)
Bluma, L. E., Boatswain's Mate Second Class, USN
Bomar, W. W., Jr., Private First Class, USMC; Insular Patrol (*Killed on Guam*)
Bowen, C. A., Pharmacist's Mate Second Class, USN
Bowman, L. W., Pharmacist's Mate Third Class, USN
Bowman, R. O., Private First Class, USMC; Marine Barracks, Sumay
Boyle, M., Corporal, USMC; Marine Barracks, Sumay
Bright, Graham Paul, Lieutenant Junior Grade (SC), USN; Assistant Supply Officer, Island Government (*Killed on Guam*)
Brown, R. M., Storekeeper Third Class, USN
Brown, R. T., Private First Class, USMC; Marine Barracks, Sumay
Bryk, C. J., Private, USMC; Insular Patrol
Budzynski, L. R., Private First Class, USMC; Insular Patrol
Buerger, B. O., Private First Class, USMC; Marine Barracks, Sumay
Burt, William A., Private First Class, USMC; Insular Patrol (*Killed on Guam*)
Bustamente, L. R., Private First Class, USMC; Insular Patrol (*Died 16 March 1944; buried in Manila Cemetery*)
Calavecchio, F. A., Boatswain's Mate First Class, USN

Campbell, Fred L., Pay Clerk, USN; Assistant Officer in Charge, Ship's Store

Carlson, Arnold J., Lieutenant (SC), USN; Supply Officer, Island Government

Carney, Francis J., Ensign (CEC), USNR; Assistant Public Works Officer

Carrillo, A. J., Quartermaster First Class, USN

Carscallen, E. W., Pharmacist's Mate Second Class, USN

Cecha, Alvin H., Commander (MC), USN; Executive Officer, Naval Hospital

Charles, M. M., Storekeeper First Class, USN

Christiansen, L., Nurse, Naval Hospital

Chuck, H., Private First Class, USMC; Insular Patrol

Church, R. H., Private First Class, USMC; Insular Patrol

Cochran, M., Chief Machinist's Mate, USN

Cohen, S. L., Private First Class, USMC; Marine Barracks, Sumay

Combs, C. A., Private First Class, USMC; Insular Patrol

Combs, J. B., Mess Sergeant, USMC; Marine Barracks, Sumay

Copeland, F. E., Corporal, USMC; Marine Barracks, Sumay

Cramer, C. J., Radioman First Class, USN

Crichton, C. M., Private First Class, USMC; Marine Barracks, Sumay

Custer, E. M., Chief Pharmacist's Mate, USN

Cutler, J. M., Private, USMC; Marine Barracks, Sumay

Dahl, Arthur P., Pharmacist, USN; Personnel and Commissary Officer, Naval Hospital

Dahlsted, A. B., Fireman First Class, USN

Dalrymple, R. E., Private, USMC; Marine Barracks, Sumay

Damon, W. L., Mess Sergeant, USMC; Marine Barracks, Sumay

Daniels, A. L., Hospital Apprentice First Class, USN

Danielson, D. O., Field Musician First Class, USMC; Marine Barracks, Sumay

Darter, H. L., Private, USMC; Marine Barracks, Sumay

Davidson, D. W., Water Tender Second Class, USN

Davis, James E., Lieutenant Junior Grade (ChC), USN; Chaplain, Naval Station

Dean, J. R., Ship's Cook Third Class, USN

DeSaulniers, A. C., Private First Class, USMC; Marine Barracks, Sumay

Diederich, A. M., Pharmacist's Mate Second Class, USN

Dietrich, C. C., Chief Electrician's Mate, USN

Dixon, V. G., Assistant Cook, USMC; Marine Barracks, Sumay

Drollette, James A., Private Second Class, USMC; Marine Barracks, Sumay

Dullard, E. J., Radioman Second Class, USN

Dunlop, W. W., Hospital Apprentice First Class, USN

Dunn, G. G., Jr., Private First Class, USMC; Insular Patrol

Dunsmoor, Earl W., Pay Clerk, USMC; Officer in Charge, Marine
Pay Accounts

Dupuis, E. J., Field Musician, USMC; Marine Barracks, Sumay

Dutro, H. W., Fireman Second Class, USN

Eads, Lyle W., Yeoman First Class, USN

Eagan, W. E., Ship's Cook First Class, USN

Ellis, R. R., Radioman First Class, USN

Emch, R. W., Private, USMC; Marine Barracks, Sumay

Epperson, B., Radioman Second Class, USN

Eppley, James E., Lieutenant Junior Grade (MC), USN; Assistant
Medical Officer, Naval Hospital

Ercanbrack, E. B., First Sergeant, USMC; Marine Barracks, Sumay

Erdman, J., Private, USMC; Marine Barracks, Sumay

Ernst, R. W., Signalman Third Class, USN (*Killed on Guam*)

Eudy, E. F., Water Tender First Class, USN

Fabian, H., Machinist's Mate Second Class, USN

Farris, L. A., Chief Yeoman, USN

Faulkner, S. T., Radioman Second Class, USN

Feder, John G., Lieutenant Junior Grade (MC), USN; Assistant
Medical Officer, Naval Hospital

Fenn, J. L., Pharmacist's Mate First Class, USN

Fisher, W. H., Chief Boatswain's Mate, USN

Flournoy, Walter N., First Lieutenant, USMC; Marine Barracks, Sumay

Fogarty, Virginia J., Nurse, Naval Hospital

Foote, A. E., Machinist's Mate First Class, USN

Ford, C. C., Staff Sergeant, USMC; Marine Barracks, Sumay

Fraser, R. G., Boatswain's Mate First Class, USN (*Killed on Guam*)

Frederick, R. N., Fireman First Class, USMC; Marine Barracks, Sumay

French, E. W., Private First Class, USMC; Marine Barracks, Sumay

Frontis, I., Chief Pharmacist's Mate, USN

Gaines, Oliver W., Lieutenant Commander, USN; Beachmaster,
Naval Station

Garrison, J. B., Private First Class, USMC; Marine Barracks, Sumay

Gayhard, C. I., Electrician's Mate First Class, USN

Giles, D. B., Private First Class, USMC; Marine Barracks, Sumay

Giles, Donald T., Commander, USN; Vice Governor and Executive
Officer, Naval Station

Goebel, D. W., Private First Class, USMC; Insular Patrol

Goetz, H. C., Pharmacist's Mate First Class, USN

Golich, G. C., Corporal, USMC; Marine Barracks, Sumay

Gordy, T. W., Radioman First Class, USN

Gottlieb, Mack L., Lieutenant (MC), USNR; Assistant Medical Officer, Naval Hospital

Graf, Paul, Lieutenant Commander, USN; Head, Executive Department

Guith, F. G., Printer First Class, USN

Gwinnup, R. W., Electrician's Mate First Class, USN

Hagood, F. M., Corporal, USMC; Marine Barracks, Sumay

Hale, E. O., Electrician's Mate Second Class, USN

Handy, H. G., Storekeeper First Class, USN

Hanson, K. C., Private First Class, USMC; Insular Patrol

Hanzsek, J., Machinist's Mate First Class, USN

Harrod, R. D., Pharmacist's Mate Second Class, USN

Haskins, T. T., Seaman Second Class, USN

Haun, Robert C., Pay Clerk, USN; Assistant Officer in Charge, Ship's Store

Haviland, James W., III, Lieutenant, USN; Commanding Officer, USS *Penguin*

Hellmers, John A., Chief Commissary Steward, USN

Herd, L., Assistant Cook, USMC; Marine Barracks, Sumay

Hernandez, P. R., Private First Class, USMC; Marine Barracks, Sumay

Hetzler, M. R., Pharmacist's Mate Second Class, USN

Higgin, W. D., Private First Class, USMC; Marine Barracks, Sumay

Hinkle, R. W., Private First Class, USMC; Insular Patrol

Hinton, C. E., Construction Mechanic First Class, USN

Holmes, J. G., Chief Machinist's Mate, USN

Honan, T. R., Sergeant, USMC; Marine Barracks, Sumay

Howard, E. N., Water Tender Second Class, USN

Humphrey, H. J., Private First Class, USMC; Marine Barracks, Sumay

Hurd, S. G., Signalman Third Class, USN (*Killed on Guam*)

Huston, J. L., Private First Class, USMC; Marine Barracks, Sumay

Iannarelli, A. N., Pharmacist's Mate Second Class, USN

Jackson, Wilma Leona, Nurse, Naval Hospital

Jaspits, J., Corporal, USMC; Marine Barracks, Sumay

Jelinski, J. G., Chief Machinist's Mate, USN (*Surrendered 12 December 1941*)

Johnston, A. G., Chief Storekeeper, USN

Johnston, C. B., Machinist's Mate First Class, USN

Jones, A. W., Private First Class, USMC; Marine Barracks, Sumay

Jones, H. A., Yeoman First Class, USN

Jones, J. H., Private First Class, USMC; Marine Barracks, Sumay

Jones, R. D., Pharmacist's Mate First Class, USN

Jones, R. W., Aerographer Second Class, USN

Jones, Y. Y., Yeoman Second Class, USN

Joslin, H. E., Radioman Second Class, USN

Kallgren, H. M., Private, USMC; Marine Barracks, Sumay

Kauffman, J., Private First Class, USMC; Marine Barracks, Sumay (*Killed on Guam*)

Keck, T. W., Pharmacist's Mate First Class, USN

Kellogg, H. G., Radioman First Class, USN (*Died at Zentsuji 25 March 1943*)

King, L. S., Private First Class, USMC; Marine Barracks, Sumay

Knighten, J. W., Supply Sergeant, USMC; Marine Barracks, Sumay

Kozlowski, L. S., Private First Class, USMC; Marine Barracks, Sumay

Krump, M. L., Chief Machinist's Mate, USN

Kucharski, L. F., Boatswain's Mate First Class, USN

Kuenen, C. R., Private First Class, USMC; Marine Barracks, Sumay

Laboritz, H. B., Pharmacist's Mate First Class, USN

LaCasse, J. J., Pharmacist's Mate Third Class, USN

LaChappa, J. E., Private First Class, USMC; Marine Barracks, Sumay

LaGrone, H., Private, USMC; Insular Patrol

Lake, O. S., Chief Quartermaster, USN

Lane, Robert Bruce, Chief Boatswain's Mate, USN

Larsen, W. K., Private, USMC; Marine Barracks, Sumay

Laser, H. F., Supply Sergeant, USMC; Marine Barracks, Sumay

Law, P. A., Assistant Cook, USMC; Marine Barracks, Sumay

Lee, R. J., Corporal, USMC; Marine Barracks, Sumay

Legato, A., Corporal, USMC; Marine Barracks, Sumay

Leininger, J., Water Tender First Class, USN

Lewis, C. W., Private, USMC; Insular Patrol

Ligon, L. E., Private, USMC; Marine Barracks, Sumay

Lineberry, William T., Commander (MC), USN; Commanding Officer, Naval Hospital

Linn, F. K., Machinist's Mate Striker, USN

Lufkin, S. R., Corporal, USMC; Marine Barracks, Sumay

Lumpkin, F., Fireman First Class, USN

Lyles, J. H., Sergeant, USMC; Marine Barracks, Sumay

McCunes, D. L., Radioman Second Class, USN

McFarlane, J. G., Chief Water Tender, USN

McGee, Thomas, Lieutenant Junior Grade, USNR; Censor, Naval Government

McInnis, Harry B., Lieutenant Junior Grade (DC), USN; Dental Officer, Naval Hospital

McKenzie, L. W., Fireman Second Class, USN

McLeod, M. D., Hospital Apprentice First Class, USN

McMillin, George J., Captain, USN; Governor and Commandant, Naval Station

McMurray, C. C., Sergeant, USMC; Marine Barracks, Sumay (*Killed September 1944*)

MacNulty, William K., Lieutenant Colonel, USMC; Commanding Officer, Marine Detachment

Madsen, Elwood C., Lieutenant, USN; Communication Officer, Island Government

Magelssen, W., Seaman First Class, USN

Malloy, G. D., Sergeant, USMC; Marine Barracks, Sumay

Malone, C. B., Pharmacist's Mate Second Class, USN

Maloof, G. M., Boatswain's Mate First Class, USN

Manning, D. K., Assistant Cook, USMC; Marine Barracks, Sumay

Markowitz, Herbert A., Lieutenant Junior Grade (MC), USN; Medical Officer, Marine Barracks, Sumay

Marks, Herbert A., First Lieutenant, USMC; Marine Barracks, Sumay

Marshall, P. B., Jr., Pharmacist's Mate Third Class, USN

Martin, Joseph, Ensign, USNR; Assistant Supply Officer

Martin, M. H., Private First Class, USMC; Insular Patrol

Mellon, Hugh R., Ensign, USNR; Assistant Supply Officer

Merritt, L. C., Chief Pharmacist's Mate, USN

Miller, A. R., Private, USMC; Marine Barracks, Sumay

Miller, C. J., Radioman First Class, USN

Moe, Tilden I., Lieutenant Commander (MC), USN; Chief of Medicine, Naval Hospital

Molnar, E., Seaman First Class, USN

Moore, H. D., Sergeant, USMC; Marine Barracks, Sumay

Moore, R. K., Private, USMC; Marine Barracks, Sumay

Moreno, A. J., Fireman First Class, USMC; Marine Barracks, Sumay

Morgan, Glenn D., First Lieutenant, USMCR; Marine Barracks, Sumay

Morrow, V. V., Private First Class, USMC; Marine Barracks, Sumay

Mosher, A. R., Pharmacist's Mate Third Class, USN

Moss, W. T., Private, USMC; Marine Barracks, Sumay

Mucciacciaro, J. D., Private First Class, USMC; Marine Barracks, Sumay

Mueller, J. A., Private First Class, USMC; Marine Barracks, Sumay

Musselwhite, O. W., Radioman First Class, USN

Myers, A. M., Chief Pharmacist's Mate, USN (*Surrendered 3 January 1942*)

Neal, G., Private First Class, USMC; Insular Patrol

Nells, N. C., Pharmacist's Mate Second Class, USN

Nestor, John L., Lieutenant, USN; Commanding Officer, USS *R. L. Barnes*

Nettles, H., Private, USMC; Marine Barracks, Sumay

Newman, Samuel A., Lieutenant Commander, USNR; Engineer Officer, Island Government

Newton, R. A., Corporal, USMC; Marine Barracks, Sumay
Nichols, F., Private First Class, USMC; Marine Barracks, Sumay
Nichols, G. E., Corporal, USMC; Marine Barracks, Sumay
Nixon, H. C., Private First Class, USMC; Marine Barracks, Sumay
O'Brien, R. W., Chief Boatswain's Mate, USN
Odom, J. C., Pharmacist's Mate Second Class, USN
Olds, Marion B., Chief Nurse, Naval Hospital
Olivia, H. O., Officers Steward Second Class, USN
Olson, G. E., Pharmacist's Mate Second Class, USN
Olson, R. T., Fireman First Class, USN
O'Neal, H. M., Pharmacist's Mate Second Class, USN
O'Neil, F. J., Boatswain's Mate First Class, USN (*Killed on Guam*)
Ordoyne, E. J., Private, USMC; Marine Barracks, Sumay
Ormseth, R. B., Private First Class, USMC; Marine Barracks, Sumay
Orr, L. D., Private, USMC; Marine Barracks, Sumay
Osborn, M. B., Private First Class, USMC; Marine Barracks, Sumay
O'Shea, J. J., Platoon Sergeant, USMC; Marine Barracks, Sumay
Parmenter, A. W., Radioman First Class, USN
Parr, R. G., Radioman Second Class, USN
Patterson, R., Chief Water Tender, USN
Peak, M. H., Private First Class, USMC; Marine Barracks, Sumay
Pineault, L. J., Coxswain, USN (*Killed on Guam; buried in National
    Memorial Cemetery of the Pacific*)
Ploke, J. F., Pharmacist's Mate First Class, USN
Plummer, N. S., Private First Class, USMC; Marine Barracks,
    Sumay
Podlesny, J. R., Corporal, USMC; Insular Patrol
Podries, A. J., Machinist's Mate First Class, USN
Pogue, B. B., Private, USMC; Marine Barracks, Sumay
Prickett, H. J., Quartermaster First Class, USN
Ramsey, Edgar A., Corporal, USMC; Marine Barracks, Sumay
Rathbun, L. E., Radioman Second Class, USN
Ratzman, E. M., Seaman First Class, USN
Raymer, F. M., Coxswain, USN
Redenbaugh, C. E., Private First Class, USMC; Insular Patrol
Reed, R. W., Signalman First Class, USN
Reed, W. J., Fireman Second Class, USN
Rice, W. E., Pharmacist's Mate Second Class, USN
Ritthaller, P. R., Field Cook, USMC; Marine Barracks, Sumay
Roepke, F. C., Chief Pharmacist's Mate, USN
Roslansky, M. A., Private, USMC; Insular Patrol
Ross, H. D., Private First Class, USMC; Marine Barracks, Sumay
Rossetto, O., Platoon Sergeant, USMC; Marine Barracks, Sumay

Rowe, A. P., Pharmacist's Mate First Class, USN
Rucker, J. D., Private First Class, USMC; Marine Barracks, Sumay
Runck, J. F., Sergeant, USMC; Marine Barracks, Sumay
Rybicki, C. J., Corporal, USMC; Marine Barracks, Sumay
Rye, J. O., Pharmacist's Mate Second Class, USN
Sager, W. H., Aerographer First Class, USN
Salisbury, R. L., Pharmacist's Mate Third Class, USN
Sanders, P. E., Chief Boatswain's Mate, USN
Sawyer, J. W., Seaman First Class, USN
Schiffbauer, R. A., Storekeeper First Class, USN
Schlegal, A. A., Private First Class, USMC; Marine Barracks, Sumay
Schubert, A. G., Private First Class, USMC; Insular Patrol
Schwab, A. J., Pharmacist's Mate Second Class, USN
Schwartz, Jack W., Lieutenant Junior Grade (CEC), USN; Public
  Works Officer
Schweighart, J., Gunner's Mate First Class, USN (*Killed on Guam*)
Seeger, H. A., Private First Class, USMC; Insular Patrol
Senchuk, Walter E., Ensign, USNR; Engineer Officer, USS *Penguin*
Settles, E. W., Seaman First Class, USN
Seymour, C. A., Private First Class, USMC; Marine Barracks, Sumay
Shane, G. J., Sergeant, USMC; Insular Patrol
Shaul, E. W., Corporal, USMC; Marine Barracks, Sumay
Shaw, G. J., Pharmacist's Mate First Class, USN
Shipp, J. G., Pharmacist's Mate Second Class, USN
Shively, D. T., Private, USMC; Marine Barracks, Sumay
Small, V. M., Chief Machinist's Mate, USN
Smalling, H., Private First Class, USMC; Insular Patrol
Smith, E., Private First Class, USMC; Marine Barracks, Sumay
Smith, F. F., Radioman First Class, USN
Smith, J. M., Private First Class, USMC; Marine Barracks, Sumay
Smith, J. M., Jr., Fireman Second Class, USN
Smith, L. T., Private, USMC; Marine Barracks, Sumay
Smith, M. T., Radioman First Class, USN
Smoot, Malvern H., Chief Machinist's Mate, USN (*Killed on Guam*)
Snater, B. J., Machinist, USN; Assistant to Engineer Officer
Sobey, W. H., Sergeant, USMC; Marine Barracks, Sumay (*Died at
  Zentsuji 29 November 1944*)
Solley, A. A., Pharmacist's Mate First Class, USN
Spellman, E. J., Jr., Private, USMC; Marine Barracks, Sumay
Spicer, Donald, Major, USMC; Executive Officer, Marine Detachment
Sprague, J. W., Pharmacist's Mate Second Class, USN
Staff, J. W., Seaman First Class, USN
Standlea, W. D., Private, USMC; Marine Barracks, Sumay

Stansbury, C. D., Seaman Second Class, USN

Starr, Marvin T., Captain, USMC; Post Quartermaster, Marine
  Barracks, Sumay

Sterling, W. T., Pharmacist, USN; First Lieutenant, Naval Hospital

Stone, F. M., Platoon Sergeant, USMC; Marine Barracks, Sumay

Storey, J. W., Pharmacist's Mate First Class, USN

Strauch, H. E., Chief Machinist's Mate, USN

Summers, G. R., Private First Class, USMC; Marine Barracks, Sumay

Tattrie, N. J., Machinist's Mate First Class, USN

Taylor, J. L., Chief Storekeeper, USN

Taylor, M. A., Private First Class, USMC; Marine Barracks, Sumay

Thiel, R. A., Corporal, USMC; Marine Barracks, Sumay

Thomason, R. B., Chief Pharmacist's Mate, USN

Thoren, O. L., Corporal, USMC; Marine Barracks, Sumay

Todd, Charles S., First Lieutenant, USMC; Military Aide to the
  Governor

Townsend, H. L., Chief Boatswain's Mate, USN

Trasher, F. L., Private First Class, USMC; Marine Barracks, Sumay

Turk, W. H., Private First Class, USMC; Marine Barracks, Sumay

Tyson, O. J., Radioman First Class, USN

Valois, R. L., Pharmacist's Mate Second Class, USN

Van Horn, R. E., Corporal, USMC; Marine Barracks, Sumay (*Killed
  3 July 1945; buried in Manila Cemetery*)

Van Peenen, Hubert J., Lieutenant Commander (MC), USN; Chief of
  Surgery, Naval Hospital

Vontom, S. R., Sergeant, USMC; Marine Barracks, Sumay

Walker, D. R., Electrician's Mate First Class, USN

Wallace, H. E., Corporal, USMC; Marine Barracks, Sumay

Waller, C. R., Corporal, USMC; Marine Barracks, Sumay

Ward, J. S., Corporal, USMC; Marine Barracks, Sumay

Wash, J. L., Seaman First Class, USN

Watts, W. W., Private First Class, USMC; Marine Barracks, Sumay

Weaver, J. W., Private First Class, USMC; Marine Barracks, Sumay

Weaver, P. R., Fireman First Class, USN

Wells, F. P., Yeoman Third Class, USN

Wells, George B., Boatswain, USN; Assistant Beachmaster, Naval
  Station

Whitaker, K. F., Chief Water Tender, USN

White, Robert Gabriel, Ensign, USNR; Gunnery Officer, USS
  Penguin (*Killed aboard USS* Penguin)

Wickham, J. E., Private First Class, USMC; Marine Barracks, Sumay

Wilkerson, M. C., Seaman First Class, USN

Wilkinson, A. L., Pharmacist's Mate Third Class, USN
Williams, C. P., Yeoman Third Class, USN
Williams, H. B., Pharmacist's Mate Third Class, USN
Williams, Richard B., Lieutenant Junior Grade (MC), USN; Assistant Medical Officer, Naval Hospital
Wilson, E. W., Pharmacist's Mate Third Class, USN
Wilson, R. E., Coxswain, USN
Wolfsheimer, Frank, Ensign (CEC), USNR; Assistant Public Works Officer
Wood, Edwin A., Ensign, USNR; Executive Officer, USS *Penguin*
Wood, J. C., Private, USMC; Marine Barracks, Sumay
Yablonsky, A., Yeoman First Class, USN
Yetter, Doris M., Nurse, Naval Hospital
Young, E. C., Radioman First Class, USN
Young, J., Chief Radioman, USN
Young, J. C., Chief Pharmacist's Mate, USN
Young, J. R., Pharmacist's Mate Third Class, USN
Zimmer, R. W., Fireman Second Class, USN

Civilian Personnel

American Citizens of Guam

Barbour, J.
Butler, C. C.
Cox, O. T.
D'Angelo, G.
Durham, W. E.
Elliot, V.
Fall, Fred W.
Gay, E. L.
Haller, ?
Hudson, ?

Jackson, A. W.
Kerner, A.
McNulty, Sidney C., Dr. (DDS)
Manley, A. P.
Notley, W. H.
Oayne, William
Olive, ?
Scambelluri, H.
Vaughn, W. L.
Wolford, H. W.

Wusstig, ? (*Died at Zentsuji. In his letter to me of 28 October 1991, Father Mel McCormack wrote that "Wus[s]tig contracted pneumonia whilst in Zentsuji and died there in the camp. We tried to persuade him to fight the pneumonia but he seemed determined to die there and he did."*)

Dependents of Military Personnel

Hellmers, Mrs. John A., and baby

Cable Station

Foden, G.
Hanson, M.
Hemming, R. C.
MacMichael, S.
O'Connor, P.
Perry, F. (*Arrived at Zentsuji
    8 September 1942*)

Pan American Airways

Arridson, R. A.
Blackett, G. I.
Conklin, G. M.
Gregg, C. F.
Hammelef, A.
Penning, E. H.
Thomas, J. O.
Vaughn, R. J.
Wells, G. L.

Standard Oil

Huston, R. N.

Public Works Department

Brinkerhoff, H.
Bruton, B.
Encerti, D.
Fearey, J.
Flagherty, A.
Hughes, W.
Johnston, W. G. (*Died in Kobe,
    Japan*)
Kluegel, John Van R. (*Killed on
    Guam; buried in Agana
    Cemetery*)
Lowe, E. B.
Nelson, J.
Sachers, H. H.
Underwood, J. H.
Walker, C. L.

Clergy

The Catholic priests who were captured on Guam were released from Japan at the end of the war. They went first to Okinawa, then to the Philippine Islands, and finally back to the United States to recuperate. Except for Father Xavier Marquette (who was deceased), Brother Gabriel, and Brother Jesus, they all returned to Guam. Of those who returned, only Father Mel McCormack is still alive. He serves as vice chancellor of the archdiocese of Agana. In his letter to me of 1 October 1991, Father McCormack wrote that "Bishop Olano came to Guam one last time and asked to stay here. He was given permission and that day went swimming in Tumon Bay and drowned that same day. He is buried in the Cathedral."

Bishop Angel de Olano y Urteaga
Father Arnold Bendowski
Father Adelberg Donlon
Father Alexander Feeley
Father Alvin Lafeir
Father Felix Ley
Father Mel McCormack

Father Xavier Marquette
Father Marcian Pellett
Father Ferdinand Stippich
Father Theophane Toma
Brother Gabriel
Brother Jesus

Advanced Group, Pacific Base Contractors

Aitken, R.
Angell, F.
Apedaile, T. D.
Ashby, W. O.
Bacon, E.
Bendon, T.
Betz, Paul
Betz, R.
Burrows, H.
Campbell, N. D.
Chambers, L. S.
Clary, E. E.
Cludas, A. B.
Corley, N. M.
Craver, C.
Davis, Edward L.
Devine, R.
Downing, C.
Edmunds, K.
Eldridge, C. H.
Falvey, William
Farwell, G.
Fraser, K.
Gabley, M. F.
Gilbert, G.
Gordanier, William
Hardy, K.
Harris, L.
Haun, H. L.
Hermes, T. M.
Hoffstat, R.
Hubbard, R. R.
Kinnison, D. W.
Kirsch, R.
Langford, Lee

Lucke, H. S.
Maxim, E. G.
Mead, H.
Meyer, H. G.
Meyer, K. E.
Moneyhan, C.
Morganthaler, J.
Myers, E. L.
Nelson, J. C.
Neuss, L.
Occhipinti, R.
O'Leary, J.
Petrovich, J. R.
Pleitner, W. H.
Robinson, Milton
Robira, W. M.
Roskowyk, R. G.
Rupert, F.
Smith, Arthur
Smith, Roy
Sterling, B. H.
Stickels, Z.
Stubbs, W. S.
Taylor, Jack
Terry, J.
Thomas, Gomer
Wallace, Don
Waters, M. B.
West, Carl
White, A. R.
Wickhan, H. H.
Woodruff, A.
Woolliscroft, E. B.
Young, R. H.

✳ Appendix B
Emperor Hirohito's Announcement of Surrender

Emperor Hirohito's imperial rescript to the Japanese people of their surrender to the United Nations, closing the Second World War, was broadcast in a radio message, a translation of which appears below.[1] It is said to have marked the first time the Japanese people had heard the voice of their emperor:

> To Our good and loyal subjects:
> After pondering deeply the general trends of the world and the actual conditions obtaining in Our Empire today, We have decided to effect a settlement of the present situation by resorting to an extraordinary measure.
> We have ordered Our Government to communicate to the Governments of the United States, Great Britain, China and the Soviet Union that our Empire accepts the provisions of their Joint Declaration.
> To strive for the common prosperity and happiness of all nations as well as the security and well-being of Our subjects is the solemn obligation which has been handed down by Our Imperial Ancestors, and which We lay close to heart. Indeed We declared war on America and Britain out of Our sincere desire to ensure Japan's self-preservation and the stabilization of East Asia, it being far from Our thought either to infringe upon the sovereignty of other nations or to embark upon territorial aggrandizement. But now the war has lasted nearly four years. Despite the best that has been done by everyone—the gallant fighting

of military and naval forces, the diligence and assiduity of Our servants of the State and the devoted service of Our one hundred million people, the war situation has developed not necessarily to Japan's advantage, while the general trends of the world have turned against her interest. Moreover, the enemy has begun to employ a new and most cruel bomb, the power of which to do damage is indeed incalculable, taking the toll of many innocent lives. Should we continue to fight, it would not only result in the ultimate collapse and obliteration of the Japanese nation, but also it would lead to the total extinction of human civilization. Such being the case, how are We to save the millions of Our subjects, or to atone Ourselves before the hallowed spirits of Our Imperial Ancestors? This is the reason why We have ordered acceptance of the provisions of the Joint Declaration of the Powers.

We cannot but express the deepest sense of regret to Our Allied nations of East Asia, who have consistently cooperated with the Empire towards the emancipation of East Asia. The thought of those officers and men as well as others who have fallen in the fields of battle, those who died at their posts of duty, or those who met with untimely death and all their bereaved families, pains Our heart night and day. The welfare of the wounded and the war sufferers, and of those who have lost their home and livelihood are the objects of Our profound solicitude. The hardships and sufferings to which Our nation is to be subjected hereafter will be certainly great. We are keenly aware of the inmost feelings of all ye, Our subjects. However it is according to the dictate of time and fate that We have resolved to pave the way for a grand peace for all generations to come by enduring the unendurable and suffering what is insufferable.

Having been able to safeguard and maintain the structure of the Imperial State, We are always with ye, Our good and loyal subjects, relying upon your sincerity and integrity. Beware most strictly of any outbursts of emotion which may endanger needless complications, or any fraternal contention and strife which may create confusion, lead ye astray and cause ye to lose the confidence of the world. Let the entire nation continue as one family from generation to generation, ever firm in its faith of the imperishableness of its divine land, and mindful of its heavy burden of responsibilities, and the long road before it. Unite your total strength to be devoted to the construction for the future. Cultivate the ways of rectitude; foster nobility of spirit; and work with resolution so as ye may enhance the innate glory of the Imperial State and keep pace with the progress of the world.

(Imperial Signature)
(Imperial Seal)
The 14th day of the 8th month of the 20th year of Showa.

Notes

Prologue

1. Kent Roberts Greenfield, ed., *Command Decisions* (Washington, D.C.: Office of the Chief of Military History, United States Army, 1960), p. 14.

2. Samuel Eliot Morison, *History of United States Naval Operations in World War II*, vol. 3, *The Rising Sun in the Pacific, 1931–April 1942* (Boston: Little, Brown, 1948), p. 18.

3. U.S. Congress, House, *Hepburn Report*, 76th Cong., 1st sess., 27 December 1938, H. Doc. 65.

4. Greenfield, *Command Decisions*, p. 154.

Chapter 2

1. In this book I have chosen to express time as it would be in the navy, in terms of a twenty-four-hour clock. Thus, 0000 is midnight, the start of the day. Half an hour later, the time is 0030, and 1 A.M. is 0100. Noon is 1200, and 1:00 P.M. is 1300. The day ends at midnight, 2400. As stated in the text, the *Henderson* entered Agap Harbor at 0800, or 8:00 A.M.

2. The *Penguin* was a Bird-class minesweeper built in 1919. She had a length of 188 feet and a beam of 36 feet, displaced 840 tons, and was capable of 14 knots.

3. The names of those who died or were captured in the defense of Guam are given in Appendix A.

4. In addition to these officers, First Lieutenant Charles S. Todd, USMC, was assigned as military aide to the governor.

Chapter 3

1. This reduction was being accomplished by attrition. Although dependents would leave Guam when tours of duty were completed, since March no additional dependents had been permitted to accompany personnel to Guam.

2. The dates given are those associated with where the action takes place. As described in Nathaniel Bowditch, *American Practical Navigator: An Epitome of Navigation* (Washington, D.C.: United States Navy Hydrographic Office, 1958), pp. 486–87,

> Time is a measure of the rotation of the earth. . . . Places to the eastward of the observer have later time, and those to the westward have earlier time. . . . To prevent the date from being in error, and to provide a starting place for each day, a date line is fixed by international agreement. This line coincides with the 180th meridian over most of its length. In crossing this line, one alters his date by one day. . . . Thus if a person is travelling eastward . . . time is becoming later, and when the date line is crossed, the date becomes one day earlier.

Because Guam is on the opposite (western) side of the international dateline from the United States, time in Guam is one day later than in the United States. Although the 1941 Army-Navy game was played on 29 November in Philadelphia, it was 30 November in Guam.

3. In addition to normal signal fading, reception of the broadcast was hampered by a high-power French radio station located somewhere in the Far East. Its transmissions were much stronger than those from faraway Philadelphia and frequently jammed the Army-Navy game broadcast those on Guam were trying to hear.

4. The following is from a letter written to me on Sunday, 30 November, passed by censor and mailed from Guam on the afternoon of 2 December (six days prior to the Japanese attack on Guam). This was the last letter we received from my father.

> Dear Don,
>
> Another disappointing Guam day. The reception on the radio was so poor that we didn't hear much of the Army-Navy game even though it was on the air. Just another of the many advantages (?) of Guam. At 0345 the alarm went off and Dr. L. and I got up and dressed, and I drove up to the club to listen in.
>
> At 0630 they served breakfast of canned grapefruit juice, fried canned ham, scrambled eggs, buns and coffee, and shortly afterwards Dr. L. and I came back home. We've been dopey ever since, even though we took a nap for a couple of hours this afternoon. I expect to get a write-up on the game via radio (dot-dash).
>
> I read the Sat. Post after coming back down from the club after breakfast, and then Dr. L. and I drove to the northern end of the island just to get out and not be in all day.

It's now 4 P.M. We just got up. After I finish this I expect I'll read some more and perhaps get some more news on the radio tonight. We have a real exciting time in Guam, you can readily see. We do have an invitation out to the supply officers' house for venison dinner Tues. night (3 junior supply officers are living together). Practically all the officers out here now except the tops are either ensigns or lieut (jg)—many are reserves.

We expect to have a plane in Tues. (both ways), so this should leave here Wed. for the States—weather permitting. We expect a couple of ships in this week, which should bring more magazines.

Chapter 4

1. Because Guam is on the opposite (western) side of the international dateline from the United States, time in Guam is one day later than in the United States. When the *Penguin* set out on the patrol referred to in the text, it was 7 December Guam time but 6 December in the United States; and when the Japanese attacked Guam on 8 December Guam time, it was 7 December in the United States. See discussion in the previous chapter, note 2.

2. Fortunately, when war broke out the *Gold Star* was coaling at Malangas, in the Philippines. Admiral Hart ordered her to proceed to Balikpapan, Borneo, where she provisioned units of the Asiatic Fleet before joining a convoy led by the USS *Houston* to Darwin, Australia. Here she served as a coastal cargo ship for the duration of the war.

3. The Japanese who were interned included Kaneki Sawada, Takekuna Shinohara, and José Shimizu. Mrs. Sawada was a prominent businesswoman on Guam with strong Japanese ties, and Mr. Shinohara was president of the Japanese Society of Guam. They had demonstrated the strength of their feelings toward Japan in November by visiting with Special Envoy Saburo Kurusu when he spent the night on Guam en route to Washington. Mr. Shimizu was a large-scale copra exporter from Guam, his ship, the *Mariana Maru,* making frequent trips to Saipan and Japan.

4. Major Donald Spicer, Prison Notebook no. 1, pp. 25, 26. While at Zentsuji and Roku Roshi Major Spicer kept a diary that was separated into three parts, which he labeled Prison Notebook nos. 1, 2, and 3. These notebooks are kept by his daughter, Mrs. Nancy Cross, who allowed me to read and use information from them.

5. Reginald W. Reed, "Saga of a Sacrificial Goat, USN" (unpublished manuscript, 1972), p. 36C12.

6. Ibid., p. 37C13.

7. Spicer, Prison Notebook no. 1, pp. 35, 36.

8. The command post remained intact right up to the surrender. Some three years later, in recapturing the island from the Japanese our forces completely eliminated this ancient structure, doubtless by naval gunfire. On my father's return to Guam after the war, the only significant portion of the building left was a stone wall, part of the foundation.

9. Spicer, Prison Notebook no. 1, pp. 57, 58.

10. After Guam was retaken but before the end of the war, war crimes trials were convened on Guam. Shinohara was tried, found guilty of treason against the United States, and sentenced to death. This sentence was commuted to life imprisonment, and he was incarcerated in Tokyo's Sugamo Prison. After six years he was released from prison and returned to Guam.

Chapter 5

1. The force that invaded Guam consisted of a fifty-five-hundred-man regimental combat team (RCT) commanded by Major General Tomitaro Horii and a detachment of four hundred sailors, trained as marines, commanded by Commander Hiroshi Hayashi (the Hayashi Detachment). General Horii planned to seize Guam through a multipronged attack. The northern prong of his attack was composed of a reinforced battalion (the Tsukamoto Force) and the Hayashi Detachment. The Tsukamoto Force and the Hayashi Detachment were brought to Guam in two different transports, thereby increasing the difficulty of coordination. After landing at 0230 through an opening in the reef at Tumon Bay, these troops were to move rapidly down a coastal road and seize Agana. Then the Hayashi Detachment would move on and occupy the Orote Peninsula. The Tsukamoto Force found the hole in the reef and landed on the beach at Tumon Bay as scheduled. Their landing was undetected. The Hayashi Detachment, however, did not find the opening. Searching for another way through the reef, they worked their way southward along the reef and around the rocky cliffs separating Tumon and Agana bays. Using flares as they entered Agana Bay, they found an opening and landed on Dungca's Beach at about 0330. They did not wait for the Tsukamoto Force—which had landed to their north at Tumon Bay—but proceeded independently toward Agana.

2. Apurguan (now lower Tamuning) is immediately south of Dungca's Beach.

3. In volume 1 of the *History of U.S. Marine Corps Operations in World War II* (Washington, D.C.: Headquarters, U.S. Marine Corps, Historical Branch, G-3 Division, 1958), Lieutenant Colonel Frank O. Hough, USMCR, says that landings occurred on the beach north of Tumon Bay (an infantry battalion), at Dungca's Beach (a naval infantry battalion), at Talafofo (an infantry battalion), and north of Merizo (an infantry regiment). He says that this latter force split, with part turning south to Merizo and the other part moving north toward Umatac and Agat. The landing that my father reported as taking place at Agat could have been that part of the infantry regiment Hough reports as moving north from Merizo. Moreover, the landing my father reported as occurring at Togcha was probably the infantry battalion Hough reports as landing at Talafofo.

4. The heavy cruiser *Aoba* and the destroyers *Kikuzuki, Obori, Uzuki,* and *Yuzuki.*

5. I have seen no other reference to landings at Pago or Inarajan and believe that the patrol reports regarding these landings must have been in error. The reported landing at Merizo was probably the infantry regiment to which

Hough refers (see note 3), and the reported landing at Umatac was probably that part of the Merizo infantry unit Hough refers to as moving north toward Umatac and Agat.

6. The Japanese had estimated the Insular Guard's strength to be fifteen hundred, whereas this force was in fact composed of only about one hundred Chamorro.

7. Walter Karig and Welbourn Kelley, *Battle Report: Pearl Harbor to Coral Sea* (New York: Farrar and Rinehart, 1944), p. 109.

8. Memorandum from Colonel Donald Spicer, USMC, to Major Keith, 10 June 1949. A copy of this memorandum is among Colonel Spicer's papers, which are kept by his daughter, Mrs. Nancy Cross.

9. Andrew James Carrillo, Quartermaster First Class, USN, *Deposition to Japanese War Crimes Trials*, 2 August 1946. A copy of this deposition is on file at the U.S. National Archives, Suitland, Maryland.

10. Reginald W. Reed, "Saga of a Sacrificial Goat, USN" (unpublished manuscript, 1972), pp. 42C18, 43C19.

11. Ibid., p. 44C20.

Chapter 6

1. H. J. Van Peenen, "Touchstone from Zentsuji," *The Retired Officer* (Retired Officers Association, Alexandria, Va.), December 1986, p. 34.

2. The five navy nurses were each allowed to bring one suitcase.

3. Van Peenen, "Touchstone from Zentsuji," p. 34.

4. Major Donald Spicer, Prison Notebook no. 1, p. 66. In his diary Major Spicer mentions particularly the following Chamorro: Mrs. Mesa, Mrs. Johnson, the Vellardis, Frank Garrido, Joe Torres, and Felix and Haullah (?) Torres.

5. Mrs. Hellmers's baby daughter was born in Agana on 21 November 1941.

6. Three Americans were left behind: Chief Yeoman Blaha, a marine, and Mr. Perry, a civilian Cable Station employee. They were so badly wounded that they could not leave the island when we did. They joined the other prisoners in Japan later.

7. The M/S *Argentina Maru* was 167 meters long, displaced 12,755 gross tons, and had a maximum speed of 21.5 knots. She had accommodations for 101 first-class and 800 third-class passengers. She was launched in late 1938, was converted to an aircraft carrier (*Kaiyo*) in 1943, and was sunk in Beppu Bay, Japan, by U.S. aircraft in mid-1945.

Chapter 7

1. Walter Karig and Welbourn Kelley, *Battle Report: Pearl Harbor to Coral Sea* (New York: Farrar and Rinehart, 1944), pp. 107, 108.

2. I cannot understand why Domei permitted this statement by Governor McMillin to be transmitted, unless they did not understand it. Note that the

report about Captain McMillin's means of transportation is incorrect, inasmuch as he accompanied all of the Guam prisoners to Japan aboard the M/S *Argentina Maru.*

3. Whenever I listen to this recording, I still feel the heart-wrenching finality of my father's closing, "to all my friends in America, I say goodbye."

Chapter 8

1. The location of Zentsuji is shown on map 3. It is in northern Shikoku on rail lines to Tadotsu and Takamatsu, one of the major cities on Shikoku. Although connected to Honshu and Kyushu by boats that plied the Inland Sea, in the 1940s Shikoku was relatively isolated from other parts of Japan. Zentsuji is situated on a coastal plain between the Inland Sea and a range of mountains that rise to an elevation of thirty-five hundred feet, geographical features that further isolate the area. Because most of Shikoku is mountainous, flat areas were cultivated heavily. As in other parts of Japan, hilly areas were terraced intensively to increase the farmable area. The area around Zentsuji was planted in rice and double-cropped with winter wheat and barley.

2. Joseph D. Kwiatkowski, Major, USA, *Deposition to Japanese War Crimes Trials.* A copy of this deposition is on file at the U.S. National Archives, Suitland, Maryland.

3. Butaritari is an island in the Marshalls north of Tarawa.

Chapter 9

1. Report from Colonel Donald Spicer, USMC, to the Commandant, U.S. Marine Corps, 19 July 1946.

2. *Oakland Tribune,* 19 September 1945.

3. In the diary that he kept while a prisoner, Reginald Reed falsified the content of some entries, fearing reprisal if the diary were found. After repatriation, when he wrote his manuscript "Saga of a Sacrificial Goat, USN," he corrected these entries. In that manuscript Reed detailed an "indictment of the armed forces of Japan and others, living or dead, who deliberately mistreated and tortured allied prisoners of war and internees entrusted to their custody during World War II."

4. In English the Japanese word *benjo* translates as bathroom, john, or, in navy terminology, head.

5. H. L. Townsend, Chief Boatswain's Mate, USN, *Deposition to Japanese War Crimes Trials.* A copy of this deposition is on file at the U.S. National Archives, Suitland, Maryland.

6. H. J. Van Peenen, "Touchstone from Zentsuji," *The Retired Officer* (Retired Officers Association, Alexandria, Va.), December 1986, p. 36.

7. Reed, "Saga of a Sacrificial Goat, USN," p. 71C47.

8. Both the *hakama* and the *haori* are traditional-style clothing worn by men. My father was wrong in his description of the *hakama.* It is a long, wide, divided skirt. Although he describes it as being worn in Zentsuji in the 1940s,

at the present time it is worn mainly for ceremonial occasions and ancestral rites. When my wife and I returned to Japan for a brief visit in 1985 (see Epilogue), we were greeted at the Togo Memorial Club by a retired senior admiral of the Imperial Japanese Navy who was dressed in *hakama*.

9. Reed, "Saga of a Sacrificial Goat, USN," p. 66C42.

10. The civilian construction workers had been on Guam for preliminary planning to dredge the harbor and construct airfields and other military installations recommended by the Hepburn Board in 1938.

11. In Kobe the Catholic priests were kept first at the Seamen's Institute and then at the Canadian Academy. Finally they were moved to the foothills of Futatabi-san, a mountain that rises directly north of the harbor.

12. *Washington Post,* 30 August 1942.

13. *Oakland Tribune,* 19 September 1945.

14. Griffith had been stationed at the American Consulate in Tsingtao, China, where he had been serving with diplomatic status.

15. On the way home aboard the *Gripsholm* Miss N. V. Fogarty met and married a member of the American Consular Service. She remained with him at his new station in Africa. The other nurses (Miss L. Christiansen, Miss Wilma Leona Jackson, Miss Marion B. Olds, and Miss D. Yetter) and Mrs. Hellmers and her infant daughter arrived in New York on 25 August 1942.

16. Reed, "Saga of a Sacrificial Goat," p. 65C41.

Chapter 10

1. Some of the men who were captured had been assigned to a COMINT listening station on Guam. The Japanese were unaware of this, and fortunately for these prisoners, the nature of their assignment was never discovered.

2. The Japanese advertised the Greater East Asia Co-prosperity Sphere as a partnership with the people of East Asia whose countries they had seized. In reality it was designed to serve as a Japanese economic and geopolitical bloc in East Asia.

3. Samuel Eliot Morison, *History of U.S. Naval Operations in World War II,* vol. 3, *The Rising Sun in the Pacific: 1931–April 1942* (Boston: Little, Brown, 1948), p. 234.

4. Commander Campbell Keene, USN, was captured when Wake Island was surrendered to the Japanese on 23 December 1941. He arrived at Zentsuji with other prisoners from Wake on 29 January 1942.

5. Reginald W. Reed, "Saga of a Sacrificial Goat, USN" (unpublished manuscript, 1972), p. 58C34.

6. Major Donald Spicer, Prison Notebook no. 1, pp. 74–76.

7. Reed, "Saga of a Sacrificial Goat, USN," p. 76C50.

Chapter 11

1. Lyle W. Eads, *Survival amidst the Ashes* (Marble Hill, Mo.: Stewart Printing and Publishing, 1985), p. 105.

2. Occasionally the prisoners at Zentsuji were permitted to write letters. These were always brief and the subject matter was restricted, not just by the Japanese but also by the writer himself, for his own protection. The letters we received in Annapolis came via Switzerland. A copy of the envelopes for two of the letters we received is shown in figure 19. Note that one of the envelopes bears the postmark 17.9.1. In Japan, years are numbered within an era. Each era corresponds with the reign of an emperor and is given a name. For example, the era of Emperor Hirohito (from 1926 to 1988) is called Showa ("Radiant Peace"). Thus, the year 1926 is numbered Showa 1, the year 1927 is numbered Showa 2, and so on. The postmark 17.9.1 indicates that the letter had been sent on September 1 in the year Showa 17 (i.e., 1943).

3. The USS *Guam* was launched at the New York Shipbuilding Corporation in Camden, New Jersey, on 12 November 1943. Mrs. McMillin was her sponsor; my mother, Mrs. Todd (the wife of Captain McMillin's aide), and I were there. The *Guam* was commissioned on 17 September 1944 and joined Task Force 58 on 14 March 1945.

4. At the war crimes trials held in Yokohama in the late 1940s Captain Hosotani was convicted of "Withholding Red Cross Packages from Prisoners at Zentsuji" and sentenced to serve five years in prison.

5. During the war years the Japanese yen was worth about 50 cents. Whereas a major was paid 2.5 yen a day (or about $1.25), an enlisted man was paid 0.7 yen a day (or about 35 cents) for his hard manual labor.

6. An additional 20 percent was withheld as a "rainy-season fund."

Chapter 12

1. There were 100 sen to the yen, and during the war years a yen was worth about 50 cents.

2. Kendo, or *ken-jutsu,* is an ancient Japanese form of fencing. Mere skill in striking an antagonist is not prized as much as exhibitions of coolness and presence of mind. Attempting to unnerve his opponent, a player frequently precedes his blows with blood-curdling yells—not unlike those heard by our forces during Japanese banzai charges.

3. Reginald W. Reed, "Saga of a Sacrificial Goat, USN" (unpublished manuscript, 1972), p. 61C37.

4. Ibid., p. 72C48.

5. Report from Colonel Donald Spicer, USMC, to the Commandant, U.S. Marine Corps, 19 July 1946.

6. Reed, "Saga of a Sacrificial Goat, USN," p. 72C48.

7. Ibid., p. 72C48.

Chapter 13

1. In his deposition to the Japanese War Crimes Trials, Dr. H. J. Van Peenen stated that there were thirteen deaths in camp. A copy of this deposition is on file at the U.S. National Archives, Suitland, Maryland.

Chapter 14

1. Somehow the rumor of the move to Hiroshima reached Annapolis, where a navy wife whose husband was not a POW spread it with unwarranted authority. Not having been informed of the move officially, my mother tried to discount the rumor. Rumors are always potentially dangerous, and after the atomic bombing of Hiroshima, we in Annapolis suffered several weeks of uncertainty and fear.

2. The camp is called Roku Roshi (two words) in all the American references I have found. On Japanese maps and in those few Japanese publications that refer to the town or area, however, it is called Rokuroshi (one word). The approximate location of the camp is shown in maps 3 and 4.

3. Major Donald Spicer, Prison Notebook no. 3, pp. 62, 63.

4. H. J. Van Peenen, "Touchstone from Zentsuji," *The Retired Officer,* December 1986, p. 37.

5. In his book *Bataan and Beyond: Memories of an American POW* (College Station: Texas A&M University Press, 1978), John S. Coleman, Jr., says that they detrained at a place called Chio. The U.S. Defense Mapping Agency gazetteer of Japan does not identify any town by this name, and neither the Japanese Embassy nor officials of the Fukui prefectural government could identify such a town. It is possible that Mr. Coleman was mistaken, or that the name of the town has been changed. I believe the rail journey ended at Nishi-Kadowara (or Nishi-Kadohara). Nishi-Kadowara is on a rail line from Fukui that passes south of the area of Rokuroshi. It is approximately twenty-five miles from Fukui and at the foot of a steep secondary road that leads toward an area called Rokuroshi *shikogen* (Rokuroshi heights). Rokuroshi *shikogen* includes the Rokuroshi *skijo* (ski area) and the Rokuroshi *kokumin kyuyochi* (rest place)—a name that in no way describes what was there in 1945. The road from Nishi-Kadowara to Rokuroshi *shikogen* closely parallels a mountain stream (which my father mentions hearing as the prisoners made their way up the mountainside). In a distance of about fifteen kilometers the road climbs from an elevation of fifteen hundred feet to about three thousand feet.

6. Van Peenen, "Touchstone from Zentsuji," p. 37.

7. On the basis of information contained in POW debriefing reports, the first group of POWs arrived at Roku Roshi on 15 April 1945. This group consisted of American, Dutch, and British enlisted men in addition to two civilians who had been captured on Wake. In June, when the prisoners from Zentsuji arrived, there were 365 prisoners at Roku Roshi: U.S. Army 266, U.S. Navy 60, U.S. Marine Corps 19, U.S. civilians 10, British military 5, and Dutch military 5. The camp commandant was a Captain Habe, whom Colonel Spicer described in his debriefing report as a brute and a liar. Other Japanese at the camp were an interpreter named Fujimoto and two camp stewards named Nakada and Ishida, both of whom Colonel Marion D. Unruh, USA, the senior officer among the prisoners at Roku Roshi, described in his debriefing report as brutal.

8. Some of the prisoners had a different name for Roku Roshi. It was Roku Sukoshi, *sukoshi* meaning "scarce" in Japanese. That was marginally descrip-

tive of the amount of food they were getting. A more accurate name would have used a term whose meaning approached "not any." In his report of 19 July 1946 to the Commandant, U.S. Marine Corps, Major Spicer wrote that those who did not work were fed about 800 calories a day. Those who accepted the alternative of working four hours a day on the "voluntary" agricultural project were fed about 1,100 calories a day.

9. Van Peenen, "Touchstone from Zentsuji," p. 37.

10. Fukui was roughly to the west of Roku Roshi. If the fires were toward the south, as my father wrote, it might have been that the port of Tsuruga, approximately forty miles to the southwest, was under attack.

11. Although my father did not document it, he told me that one day one of the Japanese officers came to him and said something to the effect that the Japanese sun had ceased to rise and that he was very sad.

12. See, for example, Emperor Hirohito's official announcement to the Japanese people in Appendix B.

13. The *Lisbon Maru* was a Japanese commercial ship of 7,050 tons' displacement taken over by the Japanese navy for use as a troop transport. On 1 October 1942 she was torpedoed and sunk by the U.S. submarine *Grouper* one hundred miles off Ning-po, China (ninety miles south of Shanghai).

14. Memorandum from Colonel Donald Spicer, USMC, to Major Keith, 10 June 1949. A copy of this memorandum is among Colonel Spicer's papers, which are kept by his daughter, Mrs. Nancy Cross.

15. Handwritten note by Colonel Donald Spicer, undated. This note is among Colonel Spicer's papers, which are kept by his daughter, Mrs. Nancy Cross, who allowed me to use it.

16. Memorandum from Spicer to Keith, 10 June 1949.

17. Handwritten note by Spicer, undated.

18. While a prisoner at Zentsuji my father was told by incoming prisoners that he had been selected for promotion to captain, U.S. Navy, in mid-1942. But in prison camp there was no one who could administer the oath and swear him in to that rank. Knowing that he had been selected for promotion, however, many of his fellow prisoners addressed him as "Captain."

Chapter 15

1. When weighed during this preliminary physical examination, my father found that he had lost seventy-five pounds.

2. Captain Old was a member of the Naval Academy class of 1920.

Chapter 16

1. After her tour of duty on Guam Nurse Jackson was commissioned a captain and became head of the Navy Nurse Corps.

2. Some Japanese soldiers remained hidden in the jungle for years after the war ended, continuing to brutalize the Chamorro as they had all during the Japanese occupation of Guam. One example—albeit an extreme one—of such

brutality was that committed by Superior Private Kiyoshi Takahashi and Seaman First Class Koju Shoji, who managed to escape capture for six months. In January 1945 Takahashi and Shoji kidnapped a Chamorro man and his child, both of whom they then killed and ate. After being captured, they were tried and convicted of first-degree murder on 20 August 1945 by a military commission convened on Guam. They were hanged on 19 June 1947.

3. Peddicord's was a tailor shop on Maryland Avenue, about three blocks from the Naval Academy Main Gate. Although Mr. Peddicord was well known for hand-tailored civilian suits, his primary business was making uniforms and providing caps and insignia for naval officers.

Chapter 17

1. Exactly who issued the questionnaire, whether the results were ever published, or where the original report resides if still extant are not known. My father's papers do not reveal this—only that they sent by military authorities. In the late 1940s access to such data was not as tight as now. I can only surmise he got the results from a friend in the Navy Department.

Appendix B

1. Papers of Donald T. Giles, Sr. Source unknown.

✳ Glossary

ACCOMMODATION LADDER. A portable flight of steps suspended at the side of a vessel to permit access to and from boats or a pier.

ACEY-DEUCY. A form of backgammon.

AFT. Toward the stern of a ship.

ARMORY. Room aboard ship in which small arms are stowed and serviced.

BAMBOO RADIO. Covert source of information within prison camp.

BANGO. Japanese expression meaning to count off, as during a muster.

BANZAI. A Japanese battle cry or patriotic cheer.

BAR. Browning automatic rifle.

BASU BARU. Japanese phonetic expression for baseball.

BENJO. Japanese term for privy.

BERIBERI. A disease of the peripheral nerves caused by a deficiency of vitamin B and characterized by severe emaciation and swelling of the body.

BOAT. Small ship or vessel; used in reference to submarines (e.g., pigboats).

BOONDOCKS. A remote rural area.

BULKHEAD. Interior transverse walls within a ship or boat.

BUSHIDO. The code of the samurai, stressing unquestioning loyalty and valuing honor above life.

BUTTS. Part of a rifle range where targets are manned.

CAPITAL SHIP. One of a class of the largest warships (e.g., a battleship, battle cruiser, or aircraft carrier).

CARABAO. Water buffalo.

CEC. Civil Engineer Corps.

CHAMORRO. Native(s) of the Mariana Islands, which include Guam and Saipan.

CHC. Chaplain Corps.

CHOP. An official stamp or seal on a document or letter serving to guarantee its authenticity.

CHOPPY. A term describing a slightly rough sea condition.

COALING. To take coal on board ship.

COMINT. Communications Intelligence.

CONTRAIL. A visible condensation of water droplets or ice crystals from the atmosphere occurring in the wake of an aircraft under certain conditions.

CORPSMAN. An enlisted man working as a pharmacist or hospital assistant.

COXSWAIN. Boatswain's mate third class.

DAIKON. A large variety of radish grown in Japan. The size of the daikon is partially due to the night soil in which it is grown.

DC. Dental Corps.

DEEP-SIX. To drop into the sea.

DETAIL OFFICER. Officer in the Navy Bureau of Personnel responsible for assigning officers to billets.

DRAG. Navy slang expression for "a date" or "to date."

EAGLES. Collar insignia worn by a navy captain.

FMFLANT. Fleet Marine Force, Atlantic.

FOUR-PIPER DESTROYER. Pre–World War II destroyer with four smokestacks.

FRANGIPANI. A fragrant tree or shrub found in tropical America.

GALLEY. The kitchen aboard ship.

GETA. A type of Japanese footwear; clog; an oblong wooden piece raised above the ground by crosswise wooden supports.

GOBO. Common burdock, a coarse, brown-leafed weed.

GUNBOAT. A small vessel of light draft carrying mounted guns.

GUNWALE. Top edge of the side of a small boat or launch.

HAKAMA. An old-style wide divided skirt worn by Japanese men, normally for ceremonial occasions. It is not often seen at the present time.

HAORI. A dark-colored cloaklike garment sometimes worn by Japanese men. The *haori* comes down to a little below the knees and is fastened in front by braided cords.

HARDTACK. A hard, saltless biscuit, formerly much used aboard ships.

HEAD. Slang expression used in the navy for toilet.

HIBACHI. A small Japanese charcoal stove.

HMS. His/Her Majesty's Ship.

HNLMS. His/Her Netherlands Majesty's Ship.

HOLD. Cargo space in the hull of a ship, especially between the lowermost deck and the bottom.

HOOK. Slang expression for anchor.

INLAND SEA. The long expanse of water between Honshu and the islands of Shikoku and Kyushu. It begins on the east at the Bay of Osaka and ends on the west at the Shimonoseki Strait, a distance of about 310 miles.

JIBE. To be in accord with; to agree.

KAMIKAZE. During the Second World War, a member of a corps in the Japanese air force charged with the suicidal mission of crashing his aircraft into an enemy target.

KENDO. Japanese fencing.

KEN-JUTSU. The art of handling a sword.

KUTSUSHITA. Japanese stockings.

LEE. The side or quarter away from the wind; the sheltered side.

LUGAO. A rice porridge of Philippine origin.

MARITIME SELF DEFENSE FORCE (MSDF). In order to avoid any semblance of militarism, the Japanese Constitution does not permit that country to have offensive military forces. Instead it has what are identified as self-defense forces, the navy component of which is the MSDF.

MC. Medical Corps.

MESS. A group that regularly eats together; the area in which meals are eaten.

MOOR. To secure a ship alongside a pier or to a buoy.

MOORINGS. The means by which a vessel is moored.

M/S. Motor ship.

NIGHT SOIL. Human excrement used in Japan as fertilizer.

NIPA. A palm whose foliage is used for thatching.

NISEI. A second-generation American of Japanese ancestry.

O-BENTO. A Japanese worker's lunch. Packed in a small box, it usually consists of some rice, a bit of fish, and a pickle.

OUTBOARD. Located on the exterior of a hull; located farther from the center.

PLEBE. A midshipman in his first year at the Naval Academy.

POGEY-BAIT. Slang term for candy or sweets.

POKY. Slang term for jail.

PRESS ON. To continue.

SACK OUT. A slang expression meaning to lie down.

SAKE. Japanese fermented alcoholic beverage made from rice.

S CLASS. An early class of U.S. submarines.

SCRAMBLED EGGS. Gold decoration on the visor of caps worn by senior naval officers (i.e., commander and above).

SC. Supply Corps.

SCUTTLEBUTT. Nautical term for drinking fountain or for rumors and gossip.

SEABAG. Cylindrical canvas bag used by a sailor for his gear.

SECURE. To make fast; to cease or stop.

SEN. Japanese monetary unit; one-hundredth of a yen.

SHOJI. A light screen of translucent paper, used as a sliding door or room divider in Japanese homes.

SHORE UP. To brace up something.

SPUDS. Slang expression for potatoes.

S/S. Steamship.

STEERAGEWAY. Sufficient speed to permit a vessel to be maneuvered.

SURVEY. To expend accountable material from the records. To throw away something that is no longer needed.

TABI. Japanese socks having a separation for the big toe so that they can be worn with geta.

TAKA GETA. Tall geta worn in inclement weather to raise the feet above standing water or mud.

TATAMI. Straw mats that form the floor of a Japanese house. In this book tatami refers to a thin straw pad.

TOFU. A soft, bland, cheeselike food made from curdled soybean milk.

TOPSIDE. The upper side; of, pertaining to, or located on the topside; up on the deck.

TORII. A wooden gateway erected at the approach to every Shinto shrine. The most primitive kind consists of two upright posts and two crossbars.

TRAWLER. A vessel used in fishing with a trawl net (i.e., with a strong fishing net for dragging along the sea bottom).

UNCOVER. To remove one's hat or cap.

UNDER WAY. In motion.

WARDROOM. The area aboard ship serving as living quarters for all commissioned officers except for the commanding officer.

WARDROOM MESS. Officers aboard ship who regularly take meals together in the wardroom.

WEATHER DECKS. Decks of a ship that are exposed to the weather.

WHITE HAT. Slang expression for a sailor.

YEN. Japanese monetary unit. In 1942 the value of a yen was approximately 50 cents.

YOUNGSTER. A midshipman in his second year at the Naval Academy.

YP. Yard patrol boat.

ZIGZAG. A course characterized by sharp turns, first to one side and then to the other; used to complicate torpedo attacks by enemy submarines.

✳ Bibliography

Alden, John D. *U.S. Submarine Attacks during World War II*. Annapolis: Naval Institute Press, 1989.

Aurthur, Robert A., and Kenneth Cohlmia. *The Third Marine Division*. Edited by Robert T. Vance. Washington, D.C.: Infantry Journal Press, 1948.

Beardsley, Charles. *Guam Past and Present*. Rutland, Vt.: Charles E. Tuttle, 1964.

Benedict, Ruth. *The Chrysanthemum and the Sword*. Boston: Houghton Mifflin, 1946.

Bourke-White, Margaret. *Shooting the Russian War*. New York: Simon and Schuster, 1942.

Bowditch, Nathaniel. *American Practical Navigator: An Epitome of Navigation*. Washington, D.C.: United States Navy Hydrographic Office, 1958.

Carano, Paul, and Pedro Sanchez. *A Complete History of Guam*. Rutland, Vt.: Charles E. Tuttle, 1964.

Christopher, Robert C. *The Japanese Mind: The Goliath Explained*. New York: Linden Press/Simon and Schuster, 1983.

Coleman, John S., Jr. *Bataan and Beyond: Memories of an American POW*. College Station: Texas A&M University Press, 1978.

Costello, John. *The Pacific War*. New York: Rawson, Wade, 1981.

Craig, William. *The Fall of Japan*. New York: Dial Press, 1967.

Dull, Paul S. *A Battle History of the Imperial Japanese Navy (1941–1944)*. Annapolis: Naval Institute Press, 1978.

Eads, Lyle W. *Survival amidst the Ashes*. Marble Hill, Mo.: Stewart Printing and Publishing, 1985.

Farrell, Don A. *The Pictorial History of Guam: Liberation–1944.* Tamuning, Guam: Micronesia Productions, 1984.

———. *Guam 1898–1918.* Tamuning, Guam: Micronesia Productions, n.d.

Greenfield, Kent Roberts, ed., *Command Decisions.* Washington, D.C.: Office of the Chief of Military History, United States Army, 1960.

Grover, David H., and Gretchen G. Grover. *Captives of Shanghai: The Story of the President Harrison.* Napa, Calif.: Western Maritime Press, 1989.

Hough, Frank O. *The Island War.* Philadelphia and New York: J. B. Lippincott, 1947.

Hough, Frank O.; Verle E. Ludwig; and Henry I. Shaw, Jr. *History of U.S. Marine Corps Operations in World War II.* Vol. 1, *Pearl Harbor to Guadalcanal.* Washington, D.C.: Headquarters, U.S. Marine Corps, Historical Branch, G-3 Division, 1958.

Hoyt, Edwin P. *Japan's War: The Great Pacific Conflict.* New York: McGraw-Hill, 1986.

Ienaga, Saburo. *The Pacific War: World War II and the Japanese, 1931–1945.* New York: Pantheon Press, 1980.

Japan Travel Bureau. *Japan: The Official Guide.* Tokyo: Japan Travel Bureau, 1954.

Johnson, L. W. "Guam before 1941." U.S. Naval Institute *Proceedings* 68 (July 1942): 998.

Karig, Walter, and Welbourn Kelley. *Battle Report: Pearl Harbor to Coral Sea.* New York: Farrar and Rinehart, 1944.

Kerr, E. Bartlett. *Surrender and Survival: The Experience of American POWs in the Pacific, 1941–1945.* New York: William Morrow, 1985.

Layton, Edwin T.; R. Pineau; and J. Costello. *And I Was There: Pearl Harbor and Midway—Breaking the Secrets.* New York: William Morrow, 1985.

Lodge, O. R. *The Recapture of Guam.* Washington, D.C.: Headquarters, U.S. Marine Corps, Historical Branch, G-3 Division, 1954.

McMillin, G. J. *Surrender of Guam to the Japanese.* Official Report to Chief of Naval Operations. Washington, D.C.: Navy Department, 11 September 1945.

Morison, Samuel Eliot. *History of U.S. Naval Operations in World War II.* Vol. 1, *The Battle of the Atlantic: 1939–1943.* Boston: Little, Brown, 1947.

———. *History of U.S. Naval Operations in World War II.* Vol. 3, *The Rising Sun in the Pacific: 1931–April 1942.* Boston: Little, Brown, 1948.

———. *History of U.S. Naval Operations in World War II.* Vol. 8, *New Guinea and the Marianas: March 1944–August 1944.* Boston: Little, Brown, 1975.

Palomo, Tony. *An Island in Agony.* Privately published, 1984.

Portusach, Frank. "History of the Capture of Guam by the United States Man of War *Charleston* and Its Transports." U.S. Naval Institute *Proceedings* 43 (April 1917): 707–18.

Price, Willard. "Guam without Regrets." *Pacific Profile,* July 1964, p. 22.

Reed, Reginald W. "Saga of a Sacrificial Goat, USN." Unpublished manuscript, 1972.

Roscoe, Theodore. *United States Submarine Operations in World War II.* Annapolis: U.S. Naval Institute, 1949.

Schratz, Paul R., Captain, USN (Ret.). *Submarine Commander*. Lexington: University Press of Kentucky, 1988.

Thompson, Robert Smith. *A Time for War*. New York: Prentice-Hall, 1991.

Toland, John. *But Not in Shame*. New York: Random House, 1961.

———. *The Rising Sun*. New York: Random House, 1970.

Tolley, Kemp. *Cruise of the Lanikai: Incitement to War*. Annapolis: Naval Institute Press, 1973.

Tweed, George Ray (as told to Blake Clark). *Robinson Crusoe, USN*. New York and London: Whittlesey House, McGraw-Hill, 1945.

U.S. Congress. House. *Hepburn Report*. 76th Cong., 1st sess., 27 December 1938. H. Doc. 65.

U.S. Navy Department. *U.S. Naval Report on Guam, 1899–1950*. Washington, D.C.: U.S. Government Printing Office, 1951.

Van Peenen, H. J. "Touchstone from Zentsuji." *The Retired Officer* (Retired Officers Association, Alexandria, Va.), December 1986, pp. 34–37.

Wilds, Thomas. "Japanese Seizure of Guam." *Marine Corps Gazette* (Marine Corps Association, Quantico, Va.) 39 (July 1955): 20–23.

Willmott, H. P. *Empires in the Balance: Japanese and Allied Pacific Strategies to April 1942*. London: Orbis, 1982.

Yamaguchi, K. W. *We Japanese*. Yokohama: Yamagata Press, 1950.

Index

Note: Boldface type refers to drawings; italic type to photographs. Numbers in parentheses following a note number indicate the text page on which that note appears.

About the Authors

Donald T. Giles, Sr., graduated from the U.S. Naval Academy (class of 1921) and received a graduate degree in mechanical engineering from Columbia University. He had three tours of duty in submarines and served aboard the USS *Maryland,* USS *Utah,* USS *Dent,* and USS *Wichita.*

In February 1941 Commander Giles was assigned as Vice Governor, and Executive Officer of the Naval Station, Guam. In December of that year, when Guam fell to the Japanese, he and the other military personnel stationed there were captured and interned in Japan for the duration of the war. He was awarded the Bronze Star Medal with Combat V for his wartime service.

After rehabilitation, he continued his naval career in the Office of the Assistant Secretary of the Navy and then as Supervising Inspector of Naval Material at Atlanta, Georgia.

He retired as a rear admiral in 1953. In the 1970s Rear Admiral Giles reconstructed his wartime experiences in a memoir. He died on 28 February 1983 and is buried in the U.S. Naval Academy cemetery in Annapolis.

Donald T. Giles, Jr., graduated from the U.S. Naval Academy (class of 1948) and holds graduate degrees from Georgetown University and Loyola College. In 1955 he graduated from the Naval Intelligence School and the Navy Language School (Chinese), at which point he was ordered to duty as assistant naval attaché at the American Embassy in Tokyo. As a diplomat in Japan, he experienced a lifestyle vastly different from what his father had experienced as a prisoner of war ten years earlier.

Mr. Giles retired in 1989 from the Central Intelligence Agency. He and his wife live in Hollin Hills, a suburb of Alexandria, Virginia.

The **Naval Institute Press** is the book-publishing arm of the U.S. Naval Institute, a private, nonprofit society for sea service professionals and others who share an interest in naval and maritime affairs. Established in 1873 at the U.S. Naval Academy in Annapolis, Maryland, where its offices remain, today the Naval Institute has more than 100,000 members worldwide.

Members of the Naval Institute receive the influential monthly magazine *Proceedings* and discounts on fine nautical prints and on ship and aircraft photos. They also have access to the transcripts of the Institute's Oral History Program and get discounted admission to any of the Institute-sponsored seminars offered around the country.

The Naval Institute also publishes *Naval History* magazine. This colorful bimonthly is filled with entertaining and thought-provoking articles, first-person reminiscences, and dramatic art and photography. Members receive a discount on *Naval History* subscriptions.

The Naval Institute's book-publishing program, begun in 1898 with basic guides to naval practices, has broadened its scope in recent years to include books of more general interest. Now the Naval Institute Press publishes more than seventy titles each year, ranging from how-to books on boating and navigation to battle histories, biographies, ship and aircraft guides, and novels. Institute members receive discounts on the Press's nearly 400 books in print.

For a free catalog describing Naval Institute Press books currently available, and for further information about subscribing to *Naval History* magazine or about joining the U.S. Naval Institute, please write to:

Membership & Communications Department
U.S. Naval Institute
118 Maryland Avenue
Annapolis, Maryland 21402-5035

Or call, toll-free, (800) 233-USNI.